# low-carb meals in minutes

linda gassenheimer

Bay Books

To Harold – for his love, support, and advice.

Other Books by Linda Gassenheimer
*French Cuisine*
*Simply Sauces*
*Keys Cuisine: Flavors of the Florida Keys*
*Dinner in Minutes: Memorable Meals for Busy Cooks*
*Vegetarian Dinner in Minutes*
*More Low - Carb Meals in Minutes*



Bay Books is an imprint of Bay / SOMA Publishing
444 De Haro St., No. 130, San Francisco, CA 94107.

Cover design: Randall Lockridge
Editorial and Design: Terrace Publishing

---

Library of Congress Cataloging-in-Publication Data
Available from the Publisher

---

ISBN 1-57959-512-X
Printed in the United States of America
15 14 13 12 11

Distributed by Publishers Group West

# contents

# acknowledgments

Many, many thanks go to my husband, Harold. He has been the main force behind this book. Since his decision five years ago to adopt a low-carb lifestyle, he has stood by my work and by my side. He encouraged me to create the recipes, helped to test and taste them, and edited every word.

I'd like to thank my assistant, Jackie Murrill, for her patience and help in testing these recipes. She spent hours on her feet working with me—and always with a smile.

James Connolly, President and Publisher of Bay Books, deserves a big thank you. He has supported this project and worked very hard to bring it to print in what must be record time.

Much thanks goes to Terrace Partners—Martha Hopkins, my editor who worked night and day to meet our tight schedule, and Randall Lockridge for his delightful cover design.

I'd also like to thank my family who embraced the project and supported me through it. My son James, his wife Patty, and their son Zachary, who all came for dinner with a smile knowing they would be recipe-tasting guinea pigs. My son Charles and his girlfriend Lori who tested recipes via email. My son John, his wife Jill, and their son Jeffrey who cheered me on. My sister Roberta and brother-in-law Robert who helped to edit my thoughts and words.

Thanks go to Kathy Martin, my editor at the *Miami Herald*, who has been a friend and booster for my columns and books.

Producing and hosting a weekly radio program has been a delight as well as an enormous amount of work. Thanks to the management and staff at WLRN 91.3 FM, public radio for South Florida, for their friendship and help.

I'd like to thank the many readers and students who correspond with me from all over the U.S. to say how much they enjoy the recipes and how much better they feel. This kind of encouragement makes the lonely time in front of the computer worthwhile.

Most importantly, I'd like to thank all of you who read this book and prepare the meals. I hope you enjoy them and reap the benefits as much as I've enjoyed creating the recipes and watching the wonderful results.

# introduction

Why are millions of people giving up their bagels, sandwiches, and pasta meals? After unsuccessful attempts at weight loss from low-fat, high-carb diets, they're finally getting the results they want from a low-carb lifestyle.

My experience began five years ago. My husband told me he was going to try a low-carbohydrate diet. My first reaction was, "Why? We have always eaten well-balanced meals, and most diets are just fads." But he was determined. He had never had a weight problem before, but he found the few pounds gained during a vacation weren't coming off. In addition, he had just come from the cardiologist, where he learned his triglycerides were at an all-time high and his cholesterol was creeping into an area of concern.

As I watched him struggle to put together low-carb meals, I realized that this was going to be a challenge for both of us. Bagels for breakfast and cans of sugary sodas after tennis were out. No more baked potato with his steak. And, what could he substitute for crackers and chips with drinks?

I read all of the available books on the subject and set out to create low-carb recipes and menus that suited our fast-paced lives. As I became more involved, I worked with several cardiologists, endocrinologists, and nutritionists working in the field. What I found was that the doctors and nutritionists could readily explain why this approach worked, but could not tell me how to adapt it to my busy life. In fact, when I attended medical lectures, the reception for the diet was highly enthusiastic, but the questions at the end—even from the doctors in the audience were—"How do I do it? What do I eat?" I began writing articles, giving lectures, and teaching cooking classes. As I heard from readers and worked with participants in my classes, I was astounded by their weight-loss results. They were starved for additional recipes, techniques, and guidelines.

I myself was lost when I first tried to make low-carbohydrate meals. I had to fundamentally rethink my approach to shopping and cooking. I started by restocking the pantry and refrigerator. The changes were dramatic.

## off the list were:

- Low-fat processed foods, such as fat-free cookies, cakes, and other sugary desserts.
- Fat-free mayonnaise, salad dressings, cream cheese, and sour cream.
- Condiments, sauces, and salsas where sugar is one of the first five ingredients.
- Pancakes, bagels, and waffles.

- Jams and jellies.
- Pizza and platefuls of pasta as a main course.
- Garnished baked potato as a meal.
- Sugary sodas and fruit juices.
- Chips, pretzels, and popcorn.

## on the list were:

- Eggs, as many as four a week. We hadn't used them for breakfast for 10 years.
- Egg substitute (which is basically egg whites), as a good source of protein.
- A well-stocked vegetable drawer, including cucumbers, lettuce, celery, bell peppers, mushrooms, and tomatoes.
- Low-fat deli meats, such as turkey breast, chicken, ham, and lean roast beef.
- Brown rice and whole wheat pasta, in place of the lower fiber, less nutritious white varieties.
- High-fiber, whole-grain breads that are relatively low in carbs.
- No-sugar-added tomato sauce and salad dressings.
- Real mayonnaise made with soybean or olive oil
- High-fiber, no-sugar-added bran cereal for breakfast.
- Olive and canola oil.
- Walnuts, pecans, almonds, and peanuts.
- Eight glasses (64 ounces) of water per day.

With this list of do's and don'ts, I created recipes that are fast, fun, and delicious. My husband's response was enthusiastic: He lost his extra weight, has kept it off for five years, and lowered his cholesterol and triglyceride counts to healthy levels.

Why is this lifestyle becoming mainstream in American eating? What are the principles behind it, and why is it working for so many people?

The theory behind low-carbohydrate, high-protein diets is this: Eating lots of carbohydrates could over-stimulate insulin production, causing peaks and valleys in blood sugar levels that might, in turn, create hunger pangs. On the other hand, protein is digested more slowly, promoting more even blood sugar levels. Eating more protein, fewer carbs, and more monounsaturated fat promotes weight loss by decreasing fat storage, increasing fat burning, and delaying the onset of hunger pangs.

The major low-carbohydrate books, such as *The Zone, Protein Power, Sugar Busters, Dr. Atkins' New Diet Revolution,* and *The Carbohydrate Addict's Diet,* differ in their approaches, but their central idea is to use diet to moderate insulin levels for the reasons explained above. All of the recipes in this book fit into the low-carbohydrate guidelines outlined in these books (and others on the subject).

Several cardiologists steered me away from diets that call for high levels of saturated fat. I also found that many of the diets are based on gimmicks—always recipes for disaster. My husband and I, as well as my listeners and readers, like to go out and enjoy our meals. We don't want to be oddities at the dinner table, especially in business situations. We want to be part of the mainstream, and we've found that special timing and food combination requirements are unnecessary. They're difficult to follow and stick with on a prolonged basis, and they're not necessary for a successful low-carb lifestyle.

So how do you get started? *Low-Carb Meals in Minutes* follows my "Dinner in Minutes" promise: attractive, delicious, fun, healthful, "no brainer" meals that are quick and easy to make.

These menus fit our fast-paced lives. For many days of the week, we eat breakfast on the run, if at all, lunch at our desks or at a fast food restaurant, and dinner is take out, home delivered, or restaurant fare. So, in addition to quick and easy menus, I've included recipes based on assembling bought, prepared foods, and a guide to eating out and ordering in.

I developed these techniques after many years of juggling my family, career (founding and running a cooking school, guiding a gourmet supermarket as its Executive Director, writing a food column for newspapers and magazines, and hosting a radio talk show), and a desire for good food.

It's a method that covers all aspects of food, from purchasing to preparing ingredients to presenting complete meals. There's no need to think about how to cook a dish or what goes with it.

"Dinner in Minutes" has simple, easy-to-follow recipes. I've learned to use classic techniques and familiar combinations to produce delicious results while cutting the cooking time.

"Dinner in Minutes" defines the organization of your kitchen. An efficient kitchen with all equipment in reach and in its place, uncluttered countertops, and a clean sink can save 10 to 15 minutes of preparation time.

And presentation is as important as preparation. If it doesn't look attractive and taste delicious, nothing else matters.

Consider "Dinner in Minutes" a blueprint that you can use for everyday meals or dressed up for parties or special occasions.

## shopping list

This blueprint contains a shopping list based on how the food is bought in the market.

- Quick shopping is as important as quick cooking. You won't have to think about how many mushrooms to buy. I've given you the amount.
- I list the ingredients by supermarket departments to help you navigate the aisles with ease.
- I've included tips on how to get in and out of the supermarket fast and how to take advantage of today's timesaving prepared foods.

- My 13-year-old "Dinner in Minutes" syndicated column is known as the one with the shopping list. People have told me that the list saves them both time and money since they buy only what they need.
- The Staples list helps them organize their cabinets so that they are not filled with extraneous items. To help you plan your pantry I have included a separate section using the staples listed in the book. You will already have many of the ingredients for the recipes and only need to buy a few fresh items.

## helpful hints and countdown

Each meal contains Helpful Hints on shopping, cooking, and substitutions, as well as a Countdown so you can get the whole meal on the table at the same time.

- You can hit the kitchen on the run without having to plan or think about each step.
- In my home, the dinner preparation starts the minute I turn on the light in the kitchen until the plates are brought to the table.
- The Helpful Hints tell you what to buy, how to buy it, and what you can substitute. They include tips on the best preparation method and quick-cooking techniques, as well as time-saving clean-up tips.
- *Low-Carb Meals in Minutes* doesn't mean broiled chicken every night. You will find a wide variety of delicious meals covering many ethnic flavors.
- A week of meals can include an Italian meatball minestrone, a French steak au poivre, a San Francisco cioppino, a Thai peanut-rub pork, or a Jamaican chicken salad. Wherever I travel throughout the world, I go to street markets with chefs, taste their foods, and bring back their flavors to add to the repertoire of simple, low-carb recipes.

A blueprint means that it is totally flexible.

- When you chose a fish recipe, you can buy the freshest looking fish in the market rather than the fish called for in the recipe.
- You can use the best sirloin, filet, strip steak, or more economical cuts like flank and skirt steaks.
- All of the recipes were tested and produced delicious results with products you can readily buy with one stop shopping in your local supermarket.
- Branching out to use the freshest and best ingredients like a favorite gourmet infused olive oil or aged balsamic vinegar will add even more flavor and zip to these recipes.
- You can use the ingredients called for or change them within the blueprint guidelines to suit your taste. The California Chef's Salad calls for ham, turkey, roast beef, and Swiss cheese. You can create fun, tempting, endless variations by using Black Forest ham, Cajun roast beef, or mesquite-smoked turkey breast.
- This flexible approach lets you choose whatever is in season, on sale, or just fits your mood.

Low-carbohydrate programs are normally divided into three phases: an initial phase of significant carbohydrate reduction, an intermediate phase for reintroduction of carbs, and a maintenance phase of balanced eating.

## quick start: reducing carbohydrate intake for maximum weight loss

The first step to successful eating in this plan calls for a reduction of carbohydrates. While differences exist, most proponents of lower carb levels advise an intake of about 30 to 40 grams of carbs a day. My Quick Start section maintains that level through healthful recipes containing vegetables and lean proteins. Follow the 14-day meal plan for this phase and you will enjoy meals like Pesto Scramble and Smoked Chicken and Cheddar Grill. My students tell me breakfast presents the greatest challenge to adapting to low-carb eating. This two-week meal plan gives you a variety of easy recipes including some quick-takes for breakfast on the run. The others can be completed in 15 to 20 minutes. Salads and wraps fit the bill for lunches. Try the Mozzarella Tomato Tower over Mesclun Greens or Smoked Trout Salad with Field Greens. All are quick. Many are available on restaurant menus, and you can use the recipe for proportion guidelines. Dinner can be Southern Comfort Pecan-Crusted Grouper with Vegetable Creole or Pacific Rim Pork with Ginger-Garlic Stir-Fry Vegetables and Pickled Daikon Radish Salad that take only minutes to make.

## which carbs: reintroducing carbohydrates while continuing to lose weight

Listening to the questions from the participants in my low-carb classes, I realized the second phase is the most difficult. They are afraid that returning to higher levels of carbohydrates will negate all of the benefits they've achieved. In Which Carbs, I reintroduce carbohydrates in the form of high-fiber, low–simple sugar carbohydrates. The Which Carbs 14-day meal plan will help you sail through without having to question what you're eating. High-fiber cereal helps start the day the low-carb way. Add to this dishes like Microwave Cheddar Scramble with Bran Cereal or a scrumptious Raspberry-Red Smoothie (which has become a must for my husband). Nuevo Tex-Mex Layered Salad or Roast Turkey Sandwich with Greek Sadziki Sauce and Pistachios fill the lunch bill. How does Chicken Provençal, Neapolitan Steak Pizzaiola, or Seared Sesame Tuna sound for dinner?

## right carbs: permanent level with great food for a healthy lifestyle

The third stage leaves you permanently with the Right Carbs. So, what should you eat to maintain your weight loss? Right Carbs has the answers. This section achieves a well-balanced lifestyle of approximately 40 percent of calories from carbohydrates, 30 percent of calories from lean proteins, and 30 percent of calories from fat (primarily monounsaturated.)[1] Vietnamese Pancakes, Shrimp Caesar Wrap, and Chicken Parmesan are a breakfast, lunch, and dinner that are quick to make, fit the guidelines, and most important of all, taste fabulous!

Does it mean you can't have desserts? No. Some of the meals include a dessert. In addition, I have created a guilt-free Dessert chapter to satiate your sweet tooth. When you want to take the time to make a special dessert, try Strawberry Pecan Whip or Mocha Fudge Cake.

So how does my husband handle vacations and blow-out weekends? No need to worry here. Remember, balance is the key. We have found that you can splurge on special occasions without negative effects when you come back to the Right Carbs. In fact, one cardiologist advisor said that varying from a good base once in a while still leaves you much better off than if you don't have that base at all. In other words, the low-carbohydrate approach is forgiving. Following the program even with some deviations will produce a good result. My husband found that returning to the Right Carbs is easy because it takes so little effort and the menus are so appealing. Any time you want to restart weight loss, you can go back to Quick Start for a week or two and work yourself back up to Right Carbs.

The 14-day meal plans in each of the three sections are organized to provide a day-to-day guide to low-carb eating. The breakfasts, lunches, and dinners are presented as entire meals. While you can mix and match if you prefer a different side dish, the meals have been created to achieve the nutritional priorities of that phase. By all means, if you don't like or can't eat a particular food, simply replace that meal with a meal from the same section. Regardless of the section, feel free to substitute fish or chicken for the other.

*Low-Carb Meals in Minutes* is for all of you who want to eat healthfully and be able to fit a low-carbohydrate weight-loss program into your time-starved lives. The low-carb lifestyle has certainly changed our lives. My husband and I no longer think about what is and isn't low-carb—we just consider it good food that fits into our busy schedule.

Before starting a program of this type, it is always best to check with your doctor first. This is especially true if you are taking any medication under a doctor's care—particularly if being treated for diabetes. It might be interesting to look at your cholesterol and related blood tests before and after to compare your results.

These meals have been made by my many students and readers from all over the United States. Wherever I travel and lecture, they tell me how well they work. I get hundreds of emails on how well they're doing and how these easy meals have changed their lives. They love the variety that comes from my travels around the world. My goal in sharing these recipes with you is to help you enjoy good food for good health. My husband and I love good food. Now, with these recipes, we can live to eat and eat to live. We hope you enjoy them, too.

Bon Appétit.

[1] *Why 40-30-30? All foods contain only these three components (carbohydrates, protein and fat) and all are essential for your well being. While there are differences of opinion, it is generally agreed that fat levels (primarily monounsaturated) should make up to 30 percent of one's diet. Carbohydrate intake should be restricted to 30 percent more than protein intake. So if the calories from protein are 30% of diet, the correct carbohydrate level should be 40%.*

# smart shopping the low-carb way

When I was the Executive Director of a gourmet grocery chain, I used to hear people say, "I hate to shop. I'd cook more if I had the ingredients at home." Here are some tips that will help get you in and out of the market quickly.

## some advice

The adage of "don't go to the store hungry" is true. It can be a disaster. If I go to the market when I'm tired and hungry, I just get to a starving point and eat anything offered to me. Go after a meal or have a snack before you go. This will help you concentrate on what you should be buying instead of what you shouldn't buy.

Try to go to the market when it isn't crowded or directly after a long day's work. Carry a cooler in your car so you can stop on the way to work, during lunch, or at other times. The cooler will protect foods from moderate heat and cold, but it won't help with extreme heat or freezing temperatures.

Many offices have refrigerators. If one is available to you, shop before work or at lunch and store your food in the refrigerator. Here's a hint: There have been many times when I've accidentally left my packages at work or at a friend's house. The best solution to this is to put your car keys in one of the shopping bags. You won't be able to go anywhere without them.

Keep the foods from the Staples list on hand. (See pages 17–18.) You will only need to pick up a few fresh items to complete your meal.

## supermarket savvy:

### let the markets help you

Supermarkets are in a "meals solution" revolution. They are constantly updating their product mix to help us get our meals on the table fast. Use the supermarket to your advantage.

### salad bars

Great for picking up a quick salad or lunch and for buying cut vegetables and fruits for cooking at home.

### deli

Look for new leaner cuts of cooked meats—all with nutritional analysis. Canadian bacon, roast beef, and ham have been made leaner without the use of high carbs.

### dairy

Reduced-fat cheese has come a long way. Gone is the rubbery cheese that won't melt. Many brands using new techniques have developed lower fat cheeses with flavors that melt well.

### prepared foods

Ask for roast chicken breast only. Ask for an ingredients list. Read the labels carefully for all prepared foods, as many have added salt and sugar.

## produce department

Bags of washed, ready-to-eat salads are one of the best conveniences I've seen. Read the labels. If they don't say ready-to-eat or washed, then you will need to wash the ingredients prior to using.

Many supermarkets have cubes of melons and pineapple ready to eat.

## meat department

Look for lower fat or lean meats. Many markets now have separate sections for lean meats or mark them with special labels. Pork and beef are now available with reduced-fat content.

There are many marinated or precooked meats available. Watch for sugar, salt, and fat content.

## grocery aisles

There are many items that make our lives easier, with more coming out each day. Low-fat, no-sugar-added salad dressings and tomato-based pasta sauces are a few of the products. In fact, there are so many available, it's best to try a few and, when you find one you like, buy several bottles to keep on hand. Again, the most important advice is to read the nutritional labels and ingredients lists. In general, an item should have no more than 12 grams of carbohydrates per cup.

## how to read the labels

It's worth a few extra minutes to read the labels on the food you're buying. They can be confusing. Here are some answers to the most frequently asked questions.

## what do "low-fat," "reduced-fat," or "light" on a label mean?

- "Low-fat" means 3 grams of fat or less per serving.
- "Reduced-fat" means at least 25 percent less fat per serving than the food it is being compared to.
- "Light" generally means that it contains 50 percent fewer calories from fat than a comparable product.
- "Sugar Free" according to the FDA must mean less than 0.5 grams per serving.

Check the serving size on the label. It can be misleading. If the serving size is 1 tablespoon, you need to think if that is the amount you will actually eat.

Ingredients must be listed in descending order by weight. Generally, if an ingredient is fifth or lower in the list, it has minimal amounts in each serving.

# staples

This is a comprehensive list of the staples listed in the recipes included in the book. Keep these staples on hand and you'll only need to pick up a few fresh items to make quick meals.

## canned or bottled goods

- No-sugar-added oil and vinegar dressing
- Canned tuna packed in water
- Low-sodium tomato or V-8 juice
- Low-sodium, no-sugar-added tomato sauce and diced tomatoes
- No-sugar-added tomato salsa
- Mayonnaise made with olive or soybean oil
- Fat-free, low-salt chicken broth
- Dijon mustard
- Canned chickpeas, black beans, navy beans, cannellini
- Canned water chestnuts
- Hearts of palm

## condiments

- Worcestershire sauce
- Hot pepper sauce
- Low-salt soy sauce

## dairy

- Parmesan cheese
- Light yogurt
- Reduced-fat Swiss, cheddar, mozzarella, and Monterey Jack cheese
- Reduced-fat cottage cheese
- Skim milk
- Eggs
- Egg substitute

## deli

- Lean ham (not honey-smoked or sugar-glazed)
- Lean Canadian bacon
- Turkey breast
- Chicken breast
- Lean roast beef

## dry goods

- Long-grain brown rice
- Quick-cooking pearl barley
- Lentils
- Whole wheat pasta
- Whole wheat flour
- High-fiber, no-sugar-added bran cereal
- Oatmeal
- Salt
- Sugar substitute

## freezer goods

Frozen, diced onion

Frozen, diced green bell pepper

## grains and breads

100% whole wheat bread

Rye bread

Multigrain bread

Whole wheat pita bread

Whole wheat tortillas

Barley

Lentils

Brown rice

Wild rice

## oils and vinegars

Olive oil

Canola oil

Olive oil spray

Balsamic vinegar

Rice vinegar

Distilled white vinegar

Red wine vinegar

## produce department

Red onions

Yellow onions

Bell peppers

Cucumbers

Celery

Tomatoes

Lemon

Garlic

## spices and herbs

Black peppercorns

Cayenne pepper

Chili powder

Dried oregano

Dried rosemary

Dried tarragon

Dried dill

Freeze-dried chives

Ground cumin

Ground cinnamon

# equipment

You really don't need a lot of special equipment to make these meals. However, the following items will speed your preparation and make your life easier.

## food processor

A food processor or mini-chop will quickly slice, chop, and blend foods together.

## garlic press

Some of the newer ones allow you to crush garlic without peeling the cloves. I also use it to crush fresh ginger.

## knives

Sharp knives are important for fast and accurate cutting. A dull knife can be dangerous. It can slip or slide when you are trying to slice. Three different types are all you really need for most cutting tasks: a 13-inch, 8-inch, and a serrated knife for fruits or tomatoes.

## meat thermometer

I love the new style probe that uses a cord. The cord is connected to a dial that sits on the counter. With the cord, it works well for items on the stove, in the oven, or on the grill.

## microwave oven

Use this fast-cooking tool. And remember, any dish that's microwave safe is dishwasher safe, too.

## pots and pans

You can make most of the meals in this book using a medium (9- to10-inch) nonstick skillet, a large (3- to 4-quart) saucepan, and a wok. Nonstick skillets are essential, as these recipes are designed using small amounts of oil. If you follow the instructions, your food will not stick.

## scale

A small kitchen scale is very handy and not expensive. Where weights are given, I've also listed measurements in cups and ounces, though it's much faster and more accurate to use a scale.

## vegetable peeler

For easy peeling, make sure yours is sharp. These are actually little knives and should be replaced as they start to dull.

# quick cooking tips and helpful hints

Each recipe has a helpful hints section. Knowing what to substitute, the best way to prepare ingredients, or some other shortcut can make a big difference in the time it takes you to get your meal on the table.

## slices and weight

To determine the weight of sliced cheese or packaged meat, divide the package weight by the number of slices.

## parmesan cheese

Buy good quality Parmesan cheese. Ask the grocer to grate it for you or chop it in the food processor yourself. Freeze extra for quick use later—simply spoon out what you need and leave the rest frozen.

## washing mushrooms

To clean whole mushrooms, wipe them with a damp paper towel.

## washing herbs

The quickest way to wash watercress, arugula, parsley, or basil is to place the bunch, head first, into a bowl of water. Leave for a minute, then lift out and shake dry. The dirt and sand will be left behind. Repeat if necessary.

## chopping fresh herbs

To quickly chop herbs, dry and snip the leaves right off the stem with scissors.

## fresh ginger

To chop fresh ginger quickly, cut it into small cubes and press through a garlic press with large holes. If using a press with small holes, just capture the juice that is squeezed out; it will give enough flavor for the recipe.

## dried spices and herbs

If using dried spices, make sure the bottle is less than 6 months old. To bring out the flavor of the dried herbs, chop them with fresh parsley. The juice from the parsley will help release the flavor of the herbs.

## shelling shrimp

Buy shelled shrimp, or ask for the shrimp to be shelled while you complete your shopping. Most stores will do this for a small fee, which is worth the time saved in shelling them yourself.

## food processor

To use the food processor for a recipe without having to stop to wash the bowl, first chop the dry ingredients (such as nuts), and then the wet ones (such as onion). You won't have to stop in the middle of preparing the ingredients.

## crisp stir-fry

For crisp, not steamed, stir-fried vegetables, start with a very hot wok or skillet. Let the vegetables sit a minute before tossing to allow the wok to regain its heat.

## timely stir-fry

To keep from looking back at a recipe as you stir-fry the ingredients, line them up on a cutting board or plate in the order of use. You will know which ingredient comes next.

## electric cooking

To get a quick high/low response from electric burners, heat two burners, one on medium high and the other on low. Move the pot back and forth between them.

## fluffy rice

I like to cook my rice like pasta, using a pot of boiling water that's large enough for the rice to roll freely. Use the method given here or follow the directions on the package of rice.

# low-carb food guidelines

After you've cooked several recipes in this book, you will begin to understand the types of ingredients and proportions that are part of a low-carb lifestyle. Use these foods to help you create your own menus.

Vegetables are an important part of a healthful eating lifestyle. You may find it hard to believe that vegetables have carbohydrates. Some have more than others. Here's a list of vegetables that are low in carbohydrates versus those with high carbs that should be eaten in smaller quantities.

## eat as many of these vegetables as you like:

Alfalfa sprouts

Artichokes

Asparagus

Beans, wax or green

Bok choy

Broccoli

Brussels sprouts

Cabbage

Cauliflower

Celery

Collard greens

Cucumber

Eggplant

Herbs, all types

Kale

Leeks

Lettuce, all types: chicory, escarole, Belgian endive, romaine, iceberg, Boston, or Bibb

Mushrooms, all types

Onions

Okra

Peppers: green, red, yellow, and all hot peppers

Radishes

Rutabagas

Scallions

Snow peas

Spinach

Swiss chard

Tomatoes

Turnips

Yellow squash

Zucchini

## eat these vegetables in measured amounts (about ½ cup per serving):

Beets

Carrots

Corn

Potatoes

Hard squash, such as acorn or butternut

## fruits

Fruits are often high in carbohydrates, and they should be avoided in Quick Start meals. They are reintroduced in the Which Carb and Right Carb sections. The amounts given are guidelines for how much should be eaten at a serving.

Apple (1 small)

Apricots (4)

Apricots dried (7 halves)

Banana (½)

Berries: strawberries, raspberries, blueberries (¾ cup)

Cantaloupe (¼ whole cantaloupe or 1 cup cubed)

Cherries (12 cherries or ⅓ cup)

Grapes (⅓ cup)

Grapefruit (½)

Honeydew (¼ whole honeydew or 1 cup cubed)

Kiwi (1)

Lemon juice (¼ cup)

Lime juice (¼ cup)

Nectarine (1)

Orange (1)

Tangerine (1)

Mango (½)

Peach (1)

Pear (1)

Pineapple (½ cup cubed)

Plums (2)

Watermelon (1 cup cubed)

## meats, poultry, and seafood

From steak to shrimp and all of the meats in between, here's a list of the leaner cuts:

### beef

Top round

Eye round

Beef tenderloin (filet mignon)

Round tip

Top loin

Sirloin

Ground sirloin

## poultry (skinless)

Turkey breast

Chicken breast

Chicken legs

Cornish game hens

Poussins

Low-fat turkey sausage—keep in freezer for a quick dinner, lunch, or breakfast

## seafood

All types of shellfish. Tuna, salmon, sardines, mackerel, halibut, and trout are high in omega-3 fatty acids. Try to eat one of these on a regular basis.

## pork

Pork tenderloin

Lean Canadian bacon

Lean ham (no honey-baked or sugar-glazed)

## veal

Top round

Veal chop

Veal cutlet

## lamb

Leg (preferred)

Chops with visible fat removed

# easy ways to make these meals "special events"

Presentation is as important as preparation. The appeal of a beautiful plate of food adds to our eating experience. Some meals are special with friends or when celebrating events and holidays. But all meals have a special dimension with these tips or your own creativity.

Use attractive dinnerware—colorful plates with matching napkins to create a warm and fun atmosphere.

Set your table with the theme of the meal in mind:

- Serve Asian dishes on Chinese-style plates and include chopsticks with the fork and knife place settings.
- Serve Southwestern dishes on earthenware plates that reflect the hot, earthy colors of the Southwest or Mexico.
- Set the table for tropical meals using tropical-colored place mats or arrange some hibiscus or tropical plants for a centerpiece.
- Mediterranean meals look great served in Italian pottery or presented on place mats and tablecloths using the blues, reds, and saffron yellows of Provence.

For recipes that use the broiler or oven, use oven-to-table ware and bring the sizzling platter to the table. The sound and smell are part of the enjoyment.

Dress up salads with some nasturtiums or other edible flowers. Place them attractively on the plate or cut the colorful petals into strips and sprinkle them over the salad.

Create attractive salads by stacking them. Place the salad ingredients on a plate and then form them into a pyramid shape to give height. Or, create layers with the salad greens as a base and top with layers of the other ingredients in alternating colors. A layer of sliced red bell peppers, for instance, can be followed by a layer of sliced cucumbers, and then topped with sliced or cherry tomatoes.

Make salads with several different colored leaves. For example, romaine, radicchio, arugula, or basil leaves add varied color and flavor. Or place pale Belgian endive with spicy, deep green watercress.

Make a plated meal look attractive by adding different colored lettuce leaves as a garnish or base for the food. For example, the Grilled Cheddar and Chicken Salad can be served on a bed of red-leaf lettuce.

When serving wraps, cut them in half crosswise on the diagonal and lay one half on its side and the other half standing on its end leaning against it. This will make an attractive pattern on the plate and show the colorful layers inside the wrap.

Use a cast-iron omelette pan, and serve the omelettes and frittatas at the table right in the pan.

Sprinkle soups with fresh green herbs, choosing the appropriate herb to go with the flavor of the dish: fresh basil or oregano for Italian meals, cilantro for a Southwestern or Caribbean touch, and chives or arugula to give a dish an extra bite.

When serving meat, fish, or poultry on a bed of salad, make an attractive fan by slicing to one narrow point on the meat, making sure not to cut through the point. Then spread the slices from that point into a fan.

These meals have been planned with color and texture in mind. For example, the Pan-Glazed Balsamic Chicken with Roasted Squash and Snow Peas combines a glazed chicken with yellow squash and bright green snow peas to make a very pretty presentation. When creating your own meals, consider these points.

# tips for eating out

One of the biggest challenges to making sure we eat healthfully is that 60 percent of our meals are prepared outside the home. We eat out, bring in, and eat on the run. Use the recipes in this book as a guide to eating out. Once you understand the types of foods and proportion sizes, you will be able to order from the menu with confidence. Here are some hints and tips to eat well in spite of your schedule:

- Avoid all deep-fried foods.
- Avoid sugary drinks. Opt for water, unsweetened ice tea, or diet soda.
- Plain, soft tacos or tortilla-filled wraps are fine as long as they aren't filled with rice and beans. Ask for whole wheat, if possible.
- Roasted or grilled meats are best. Make sure you include vegetables with your meal. Stay away from sugar-based sauces, especially barbecue sauce and most glazes.
- Many meals are loaded with carbs. Order two vegetables instead of a starch. Most restaurants are used to substituting this way.
- Ask for your salad dressing on the side. Most salads come swimming in dressing. You'll be surprised at how far 1 tablespoon of dressing will go, or just dip your vegetables into the dressing on the side.
- If you order dessert, share it with the table or make sure you don't have a starch during dinner. Better still, order a fresh fruit salad or berries.
- Have a low-carb snack (vegetables, a few nuts, a slice of low-carbohydrate cheese) before you go out to eat. This will help you avoid the basket of bread while you're waiting for your meal.
- Don't go out for drinks or attend a cocktail party on an empty stomach. One drink on an empty stomach will make you immediately hungry, and you'll eat the first thing you can find. Have a healthy snack before you go out. If you think it will be a long cocktail hour, start with sparkling water with a piece of lemon or lime or a diet soda first. Then go on to a drink or glass of wine.
- Fast food can be fine. Order grilled chicken or fish and discard the bread or roll. Or, eat it as an open sandwich using just one half of the roll. Order a salad with the dressing on the side. Stay away from fries, baked potatoes, and chips.
- Chinese food can be loaded with sugar. Order stir-fried meats and vegetables or skewered meats, and avoid soups with fried wontons, egg rolls, ribs in thick sauce, and noodles. It is refreshing to see that some restaurants are offering brown rice as an alternative to white rice.
- Italian food doesn't have to mean a plate of pasta. Order an antipasto platter or any of the meats, salads, or vegetables.
- French food can be very healthy. Order clear soups, salads, vegetables, meats, or seafood, but avoid heavy sauces and bread.
- Japanese sushi is based on rice—very often with sugar added to it. Try miso soup or any of the cooked meats and vegetables instead.

- Mexican food can be high in saturated fat and carbohydrates. Fajitas (1 tortilla) with the garnishes, grilled meats, and salads are fine. Avoid rice, refried beans, and nachos.

Watch portion size when eating out. Here's a guide to help you size up what you should be eating.

## sizing it up*

½ cup fruit, vegetable, cooked cereal, pasta, or rice . . . . . . . . . . . . .a small fist

3 ounces cooked meat, poultry, or fish . . . . . . . . . . . . . . . . . . . . . . .a deck of cards

½ bagel . . . . . . . . . . . . . . . . . . . . . . . . . . . . . . . . . . . .width of large coffee lid

1 medium apple or orange . . . . . . . . . . . . . . . . . . . . . . . . . . . . .a baseball

1½ ounces cheese . . . . . . . . . . . . . . . . . . . . . . . . . . . . . . . . .6 dice

1 tortilla . . . . . . . . . . . . . . . . . . . . . . . . . . . . . . . . . . . . . . .a small (7-inch) plate

1 muffin . . . . . . . . . . . . . . . . . . . . . . . . . . . . . . . . . . . . . . .a large egg

1 teaspoon butter . . . . . . . . . . . . . . . . . . . . . . . . . . . . . . . . . .a thumb tip

2 tablespoons peanut butter . . . . . . . . . . . . . . . . . . . . . . . . . . . .a golf ball

*Food Insight News published by IFIC
(International Food Information Council)

# quick snacks

Snacks are important little meals that will help you through the day, especially during the first Quick Start phase. They can prevent that sinking feeling at 4 or 5 p.m. when your energy is low, or the mid-morning, is-it-time-for-lunch clock watching.

Knowing what to snack on and how to have it handy can help prevent raids on the vending machine to satiate candy cravings.

## here are some ideas:

- If you've had an extra large lunch salad, take some back to the office or home and use the remainder as an afternoon snack.
- 1 ounce low-fat cheese (string cheese, stick cheese, small round individually packed wax-covered low-fat cheese)
- 1/4 cup low-fat cottage cheese
- 1 ounce nuts, such as almonds, pecans, and walnuts (1/4 cup). Keep small packages of nuts in your drawer at work, pocketbook, or brief case. They're easy to carry around and contain portion-size amounts.
- 2 ounces deli meats, such as lean ham, turkey, chicken, or roast beef
- 1 hard-boiled egg. Keep a few hard-boiled eggs on hand for snacks. They will need to be refrigerated at the office.
- 1 ounce sunflower seeds
- 6 olives
- Any vegetables such as cucumber slices, celery sticks, broccoli or cauliflower florets, and bell pepper slices

# quick start

## introduction

This two-week meal plan is designed to start you off on cutting carbs from your meals. When I give cooking classes and show these meals, the response always surprises me: "You mean I can eat all of that?" Knowing the quantities of each type of food you can eat will help you build your own recipes to fit your lifestyle.

There is a range of recipes in this section (some of them quite easy) involving only the assembly of ready-prepared foods from the supermarket. Another category involves cooking a few things to create the finished product. Still others involve cooking an entire meal in just minutes. This gives you a wide variety to choose from. Some you'll want to make on the weekend when you have more time, while others will be grab-and-go for midweek.

I have organized the menus into a meal-at-a-glance chart with some easy and quick meals midweek and those that take a little more time for the weekends. They are arranged to give variety throughout the day and over the course of the week. The meals are ordered in the chapter in the same sequence. Just follow the meals in the order given for a complete two-week plan.

## breakfasts

There's plenty of variety in these breakfasts to fit all tastes, Swiss Scramble with Spring Onions to Turkey Sausage and Denver Sauté. Pick the ones you like and use them for this two-week period.

## mid-morning snack

When you first start reducing carbs, you will need to eat a mid-morning snack. I have included a section with some suggestions. (See page 29.)

## lunch

There's a lunch for any occasion here—quick-take lunches that can be eaten at home or taken with you—and more elaborate lunches for when you have more time or friends stop by.

Enjoy a Herbed Chicken Caesar Salad, Greek Salad, or Chesapeake Shrimp Salad. These meals can be made at home and taken to work. They are commonly found on most lunch menus. If you are eating out, use these recipes as a guide for the portions you should eat and remember to ask for your dressing on the side. (See pages 27–28 for more tips on eating out.)

Make vinaigrette dressing according to the instructions provided in the recipes and keep refrigerated, or speed up preparation by buying a low-carbohydrate dressing to keep on hand. Read the labels carefully. There should be no more than 1 gram of carbohydrate per 2 tablespoon serving.

## mid-afternoon snack

When you first start reducing carbs, you will need to eat a mid-afternoon snack. (See page 29.)

## dinner

Do you feel like Chinese, Tex-Mex, French, or American food tonight? There's something from each ethnic group—Pacific Rim Pork with Ginger-Garlic Stir-Fry Vegetables and Pickled Daikon Radish Salad, Southern Comfort Pecan-Crusted Grouper with Vegetable Creole, Salsa-Smothered Tex-Mex Meat Loaf with Sliced Avocado, and Sirloin Burger and Fresh Slaw are some of the tempting meals.

Snapper Veracruz with Zucchini Parmesan and Italian Greens is a 15-minute meal. Steak au Poivre with French Green Beans and Hearts of Palm Salad and Rosemary-Roasted Pork with a Fennel Gratin and Brussels Sprouts take longer, about 30 minutes.

I've made dinner parties using these meals without telling anyone they were low-carb. No one knew and the only question asked was could they have the recipe.

How low is low-carb? It's important to reduce carbohydrate intake low enough for a period of time so that you eliminate the peaks of insulin secretion. Following the Quick Start 14-day plan, you will consume an average of 30 to 40 grams of carbohydrates per day. Carbohydrates percentage is based on carbohydrates less fiber consumed, which is the normal way of calculating carbohydrate consumption. The balance of these meals is 10 percent of calories from carbohydrates, 36 percent of calories from lean protein, 40 percent of calories from monounsaturated fat, and 11 percent of calories from saturated fat.

To achieve the correct balance, the recipes have been structured as complete meals. Whatever meal you pick, it's best to stay with the entire menu given.

# quick start 14-day menu plan

| week 1 | breakfast | lunch | dinner |
|---|---|---|---|
| sunday | Smoked Salmon Pinwheels . . . . . . . . .35 | Mozzarella Tomato Tower over Mesclun Greens . . . .50 | Shrimp Scampi with Roasted Asparagus and Italian Greens . . . . . .65 |
| monday | Salsa and Sliced Eggs . . . . . . . .36 | Quick-Take Turkey Bundles . . . . .51 | Asian Ginger Salmon with Sesame Broccoli and Yellow Bean Salad . . . . . . .67 |
| tuesday | Pesto Scramble . . . . .37 | Basil-Onion Tuna Salad Wraps . . . . . .52 | Pan-Glazed Balsamic Chicken with Roasted Squash and Snow Peas . . . . .69 |
| wednesday | Sunny-Side-Up Swiss Melt . . . . . . . . .38 | Smoked Trout Salad with Field Greens . . . . . .53 | Salsa-Smothered Tex-Mex Meat Loaf with Sliced Avocados . . . . . . . .71 |
| thursday | Sizzling Ham and Tomatoes . . . . . .39 | Spicy Roast Beef and Watercress Wraps . . . . . . . . . .54 | Chicken Marsala with Roman Spinach and Radicchio Salad . . . .72 |
| friday | Florentine Eggs and Ham . . . . . . . . . .40 | Chopped Salad with Roasted Chicken . . . . . . . . . .55 | Sirloin Burger and Fresh Slaw . . . . .74 |
| saturday | Turkey Sausage and Denver Sauté . . . . . .41 | Curried Chicken–Stuffed Tomatoes . . . . . . . . . .56 | Pacific Rim Pork with Ginger-Garlic Stir-Fry Vegetables and Pickled Daikon Radish Salad . . . . . . .75 |

| week 2 | breakfast | lunch | dinner |
| --- | --- | --- | --- |
| sunday | Sweet Pepper and Turkey Omelette . . . .42 | Salmon Balsamico on a Bed of Field Greens . . . . . .57 | Veal Scallopini with Garlic Greens and Saffron Cauliflower . . . . . . .77 |
| monday | Smoked Chicken and Cheddar Grill . . .43 | Quick-Take Ham and Cucumber Parcels . . .58 | Southern Comfort Pecan-Crusted Grouper with Vegetable Creole . . .78 |
| tuesday | Devilish Eggs . . . . . .44 | Greek Salad . . . . . .59 | Sausage-Pepper Sauté with Marinated Artichoke Salad . . . .79 |
| wednesday | Swiss Scramble with Spring Onions . . . . .45 | Grilled Cheddar and Chicken Salad . . . . .60 | Snapper Veracruz with Zucchini Parmesan and Italian Greens . . . . . .80 |
| thursday | Stuffed Endive with Ham and Cottage Cheese . . . .46 | Chesapeake Shrimp Salad . . . . . . . . . . .61 | Rosemary-Roasted Pork with a Fennel Gratin and Brussels Sprouts . . . . . . . . . .81 |
| friday | Grilled Portobello and Canadian Bacon Omelette . . . .47 | Herbed Chicken Caesar Salad . . . . . .62 | Chicken with Fresh Herbs, Pan-Roasted Asparagus, and Baby Turnips . . . . . .83 |
| saturday | Cheddar Frittata with Sausage . . . . . . . . .48 | Roasted Portobellos Stuffed with Smoked Trout and Sun-Dried Tomatoes . . . . . . . . .63 | Steak au Poivre with French Green Beans and Hearts of Palm Salad . . . . . .85 |

# quick start breakfasts

# smoked salmon pinwheels

*Smoked salmon spread with cream cheese makes an elegant, quick breakfast for midweek or the weekend.*

## smoked salmon pinwheels

- *3/4 pound smoked salmon*
- *1/4 cup low-fat cream cheese (2 ounces)*
- *1 tablespoon skim milk*
- *1 medium cucumber, sliced*
- *2 medium tomatoes, sliced*
- *Salt and freshly ground black pepper to taste*

Place salmon on a cutting board. Soften cream cheese with skim milk and mix until smooth. Spread on salmon. Roll up, slice crosswise into 1/2-inch pinwheels, and place on 2 plates. Season the cucumber and tomato slices with salt and pepper, and divide between the plates.

*Makes 2 servings.*

**ONE SERVING: 324** CALORIES, **37G** PROTEIN, **11G** CARBOHYDRATE **14G** FAT (**6G** SATURATED), **61MG** CHOLESTEROL, **1468MG** SODIUM, **1G** FIBER

### helpful hint

- *Buy good quality smoked salmon rather than lox, which can be very salty.*

### countdown

- *Slice cucumber and tomatoes.*
- *Complete recipe.*

### shopping list

*TO BUY:*

- *1 small package low-fat cream cheese (2 ounces needed)*
- *3/4 pound sliced smoked salmon*
- *1 medium cucumber*
- *2 medium tomatoes*

*STAPLES:*

- *Skim milk*
- *Salt*
- *Black peppercorns*

# salsa and sliced eggs

## helpful hint

- *Use an egg slicer to quickly slice the eggs.*

## countdown

- *Hard boil the eggs.*
- *Slice cucumbers.*
- *Assemble dish.*

## shopping list

*TO BUY:*

*1 small jar no-sugar-added tomato salsa*

*1 medium cucumber*

*STAPLES:*

*Eggs*

*Salsa makes an appetizing garnish for the eggs. Choose mild or hot, according to your tastes. Keep hard-boiled eggs on hand, and this breakfast can be put together in minutes.*

## salsa and sliced eggs

*4 eggs*

*1 medium cucumber, peeled*

*½ cup no-sugar-added tomato salsa*

Place eggs in a small saucepan and cover with cold water. Bring to a boil. Reduce the heat and gently simmer for 12 minutes. Drain and rinse eggs under cold water. Peel and slice with an egg slicer or cut in half lengthwise.

Slice the cucumber in half crosswise; cut into 4 pieces lengthwise. Divide the egg slices between 2 plates and spoon with salsa. Arrange the cucumbers around the eggs and serve.

*Makes 2 servings.*

**ONE SERVING: 201** CALORIES, **15G** PROTEIN, **12G** CARBOHYDRATE **11G** FAT (**3G** SATURATED), **426MG** CHOLESTEROL, **511MG** SODIUM, **3G** FIBER

# pesto scramble

*Fresh basil, parsley, pine nuts, and Parmesan cheese are the ingredients of a good pesto. Using a pesto store-bought in the supermarket, you can make these scrambled eggs in just minutes. They can even be made in the microwave. • There are several very good varieties of pesto on supermarket shelves. Some are in jars, and others are located in the refrigerated case. Look for a pesto made with olive oil. • The eggs are served on a bed of wilted lettuce. Most people don't think of cooking lettuce. It develops a tasty, nutty flavor.*

## pesto scramble

*5 ounces washed, ready-to-eat, Italian-style salad (6 cups)*
*1 cup egg substitute*
*¼ cup prepared pesto*
*2 teaspoons olive oil*
*2 tablespoons freshly grated Parmesan cheese*

Place the lettuce in a microwave-safe bowl and microwave on high for 3 minutes. Place on 2 plates. Mix egg substitute and pesto together. Heat the oil in a medium-size nonstick skillet on high. Reduce the heat to low or remove the pan from the heat; add the egg mixture. Scramble about 1 minute, or until desired doneness. Serve over the lettuce. Sprinkle with Parmesan cheese.

*Makes 2 servings.*

**ONE SERVING: 279** CALORIES, **18G** PROTEIN, **10G** CARBOHYDRATE **18G** FAT (**5G** SATURATED), **236MG** CHOLESTEROL, **147MG** SODIUM, **1G** FIBER

## helpful hints

- *If you don't have a microwave oven, sauté the lettuce for about 1 minute in a skillet, remove to a plate, and scramble the egg in the same skillet.*
- *Buy good quality Parmesan cheese and ask the grocer to grate it for you or chop it in the food processor yourself. Freeze extra for quick use later—simply spoon out what you need and leave the rest frozen.*
- *Any type of washed, ready-to-eat lettuce can be used.*

## countdown

- *Microwave lettuce.*
- *Make scrambled eggs.*

## shopping list

*TO BUY:*

*1 small container prepared pesto*
*1 bag washed, ready-to-eat, Italian-style salad (5 ounces needed)*

*STAPLES:*

*Olive oil*
*Egg substitute*
*Parmesan cheese*

# sunny-side-up swiss melt

*Eggs sunny side up are an American tradition. Here's a variation on the theme.*

## sunny-side-up swiss melt

- *Several leaves washed, ready-to-eat lettuce (about 1 cup)*
- *1 cucumber, peeled and sliced*
- *2 teaspoons olive oil*
- *2 large eggs*
- *Salt and freshly ground black pepper to taste*
- *4 slices reduced-fat Swiss cheese (3 ounces)*

Place the lettuce on a plate and microwave on high for 1 minute. Divide the lettuce and cucumber between 2 plates, and heat the olive oil in a medium-size nonstick skillet on medium high. Break the eggs into the skillet, and sprinkle with salt and pepper to taste. Cover and cook for 2 minutes. Remove the lid and place the cheese over the egg yolks. Cover and cook 1 minute. Serve the eggs on the cooked lettuce. *Makes 2 servings.*

**ONE SERVING: 265** CALORIES, **23G** PROTEIN, **8G** CARBOHYDRATE, **17G** FAT (**6G** SATURATED), **236MG** CHOLESTEROL, **147MG** SODIUM, **1G** FIBER

### helpful hints

- *If you like your egg yolk cooked through, flip the egg over before adding the cheese.*
- *To determine the weight of each slice of cheese, divide the package weight by the number of slices. With most brands, 1 slice equals 3/4 ounce.*

### countdown

- *Microwave lettuce.*
- *Slice cucumber.*
- *Cook egg.*

### shopping list

*TO BUY:*

*1 package sliced reduced-fat Swiss cheese (3 ounces needed)*

*1 package washed, ready-to-eat lettuce*

*1 medium cucumber*

*STAPLES:*

*Olive oil*

*Eggs*

*Salt*

*Black peppercorns*

# sizzling ham and tomatoes

*This is a quick, 5-minute breakfast that can be made in a skillet, toaster oven, broiler, or microwave oven.*

## sizzling ham and tomatoes

*1/2 pound sliced lean ham*
*2 small tomatoes, sliced*
*2 teaspoons olive oil*
*Salt and freshly ground black pepper to taste*

Sauté the ham in a medium-size nonstick skillet over medium-high heat for 2 minutes, or until ham begins to brown. Place tomatoes on 2 plates and drizzle with olive oil. Sprinkle with salt and pepper to taste. Divide the ham between the plates and serve. *Makes 2 servings.*

**ONE SERVING: 305** CALORIES, **30G** PROTEIN, **12G** CARBOHYDRATE **16G** FAT (**5G** SATURATED), **136MG** CHOLESTEROL, **797MG** SODIUM, **3G** FIBER

### helpful hint

- *Look for low-fat ham in the deli. Stay away from honey-baked ham.*

### countdown

- *Preheat broiler.*
- *Broil ham.*
- *Assemble dish.*

### shopping list

*TO BUY:*

*1/2 pound sliced lean ham*
*2 small tomatoes*

*STAPLES:*

*Olive oil*
*Salt*
*Black peppercorns*

# florentine eggs and ham

## helpful hint

- *Buy good quality Parmesan cheese and ask the grocer to grate it for you or chop it in the food processor yourself. Freeze extra for quick use later—simply spoon out what you need and leave the rest frozen.*

## countdown

- *Make spinach.*
- *Make ham and eggs.*

## shopping list

*TO BUY:*

*1/2 pound sliced lean ham*

*1 bag washed, ready-to-eat fresh spinach (10 ounces needed)*

*STAPLES:*

*Eggs*

*Parmesan cheese*

*Olive oil*

*Salt*

*Black peppercorns*

*Cooking the washed, ready-to-eat spinach in a microwave oven makes this a 15-minute breakfast.*

## florentine eggs and ham

*8 cups washed, ready-to-eat fresh spinach (10 ounces)*

*2 tablespoons freshly grated Parmesan cheese*

*Salt and freshly ground black pepper to taste*

*1/2 pound sliced lean ham (about 8 slices), cut into strips*

*2 teaspoons olive oil*

*2 eggs*

Place the spinach in a microwave-safe bowl and microwave on high for 5 minutes. Sprinkle with the Parmesan cheese, and season with salt and pepper to taste. Chop the cooked spinach into bite-size pieces, and divide between 2 plates.

Set a medium-size nonstick skillet over medium heat. Add the ham and sauté 2 minutes, or until slightly browned. Divide evenly over the beds of spinach

Add the olive oil to the same skillet. Break the eggs into the skillet and fry until set, about 1 minute. Using a spatula, gently turn the eggs over. Sprinkle with salt and pepper to taste. Serve the eggs over the ham and spinach.

*Makes 2 servings.*

**ONE SERVING: 337** CALORIES, **37G** PROTEIN, **10G** CARBOHYDRATE **19G** FAT (**5G** SATURATED), **270MG** CHOLESTEROL, **1501MG** SODIUM, **7G** FIBER

# turkey sausage and denver sauté

*Here's a tasty breakfast made without eggs. Frozen, diced onions and green bell peppers are available in most markets. I use them when really pressed for time. The flavor and texture are slightly different, but the results are good and save chopping time.*

## turkey sausage and denver sauté

- *8 cups washed, ready-to-eat fresh spinach (10 ounces)*
- *Salt and freshly ground black pepper to taste*
- *2 teaspoons olive oil*
- *2 low-fat turkey sausage links, cut into ½-inch slices (6 ounces)*
- *4 slices yellow onion (½ cup)*
- *1 medium-size green bell pepper, seeded and sliced (1 cup)*
- *6 button mushrooms, sliced (1 cup)*

Place the spinach in a microwave-safe bowl and microwave on high for 5 minutes. Add salt and pepper to taste. Divide the spinach between 2 plates. Heat the olive oil in a nonstick skillet on medium high. Add sausages, onion, bell pepper, and mushrooms. Sauté 5 minutes or until sausages are cooked through. Season with salt and pepper to taste. Spoon over spinach.

*Makes 2 servings.*

**ONE SERVING: 271** CALORIES, **22G** PROTEIN, **18G** CARBOHYDRATE, **13G** FAT (**3G** SATURATED), **45MG** CHOLESTEROL, **715MG** SODIUM, **7G** FIBER

### helpful hints

- *There are several types of low-fat turkey sausage links available in the supermarkets, ranging in flavor from mild to spicy-hot. Choose whichever type fits your palate. To determine the weight of each sausage, divide the package weight by the number of sausages.*
- *To save time, buy sliced mushrooms.*
- *If using whole mushrooms, clean them with a damp paper towel.*

### countdown

- *Microwave spinach.*
- *Sauté sausage and vegetables.*

### shopping list

*TO BUY:*

- *1 small package low-fat turkey sausage links (6 ounces needed)*
- *1 small bag washed, ready-to-eat fresh spinach*
- *1 medium-size green bell pepper*
- *1 small package button mushrooms*

*STAPLES:*

- *Yellow onion*
- *Olive oil*
- *Salt*
- *Black peppercorns*

# sweet pepper and turkey omelette

## helpful hints

- *To speed cooking the bell peppers, place them in a microwave-safe bowl and microwave on high for 2 minutes, and then sauté them with the turkey a few seconds before adding the eggs.*
- *Any mixture of bell peppers can be used for a colorful effect: red, yellow, green, orange, or purple. Make sure you have at least 4 cups of sliced peppers.*

## countdown

- *Preheat broiler.*
- *Prepare ingredients.*
- *Make omelette.*

## shopping list

*TO BUY:*

*6 ounces sliced smoked turkey breast*

*1 small bunch fresh parsley*

*1 medium-size red bell pepper*

*1 medium-size yellow bell pepper*

*STAPLES:*

*Egg substitute*

*Olive oil*

*Salt*

*Black peppercorns*

*Colorful sweet peppers flavor this tasty omelette—and it takes only 20 minutes from start to finish. The recipe can easily be doubled, saving half for the next day. Simply rewarm in a microwave for about 2 minutes on high.*

## sweet pepper and turkey omelette

*1 cup egg substitute*

*½ cup chopped fresh parsley leaves*

*Salt and freshly ground black pepper to taste*

*2 teaspoons olive oil*

*1 medium-size red bell pepper, sliced (2 cups)*

*1 medium-size yellow bell pepper, sliced (2 cups)*

*6 ounces sliced smoked turkey breast, diced*

Preheat the broiler. Combine the egg substitute and parsley. Add salt and pepper to taste.

Heat a medium-size nonstick skillet on medium high and add the oil. Sauté the bell peppers for 5 minutes. Add the egg mixture and turkey, and let set 2 minutes. Place under broiler for 3 minutes. Remove from the broiler, cut in half, slide out of the skillet, and serve hot.

*Makes 2 servings.*

**ONE SERVING: 289** CALORIES, **39G** PROTEIN, **13G** CARBOHYDRATE **8G** FAT (**2G** SATURATED), **60MG** CHOLESTEROL, **295MG** SODIUM, **0G** FIBER

# smoked chicken and cheddar grill

*This is an on-the-go breakfast that can be made in 5 minutes using a toaster oven or broiler. Any type of lean or low-fat deli meat can be used.*

## smoked chicken and cheddar grill

*2 large cucumbers, peeled and sliced on the diagonal*
*2 tablespoons mayonnaise made with soybean or olive oil*
*6 ounces sliced roasted chicken breast*
*Salt and freshly ground black pepper to taste*
*2 slices reduced-fat cheddar cheese (1 1/2 ounces)*

Preheat the broiler. Place the cucumbers on a foil-lined baking tray and spread the slices with mayonnaise. Top with the chicken slices and season with salt and pepper to taste.

Tear the cheese into pieces to cover the chicken. Place in a toaster oven or under the broiler for 1 minute or until cheese melts. Divide between 2 plates and serve.

*Makes 2 servings.*

**ONE SERVING: 351** CALORIES, **34G** PROTEIN, **9G** CARBOHYDRATE, **20G** FAT (**5G** SATURATED), **92MG** CHOLESTEROL, **329MG** SODIUM, **2G** FIBER

### helpful hints

- *Slice the cucumber on the diagonal for a larger surface area and oval-shaped slice.*
- *To determine the weight of each slice of cheese, divide the package weight by the number of slices. With most brands, 1 slice equals 3/4 ounce.*

### countdown

- *Preheat broiler or toaster oven.*
- *Complete recipe.*

### shopping list

*TO BUY:*

*1 package sliced reduced-fat cheddar cheese (1 1/2 ounces needed)*
*6 ounces sliced roasted chicken breast*
*2 large cucumbers*

*STAPLES:*

*Mayonnaise made with soybean or olive oil*
*Salt*
*Black peppercorns*

# devilish eggs

## helpful hint

- *The easiest way to chop chives is to cut them with a scissors.*

## countdown

- *Hard boil the eggs.*
- *Prepare the filling.*

## shopping list

*TO BUY:*

*1 small bunch fresh chives or 1 jar freeze-dried*

*STAPLES:*

*Celery*
*Eggs*
*Mayonnaise*
*Dijon mustard*
*Cayenne pepper*
*Salt*
*Black peppercorns*

*Deviled eggs are a classic comfort food that are coming back into style. They can be made ahead, stored in the refrigerator, and easily carried with you for a breakfast or lunch on the run. In fact, it's a good idea to keep a few hard-boiled eggs on hand for quick meals or snacks.*

## devilish eggs

*6 eggs (only 2 yolks used)*
*2 tablespoons mayonnaise made with soybean or olive oil*
*2 teaspoons Dijon mustard*
*Large pinch of cayenne pepper*
*2 tablespoons snipped fresh chives*
*Salt and freshly ground black pepper to taste*
*8 celery stalks, cut into 4-inch pieces*

Place the eggs in a small saucepan and cover with cold water. Set over medium-high heat and bring to a boil. Reduce the heat to low and gently simmer for 12 minutes. Drain, and then fill the pan with cold water. When the eggs are cool to the touch, peel and cut in half lengthwise. Remove and discard the yolks from 4 of the eggs. Set the egg whites on 2 plates. Place the remaining 2 whole eggs in the bowl of a food processor or mash with a fork in a mixing bowl. Add the mayonnaise, mustard, cayenne pepper, and chives. Season with salt and pepper to taste. Process until smooth. Fill the egg whites with the mixture. Serve with celery.

*Makes 2 servings.*

**ONE SERVING: 251** CALORIES, **16G** PROTEIN, **14G** CARBOHYDRATE, **18G** FAT (**3G** SATURATED), **218MG** CHOLESTEROL, **653MG** SODIUM, **4G** FIBER

# swiss scramble with spring onions

*This breakfast can be made in 15 minutes or less. Swiss cheese, bell peppers, and scallions add flavor and color to the light eggs.*

## swiss scramble with spring onions

- *2 teaspoons olive oil*
- *2 medium-size green bell peppers, sliced (2 cups)*
- *2 whole eggs*
- *6 egg whites*
- *2 cups sliced scallions*
- *4 slices reduced-fat Swiss cheese (3 ounces), torn into small pieces*
- *Salt and freshly ground black pepper to taste*

Heat the oil in a medium-size nonstick skillet. Add the bell peppers and sauté for 3 minutes. Combine the whole eggs, egg whites, scallions, and Swiss cheese in a medium-size bowl, and season with salt and pepper to taste. Add to the skillet and scramble 2 minutes, or until cooked to desired doneness. Spoon onto 2 plates and serve.

*Makes 2 servings.*

**ONE SERVING: 346** CALORIES, **35G** PROTEIN, **15G** CARBOHYDRATE **17G** FAT (**6G** SATURATED), **236MG** CHOLESTEROL, **311MG** SODIUM, **0G** FIBER

### helpful hints

- *Egg substitute can be used instead of whole eggs for this recipe.*
- *Any type of reduced-fat cheese can be used.*
- *To determine the weight of each slice of cheese, divide the package weight by the number of slices. With most brands, 1 slice equals 3⁄4 ounce.*

### countdown

- *Prepare all ingredients.*
- *Make spinach.*
- *Make eggs.*

### shopping list

*TO BUY:*

*1 package sliced reduced-fat Swiss cheese (3 ounces needed)*

*2 medium-size green bell peppers*

*2 bunches scallions (16 scallions needed)*

*STAPLES:*

*Olive oil*

*Eggs*

*Salt*

*Black peppercorns*

# stuffed endive with ham and cottage cheese

## helpful hints

- *Buy large heads of endive. The larger leaves are easier to fill.*
- *The best way to clean endive is to wipe the outer leaves with a damp paper towel. Try not to soak the leaves in water, as they tend to brown.*

## countdown

- *Chop ham, walnuts, and cheese.*
- *Fill endive.*

## shopping list

*TO BUY:*

*1 carton low-fat cottage cheese (8 ounces needed)*

*10 ounces sliced lean ham*

*1 small package walnut pieces (2 ounces needed)*

*2 medium heads Belgian endive*

*STAPLES:*

*Salt*

*Black peppercorns*

*Walnuts, ham, and cottage cheese make a crunchy, flavorful stuffing for endive spears. This is a good on-the-go breakfast. It takes just seconds to blend the stuffing to a creamy consistency. It's also great as hors d'oeuvres or a quick snack.*

## stuffed endive with ham and cottage cheese

*10 ounces sliced lean ham (about 10 slices)*

*24 walnuts (2 ounces)*

*½ cup low-fat cottage cheese*

*Salt and freshly ground black pepper to taste*

*2 medium heads Belgian endive, leaves separated*

Chop the ham, walnuts, and cottage cheese in a food processor. Add salt and pepper to taste.

Spread the mixture into wide base of each endive leaf.

*Makes 2 servings.*

**ONE SERVING: 432** CALORIES, **39G** PROTEIN, **11G** CARBOHYDRATE, **27G** FAT (**6G** SATURATED), **72MG** CHOLESTEROL, **1425MG** SODIUM, **2G** FIBER

# grilled portobello and canadian bacon omelette

*Canadian bacon, mushrooms, and scallions flavor this egg white omelette. Look for lean or low-fat Canadian bacon. There are several brands available in the supermarket, and they are all packaged to keep several weeks in the refrigerator. I always buy extra to have on hand for snacks or lunch.*

## grilled portobello and canadian bacon omelette

*8 egg whites*
*1 cup sliced scallions*
*Salt and freshly ground black pepper to taste*
*2 teaspoons olive oil*
*1/2 pound sliced portobello mushrooms (4 cups)*
*1/2 pound sliced lean Canadian bacon, diced*

Preheat the broiler. Combine the egg whites and scallions in a small mixing bowl; season with salt and pepper to taste. Heat the oil in a medium-size nonstick skillet on medium high. Add the mushrooms and Canadian bacon; sauté for 3 minutes. Add the egg mixture and let set for 2 minutes. Place under the broiler for 3 minutes, or until just cooked. Cut the omelette in half, slide out of the skillet, and serve. *Makes 2 servings.*

**ONE SERVING: 297** CALORIES, **40G** PROTEIN, **7G** CARBOHYDRATE, **11G** FAT (**3G** SATURATED), **53MG** CHOLESTEROL, **1208MG** SODIUM, **0G** FIBER

### helpful hints

- *Any type of mushrooms can be used for this recipe.*
- *If you prefer, cover the omelette with a lid in lieu of finishing it under the broiler.*
- *To save time, use presliced portobello mushrooms. If the slices are too large, cut them in half.*
- *Use a skillet with an ovenproof handle to go under broiler.*

### countdown

- *Preheat broiler.*
- *Make omelette.*

### shopping list

*TO BUY:*

*1/2 pound sliced lean Canadian bacon*
*1 bunch scallions (8 scallions needed)*
*1/2 pound sliced portobello mushrooms*

*STAPLES:*

*Eggs*
*Olive oil*
*Salt*
*Black peppercorns*

# cheddar frittata with sausage

## helpful hints

- *2 whole eggs plus 6 egg whites can be used instead of the egg substitute.*
- *There are several types of low-fat turkey sausage links available in the supermarkets, ranging in flavor from mild to spicy-hot. Choose whichever type fits your palate. To determine the weight of each sausage, divide the package weight by the number of sausages.*

## countdown

- *Preheat oven to 400 degrees.*
- *Prepare ingredients.*
- *Make frittata.*

## shopping list

*TO BUY:*

*1 small package shredded, reduced-fat cheddar cheese (2 ounces needed)*

*1 package low-fat turkey sausage (6 ounces needed)*

*1 can sliced water chestnuts*

*1 medium-size red bell pepper*

*1 small bunch arugula*

*STAPLES:*

*Olive oil*

*Egg substitute*

*Red onion*

*Celery*

*Salt*

*Black peppercorns*

*A frittata is a little like a crustless quiche and takes about 10 minutes to cook. It's great for breakfast, and when cooled and cut into squares, it makes great hors d'oeuvres or snacks.*

## cheddar frittata with sausage

*2 teaspoons olive oil*

*½ cup sliced red onion*

*1 medium-size red bell pepper, sliced (2 cups)*

*2 celery stalks, sliced (1 cup)*

*2 low-fat turkey sausage links, cut into ½-inch slices (6 ounces)*

*1 cup sliced and drained water chestnuts*

*1 cup egg substitute*

*1 cup arugula, washed and sliced*

*½ cup shredded, reduced-fat cheddar cheese (2 ounces)*

*Salt and freshly ground black pepper to taste*

Preheat the oven to 400 degrees. Heat the olive oil in a medium-size nonstick skillet on medium high. Sauté the onion, bell pepper, celery, sausages, and water chestnuts on high 3 minutes. Combine the egg substitute, arugula, and cheese in a medium-size bowl; season with salt and pepper to taste. Reduce the heat to medium, and pour the egg mixture into skillet. Swirl in the pan to cover vegetables. Let set for 3 minutes. Transfer to the oven for 7 minutes, or until the eggs set to the desired consistency. Cut the frittata in half, slide out of the skillet onto 2 plates, and serve.

*Makes 2 servings.*

**ONE SERVING: 396** CALORIES, **36G** PROTEIN, **20G** CARBOHYDRATE **19G** FAT (**7G** SATURATED), **65MG** CHOLESTEROL, **1088MG** SODIUM, **3G** FIBER

# quick start lunches

# mozzarella tomato tower over mesclun greens

## helpful hint

- *Yellow tomatoes make an attractive alternative to using red ones.*

## countdown

- *Prepare ingredients.*
- *Assemble salad.*

## shopping list

*TO BUY:*

*1 small package shredded, reduced-fat mozzarella cheese (8 ounces needed)*

*1 small package pine nuts*

*2 medium tomatoes*

*1 small bunch fresh basil*

*1 bag washed, ready-to-eat mesclun or field greens*

*STAPLES:*

*Olive oil*

*No-sugar-added oil and vinegar dressing*

*Salt*

*Black peppercorns*

*This tower is made by alternating tomato slices, mozzarella, and fresh basil until the tomato is reformed. It's a modern version of a tomato-mozzarella plate that's fun to serve and delicious, too.*

## mozzarella tomato tower over mesclun greens

*4 teaspoons olive oil, divided*

*2 medium tomatoes, cut into 1/2-inch slices*

*Salt and freshly ground black pepper to taste*

*1/2 pound shredded, reduced-fat mozzarella cheese*

*4 cups washed, ready-to-eat mesclun or field greens*

*2 tablespoons pine nuts*

*20 leaves fresh basil*

*2 tablespoons no-sugar-added oil and vinegar dressing*

Drizzle 2 tablespoons of the olive oil over the tomato slices, and season with salt and pepper to taste. Drizzle the remaining 2 tablespoons of olive oil over the cheese, tossing to coat well. Divide the field greens between 2 plates. Sprinkle with the pine nuts. Place the stem slices of the tomatoes in the center of the greens, skin side down. Sprinkle a little mozzarella on top of each. Place a few basil leaves on the mozzarella. Continue layering the tomato slices, mozzarella, and basil leaves until the tomatoes are rebuilt, ending with a sprinkling of mozzarella on top. Gently press the slices together with the palm of your hand. Drizzle the tomatoes and greens with the dressing and serve.

*Makes 2 servings.*

**ONE SERVING: 427** CALORIES, **35G** PROTEIN, **12G** CARBOHYDRATE, **24G** FAT (**6G** SATURATED), **16MG** CHOLESTEROL, **971MG** SODIUM, **4G** FIBER

# quick-take turkey bundles

*For the times when you don't have time to make a lunch, here is an idea for a quick take you can make and eat in minutes.*

## quick-take turkey bundles

- *3/4 pound sliced turkey breast*
- *18 to 20 leaves romaine or other lettuce*
- *1/2 cup deli coleslaw (3 1/2 ounces)*
- *2 small tomatoes, sliced*

Place a slice of turkey on a lettuce leaf. Add a spoonful of coleslaw and a slice of tomato. Fold the lettuce. Continue with additional lettuce leaves until all the turkey is used.

*Makes 2 servings.*

**ONE SERVING: 398** CALORIES, **52G** PROTEIN, **16G** CARBOHYDRATE **12G** FAT (**3G** SATURATED), **125MG** CHOLESTEROL, **269MG** SODIUM, **2G** FIBER

### helpful hints

- *Ask for the nutritional analysis of store-bought coleslaw, as some prepared versions have added sugar.*
- *Drain the coleslaw before use.*

### shopping list

*TO BUY:*

- *3/4 pound sliced turkey breast*
- *3 1/2 ounces deli coleslaw*
- *1 head romaine or other lettuce*
- *2 small tomatoes*

# basil-onion tuna salad wraps

## helpful hints

- *Use the tuna salad recipe given or use store-bought tuna salad. If the store-bought version is dripping in mayonnaise, drain it before using. Be sure to ask for the ingredients list of store-bought tuna salad, as some have sugar added.*
- *The easiest way to snip chives is with scissors.*

## countdown

- *Cut foil squares.*
- *Make tuna salad.*
- *Assemble wraps.*

## shopping list

*TO BUY:*

*1 (9-ounce) can tuna packed in water*
*1 head romaine lettuce*
*1 small bunch chives*
*1 small bunch basil*
*2 (6-ounce) containers alfalfa sprouts*

*STAPLES:*

*Red onion*
*Mayonnaise made from soybean or olive oil*
*Foil*
*Salt*
*Black peppercorns*

*You can find almost any type of food in wraps these days, including a whole dinner. I've used large lettuce leaves for the wrap in this recipe. These wraps are really portable and will last at least a day in the refrigerator. I take them out when we go sailing. They are a great fit for a day outside—easy to serve and very delicious.*

## basil-onion tuna salad wraps

*12 or 14 large romaine lettuce leaves, washed and dried*
*1 (9-ounce) can tuna packed in water, rinsed and drained*
*1/4 cup mayonnaise made from soybean or olive oil*
*1/2 cup snipped chives*
*1/2 cup diced red onion*
*Salt and freshly ground black pepper to taste*
*12 (11 x 4 inch) rectangles foil, parchment paper, or wax paper*
*2 cups fresh basil leaves, washed and dried*
*2 (6-ounce) packages alfalfa sprouts, tops only (2 cups)*

Crush the stems of the lettuce leaves so they lie flat. In a small mixing bowl, break the tuna up with a fork and stir in the mayonnaise, chives, and onion. Add salt and pepper to taste. Spread the foil pieces on the countertop. Place a romaine leaf on each square. Spoon some of the tuna salad on each leaf and top with the basil. Spoon the remaining tuna salad on top, and sprinkle with alfalfa sprouts. Roll up each leaf like a cigar, and wrap tightly in the foil. Seal the ends and slice in half crosswise. Use immediately or place in plastic bags and refrigerate until needed. *Makes 2 servings.*

**ONE SERVING: 421** CALORIES, **37G** PROTEIN, **12G** CARBOHYDRATE **25G** FAT (**3G** SATURATED), **66MG** CHOLESTEROL, **738MG** SODIUM, **1G** FIBER

# smoked trout salad with field greens

*It takes only a few minutes to put this tasty lunch together. A good quality smoked trout needs very little added to it to make a great meal.*

## smoked trout salad with field greens

- *6 ounces washed, ready-to-eat mesclun or field greens (6 cups)*
- *3/4 pound smoked trout*
- *2 1/2 tablespoons walnut pieces (1 ounce)*
- *2 teaspoons olive oil*
- *Salt and freshly ground black pepper to taste*

Place the mesclun on individual dishes. Flake trout into 1/2-inch pieces and place on top of the mesclun. Sprinkle with the walnuts, and drizzle with the oil. Season with salt and pepper to taste and serve. *Makes 2 servings.*

**ONE SERVING: 342** CALORIES, **31G** PROTEIN, **5G** CARBOHYDRATE, **22G** FAT (**4G** SATURATED), **77MG** CHOLESTEROL, **60MG** SODIUM, **2G** FIBER

### helpful hints

- *Any type of smoked fish can be used.*
- *Any type of lettuce can be used.*

### countdown

- *Prepare ingredients.*
- *Assemble salad.*

### shopping list

*TO BUY:*

*3/4 pound smoked trout*

*1 small package walnut pieces (1 ounce needed)*

*1 bag washed, ready-to-eat mesclun or field greens*

*STAPLES:*

*Olive oil*

*Salt*

*Black peppercorns*

# spicy roast beef and watercress wraps

## helpful hints

- *These travel well. Make them ahead, store in a plastic bag, and refrigerate until needed.*
- *Any type of lettuce can be used. Large leaves are needed.*

## countdown

- *Cut foil squares.*
- *Assemble recipe.*

## shopping list

*TO BUY:*

*3/4 pound thinly sliced lean roast beef*

*1 jar white or red horseradish*

*1 head Boston lettuce*

*1 small bunch arugula*

*1 small bunch watercress*

*STAPLES:*

*Mayonnaise made with soybean or olive oil*

*Foil*

*Arugula and horseradish give these roast beef wraps a spicy bite. Watercress adds a little crunch. Wraps are great finger food. This recipe uses large lettuce leaves instead of a tortilla to wrap around the filling.*

## spicy roast beef and watercress wraps

*12 large Boston lettuce leaves, washed and dried*

*12 (11 x 4 inch) rectangles foil, parchment paper, or wax paper*

*2 tablespoons mayonnaise made with soybean or olive oil*

*2 tablespoons horseradish*

*3/4 pound sliced lean roast beef*

*2 cups fresh arugula, washed and dried*

*12 small sprigs watercress, washed and dried*

Crush the stems of the lettuce leaves so they lie flat. Place the foil pieces on the countertop. Place one lettuce leaf on each piece of foil. Combine the mayonnaise and horseradish in a small bowl and spread on the leaves. Place one layer of roast beef on each leaf. Top with some arugula and a sprig of watercress. Roll up the lettuce into "cigars," and then wrap tightly in the foil. Seal the ends and slice in half crosswise to serve.

*Makes 2 servings.*

**ONE SERVING: 466** CALORIES, **52G** PROTEIN, **7G** CARBOHYDRATE, **24G** FAT (**6G** SATURATED), **144MG** CHOLESTEROL, **235MG** SODIUM, **1**G FIBER

# chopped salad with roasted chicken

*Here's a popular lunch or light dinner dish that appears on many restaurant menus. Cubes of vegetables and roasted chicken breast make a colorful lunch. The secret to this salad is to cut all of the ingredients into small, even cubes. This way every bite contains different flavor combinations. • This is a great way to use leftover chicken.*

## chopped salad with roasted chicken

- *2 celery stalks, chopped into 1/4-inch pieces (1 cup)*
- *1 medium-size green bell pepper, chopped into 1/4-inch pieces (1 cup)*
- *10 large red-leaf lettuce leaves, sliced into 1/4-inch pieces (4 cups)*
- *6 to 8 broccoli florets, chopped into 1/4-inch pieces (1 cup)*
- *1/4 cup no-sugar-added oil and vinegar dressing*
- *2 scallions, sliced into 1/4-inch pieces (1/4 cup)*
- *1/2 pound roasted chicken breast, skin removed and meat cut into 1/4-inch pieces*

Place the celery, bell pepper, lettuce, and broccoli in a medium-size bowl. Add the dressing and toss. Add the scallions and chicken, and toss again. Divide between 2 plates and serve.

*Makes 2 servings.*

**ONE SERVING: 401** CALORIES, **40G** PROTEIN, **14G** CARBOHYDRATE **23G** FAT (**4G** SATURATED), **96MG** CHOLESTEROL, **329MG** SODIUM, **2G** FIBER

## helpful hints

- *Several brands of roasted, skinless chicken are available already cut into small pieces. Use them for this recipe, but read the labels carefully to make sure there are no hidden carbs. Buy the original flavor rather than the honey-baked or barbecued variety.*
- *Any type of lean roasted meat can be used in the salad.*

## countdown

- *Prepare ingredients.*
- *Assemble salad.*

## shopping list

*TO BUY:*

*1/2 pound roasted chicken breast*
*1 medium-size green bell pepper*
*1 small head red-leaf lettuce*
*1 small package broccoli florets (6 or 8 florets needed)*
*1 small bunch scallions (2 scallions needed)*

*STAPLES:*

*Celery*
*No-sugar-added oil and vinegar dressing*

# curried chicken–stuffed tomatoes

## helpful hints

- *Toasting ground spices before they are used releases their natural oils and flavors. This step can be omitted if you're pressed for time.*
- *To help the tomato halves sit straight, cut a thin slice from the rounded ends.*

## countdown

- *Toast spices.*
- *Make recipe.*

## shopping list

*TO BUY:*

*6 ounces cooked chicken breast*

*1 small package slivered almonds (1 ounce needed)*

*1 jar curry powder*

*2 small tomatoes*

*1 medium-size red bell pepper*

*1 small head any type of lettuce (several leaves needed)*

*STAPLES:*

*Celery*

*Mayonnaise made with soybean or olive oil*

*Ground cumin*

*Salt*

*Black peppercorns*

*The pungent flavor of curry blends well with roasted chicken to make a tasty salad with a hint of India. Authentic curries are made with a blend of about 15 spices. For this quick salad, I use curry powder, which can be found in the spice section of the supermarket. This type of powder loses its flavor quickly and should be not used if more than three to four months old. This recipe works for any type of leftover meat. • Quick suggestion: Use deli chicken salad and add the other ingredients to it. Ask for the nutritional analysis, as some commercial chicken salads are made with sugar.*

## curried chicken–stuffed tomatoes

*1 tablespoon curry powder*

*2 teaspoons ground cumin*

*2 small tomatoes*

*2 tablespoons mayonnaise made with soybean or olive oil*

*Salt and freshly ground black pepper to taste*

*6 ounces cooked chicken breast, skin removed and meat chopped*

*1 celery stalk, diced (1/2 cup)*

*1/2 medium-size red bell pepper, diced (1 cup)*

*2 1/2 tablespoons slivered almonds (1 ounce)*

*Several lettuce leaves, washed and torn into bite size pieces*

Toast the curry powder and cumin in a toaster oven for 1 minute or microwave on high for 30 seconds. Stem the tomatoes and slice in half crosswise. Scoop the pulp, seeds, and juice from the tomato halves into the bowl of a food processor and blend until smooth. Alternatively, scoop the pulp onto a chopping board and the juice into a bowl. Chop the pulp by hand and add to the bowl. Set the tomato halves aside. Add the spices and the mayonnaise to the bowl. Add salt and pepper to taste. Combine until smooth. Stir in the chicken, celery, bell pepper, and almonds. Taste for seasoning and add more if necessary.

Divide the lettuce between 2 plates and place the tomato halves on the lettuce. Fill the tomatoes with the chicken salad and serve.

*Makes 2 servings.*

**ONE SERVING: 381** CALORIES, **34G** PROTEIN, **15G** CARBOHYDRATE **23G** FAT (**3G** SATURATED), **77MG** CHOLESTEROL, **197MG** SODIUM, **2G** FIBER

# salmon balsamico on a bed of field greens

*Rich, flavorful salmon is easy to cook and very filling. The smooth, rich texture goes well with cool, crunchy salad greens and vegetables. • Jícama is a large root vegetable with a light brown skin and white, crunchy flesh. It can be eaten raw or cooked. It's usually placed next to other root vegetables in the produce department and can easily be confused with them. Read the signs carefully or ask for help in selecting it correctly.*

## salmon balsamico on a bed of field greens

*2 teaspoons olive oil*
*1/2 pound salmon fillet*
*Salt and freshly ground black pepper to taste*
*1/2 cup balsamic vinegar*
*2 cups peeled and diced jícama*
*4 cups washed, ready-to-eat mesclun salad or field greens*
*2 tablespoons no-sugar-added oil and vinegar dressing*

Heat the oil in a small nonstick skillet on medium high. Rinse salmon and pat dry with a paper towel. Sauté the salmon 3 minutes; turn and brown 3 more minutes, or longer if salmon is more than 1 inch thick. Sprinkle the cooked salmon with salt and pepper to taste, and set aside. Add the vinegar and jícama to the skillet and reduce about 1 minute, or until the liquid is syrupy. Divide the greens between 2 plates and toss with the salad dressing. Place the salmon on top of the greens. Spoon the glaze and jícama cubes on top and serve.

*Makes 2 servings.*

**ONE SERVING: 365** CALORIES, **30G** PROTEIN, **16G** CARBOHYDRATE **20G** FAT (**3G** SATURATED), **80MG** CHOLESTEROL, **158MG** SODIUM, **6G** FIBER

### helpful hints

- *Any type of fish fillet can be used.*
- *Water chestnuts can be substituted for the jícama.*

### countdown

- *Sauté salmon.*
- *Assemble salad.*

### shopping list

*TO BUY:*

*1/2 pound salmon fillet*
*1 bulb jícama*
*1 bag washed, ready-to-eat mesclun or field greens*

*STAPLES:*

*Olive oil*
*No-sugar-added oil and vinegar dressing*
*Balsamic vinegar*
*Salt*
*Black peppercorns*

# quick-take ham and cucumber parcels

## helpful hints

- *These travel well. Make them ahead, store in a plastic bag, and refrigerate until needed.*
- *Any type of lettuce can be used. Large leaves are needed.*

## shopping list

*TO BUY:*

*3/4 pound sliced lean ham*

*1 head romaine or other lettuce*

*2 medium cucumbers*

*STAPLES:*

*Dijon mustard*

*For the days when you don't have time to make a lunch, here is an idea for a quick take you can prepare and eat in minutes.*

## quick-take ham and cucumber parcels

*3/4 pound sliced lean ham*
*18–20 leaves romaine or other lettuce*
*1/4 cup Dijon mustard*
*2 medium cucumbers, sliced*

Place 1 slice of ham on a lettuce leaf. Spread the ham with Dijon mustard. Add a few slices of cucumber. Fold the lettuce. Continue with additional lettuce leaves until all the ham is used.

*Makes 2 servings.*

**ONE SERVING: 318** CALORIES, **38G** PROTEIN, **16G** CARBOHYDRATE **11G** FAT (**3G** SATURATED), **80MG** CHOLESTEROL, **2218MG** SODIUM, **3G** FIBER

# greek salad

*With the help of the supermarket deli, you can make this salad in less than 5 minutes. A traditional Greek salad has olives, feta cheese, radishes, and good olive oil. You can also add sweet pimentos, caperberries, and anchovies, all of which can be found on the supermarket shelves. Use this recipe as the base and build your own salad with other fresh vegetables.*

## greek salad

- *2 tablespoons no-sugar-added oil and vinegar dressing*
- *2 teaspoons dried oregano or 2 tablespoons fresh*
- *6 cups washed, ready-to-eat lettuce*
- *1 medium cucumber, peeled and sliced*
- *12 black olives, chopped (preferably kalamata)*
- *8 radishes, sliced (1/2 cup)*
- *8 scallions, sliced (1 cup)*
- *1/4 cup drained capers*
- *1/2 pound medium-sliced lean deli turkey breast*
- *3 ounces crumbled reduced-fat feta cheese (2/3 cup)*
- *Freshly ground black pepper to taste*

Combine the oil and vinegar dressing and oregano together in a salad bowl. Add the lettuce, cucumber, olives, radishes, scallions, and capers. Toss well. Slice the turkey breast into 1/2-inch strips. Sprinkle on top of the salad with the crumbled feta cheese. Add pepper to taste. Divide between 2 plates and serve.

*Makes 2 servings.*

**ONE SERVING: 455** CALORIES, **41G** PROTEIN, **15G** CARBOHYDRATE **25G** FAT (**9G** SATURATED), **118MG** CHOLESTEROL, **1639MG** SODIUM, **2G** FIBER

### helpful hints

- *Dried oregano is called for in this recipe for speed. Fresh oregano (available in most supermarkets) will add a sweeter flavor to the salad. Use it if you have time.*
- *If using dried oregano, make sure it is less than six months old.*
- *Any type of washed, ready-to-eat lettuce can be used.*
- *Crumbled, domestic feta cheese works fine in the salad.*

### countdown

- *Make salad dressing.*
- *Make salad.*

### shopping list

*TO BUY:*

- *1 package crumbled, reduced-fat feta cheese (3 ounces needed)*
- *1/2 pound medium-sliced lean deli turkey breast*
- *1 jar capers*
- *1 package black olives (preferably kalamata)*
- *1 bag washed, ready-to-eat lettuce*
- *1 medium cucumber*
- *1 small bunch radishes*
- *1 bunch scallions (8 needed)*

*STAPLES:*

- *No-sugar-added oil and vinegar dressing*
- *Dried oregano*
- *Black peppercornsfff*

# grilled cheddar and chicken salad

## helpful hints

- *Chop all ingredients in a food processor.*
- *A large toaster oven can be used instead of a broiler.*
- *To determine the weight of each slice of cheese, divide the package weight by the number of slices. With most brands, 1 slice equals 3/4 ounce.*

## countdown

- *Preheat broiler.*
- *Make chicken salad.*
- *Complete recipe.*

## shopping list

*TO BUY:*

*1 package sliced, reduced-fat, aged cheddar cheese (1 1/2 ounces needed)*

*1/2 pound roasted chicken breast*

*1 medium-size green bell pepper*

*1 small bunch fresh parsley*

*2 large tomatoes*

*STAPLES:*

*Yellow onion*

*Mayonnaise made with olive or soybean oil*

*Dijon mustard*

*Salt*

*Black peppercorns*

*This lunch can be made in 5 minutes by using either leftover chicken or roasted chicken from the supermarket. The cheese melts, providing a warm covering for the cool salad. There are several brands of roasted, skinless chicken available at the grocery. Use them for this recipe, but read the labels carefully to make sure there are no hidden carbs. Buy the original flavor rather than the honey-baked or barbecued variety.*

## grilled cheddar and chicken salad

*2 tablespoons mayonnaise made with olive or soybean oil*

*2 tablespoons warm water*

*2 tablespoons Dijon mustard*

*1/2 pound roasted chicken breast, chopped*

*1 medium-size green bell pepper, seeded and chopped (1 cup)*

*1/2 cup diced yellow onion*

*1/2 cup chopped fresh parsley*

*Salt and freshly ground black pepper to taste*

*2 large tomatoes, sliced*

*2 slices reduced-fat, aged cheddar cheese (1 1/2 ounces)*

Preheat the broiler. Combine the mayonnaise, water, and mustard in a medium-size bowl. Add the chicken, bell pepper, onion, and parsley. Add salt and pepper to taste, and toss well. Place the tomato slices on an ovenproof dish or on a foil-lined baking tray, and season with a little salt and pepper. Spread with chicken salad, and tear cheese slices into small pieces to fit over the chicken salad. Broil for 2 minutes, or until the cheese melts, and serve. *Makes 2 servings.*

**ONE SERVING: 434** CALORIES, **46G** PROTEIN, **14G** CARBOHYDRATE, **22G** FAT (**6G** SATURATED), **116MG** CHOLESTEROL, **723MG** SODIUM, **0G** FIBER

# chesapeake shrimp salad

*Juicy shrimp, well seasoned, and crunchy celery make a delicious, quick lunch. Old Bay is a crab and shrimp seasoning from Maryland available throughout the U.S. It's made with a blend of spices that go well with shellfish.*

## chesapeake shrimp salad

*1/4 cup mayonnaise made from soybean or olive oil*
*1 tablespoon Old Bay or Crab Boil seasoning*
*3/4 pound cooked shrimp, cut into 1/2-inch pieces*
*8 celery stalks, finely chopped (4 cups)*
*Salt and freshly ground black pepper to taste*
*12 or 14 large romaine lettuce leaves, washed and dried*

Combine the mayonnaise and Old Bay seasoning in a medium-size mixing bowl. Add the shrimp and celery, and season with salt and pepper to taste. Mix well. Serve on a bed of lettuce leaves.
*Makes 2 servings.*

**ONE SERVING: 443** CALORIES, **38G** PROTEIN, **17G** CARBOHYDRATE **26G** FAT (3.6G SATURATED), **708MG** CHOLESTEROL, **5MG** SODIUM, **2G** FIBER

## helpful hints

- *Any type of crab or shrimp boil can be used.*
- *Any type of lettuce can be used.*
- *Buy cooked shrimp from the fish department in the supermarket or buy a good quality frozen, cooked shrimp.*

## countdown

- *Prepare all ingredients.*
- *Assemble salad.*

## shopping list

*TO BUY:*

*3/4 pound cooked shrimp*
*1 small container Old Bay or Crab Boil seasoning*
*1 head romaine lettuce*

*STAPLES:*

*Celery*
*Mayonnaise made from soybean or olive oil*
*Salt*
*Black peppercorns*

# herbed chicken caesar salad

## helpful hints

- *Use the recipe below or purchase a low-carbohydrate, Caesar-salad dressing.*
- *Toasting walnuts can be tricky, as they burn quickly. Watch them carefully.*
- *To save cleaning time, use the same baking tray to toast the walnuts and broil the chicken.*
- *Buy good quality Parmesan cheese and ask the grocer to grate it for you or chop it in the food processor yourself. Freeze extra for quick use later—simply spoon out what you need and leave the rest frozen.*

## countdown

- *Preheat broiler.*
- *Make chicken.*
- *Make dressing.*
- *Assemble dish.*

## shopping list

*TO BUY:*

*1/2 pound boneless, skinless chicken breast*
*1 small package walnut pieces (1/2 ounce needed)*
*1 tin anchovies*
*1 lemon*
*1 small head romaine lettuce*

*STAPLES:*

*Eggs*
*Parmesan cheese*
*Red onion*
*Olive oil*
*Olive oil spray*
*Garlic*
*Dried oregano*
*Worcestershire sauce*
*Salt*
*Black peppercorns*

*Caesar salads are one of the most popular American lunches. Crisp lettuce and smooth, tangy dressing provide an enjoyable, mouth-watering combination. This is a recipe that you can easily make at home. • Here's a tip when ordering a Caesar salad at a restaurant: Ask for the salad without the croutons or remove them when the salad is served. Many salads come swimming in dressing, so ask for the dressing on the side and use only 2 tablespoons on your salad.*

## herbed chicken caesar salad

*2 tablespoons walnuts (1/2 ounce)*
*6 medium-size garlic cloves, crushed (divided)*
*2 teaspoons dried oregano*
*1/4 teaspoon freshly ground black pepper*
*Pinch of salt*
*Grated rind from 1 lemon (1/2 tablespoon)*
*2 tablespoons freshly squeezed lemon juice, divided (1 lemon)*
*2 egg whites*
*1/2 pound boneless, skinless chicken breast*
*Olive oil spray*
*4 anchovies, mashed*
*4 teaspoons Worcestershire sauce*
*4 teaspoons olive oil*
*1 small head romaine lettuce, washed and cut into pieces (about 6 cups)*
*4 slices red onion (1/2 cup)*
*2 tablespoons freshly grated Parmesan cheese*

Preheat the broiler. Line a baking tray with foil. Place the walnuts on tray and broil 1 minute, or until toasted. (Watch carefully to keep from burning.) Combine 2 garlic cloves, the oregano, pepper, salt, grated lemon rind, and 1/2 tablespoon of the lemon juice in a small bowl. In a separate bowl, whisk the egg whites lightly until just frothy. Dip the chicken into the egg whites, and then roll in the garlic-lemon mixture. Spray the foil-lined baking tray with olive oil. Place the coated chicken on the baking tray, and broil about 5 inches from the heat for 5 minutes. Turn and broil another 5 minutes. Remove from oven.

To make the dressing, place the anchovies, remaining lemon juice, 4 crushed garlic cloves, Worcestershire sauce, and olive oil in the bowl of a food processor and blend thoroughly, scraping down the sides several times. Alternatively, mix the ingredients together by hand, mashing the anchovies and garlic to blend well. Place the lettuce in a salad bowl and toss with half the dressing. Divide the salad between 2 plates, add the walnuts, and top with onion slices. Sprinkle with Parmesan cheese. Cut the chicken into thin slices and place on top. Spoon the remaining dressing over the top and serve.

*Makes 2 servings.*

**ONE SERVING: 442** CALORIES, **48G** PROTEIN, **11G** CARBOHYDRATE **24G** FAT (**5G** SATURATED), **101MG** CHOLESTEROL, **708MG** SODIUM, **1G** FIBER

# roasted portobellos stuffed with smoked trout and sun-dried tomatoes

*Large portobello mushroom caps have an earthy flavor and meaty texture. They can be roasted, grilled, or sautéed. This dish can be eaten warm or at room temperature, and it only takes about 15 minutes to make. • Curly endive, sometimes mistakenly called chicory, has lacy, green-trimmed leaves, but any type of lettuce can be used for this recipe.*

## roasted portobellos stuffed with smoked trout and sun-dried tomatoes

*Olive oil spray*

*4 large portobello mushroom caps, washed (1/2 pound)*

*Salt and freshly ground black pepper to taste*

*2 tablespoons mayonnaise made with olive or soybean oil*

*1 tablespoon freshly squeezed lemon juice (about 1/2 lemon)*

*1/4 cup horseradish*

*1/2 pound smoked trout or other smoked fish*

*1 cup drained, diced sun-dried tomatoes*

*Several leaves curly endive lettuce*

Preheat the oven to 450 degrees. Line a baking tray with foil and spray with olive oil. Place the mushrooms on the tray and spray both sides with olive oil until lightly coated. Bake for 5 minutes; turn and bake for 5 more minutes. Remove from the oven, and add salt and pepper to taste. Combine the mayonnaise, lemon juice, and horseradish in a medium-size mixing bowl. Flake the smoked trout into the mayonnaise mixture. Stir in the sun-dried tomatoes, blending well. Season with salt and pepper to taste. Spoon the mixture into the mushroom caps. Divide the lettuce between 2 plates, top with the stuffed mushroom caps, and serve.

*Makes 2 servings.*

**ONE SERVING: 476** CALORIES, **33G** PROTEIN, **17G** CARBOHYDRATE **30G** FAT (**5G** SATURATED), **82MG** CHOLESTEROL, **179MG** SODIUM, **4G** FIBER

### helpful hints

- *To clean whole mushrooms, wipe them gently with a damp paper towel.*
- *The smoked fish filling can be mixed in a food processor.*

### countdown

- *Preheat oven to 450 degrees.*
- *Roast mushrooms.*
- *Assemble dish.*

### shopping list

*TO BUY:*

*1/2 pound smoked trout or other smoked fish*

*1 jar white horseradish*

*1 jar diced sun-dried tomatoes*

*4 large portobello mushrooms (1/2 pound)*

*1 lemon*

*1 head curly endive lettuce*

*STAPLES:*

*Olive oil spray*

*Mayonnaise made with olive or soybean oil*

*Salt*

*Black peppercorns*

# quick start dinners

# shrimp scampi with roasted asparagus and italian greens

*When I made this scampi for my husband, he couldn't believe it took only 5 minutes to make the sauce. The secret is red vermouth. It adds spice and depth to fresh tomatoes and goes perfectly with the shrimp. • Roasting intensifies the flavor of fresh vegetables. The roasted asparagus takes only 15 minutes.*

## shrimp scampi

*2 teaspoons olive oil*
*6 medium-size garlic cloves, crushed*
*½ cup dry red vermouth*
*1 cup diced tomatoes*
*¾ pound large shrimp, shelled and deveined*
*½ cup chopped fresh parsley*
*Several drops hot pepper sauce*
*Salt and freshly ground black pepper to taste*

Heat the olive oil in a medium-size nonstick skillet on medium high. Sauté the garlic for a few seconds, then add the red vermouth and tomatoes. Cook 5 minutes. Add the shrimp and parsley, and cook 2 to 3 minutes until the shrimp are pink. Season with hot pepper sauce, salt, and pepper to taste. Divide between 2 plates and serve.
*Makes 2 servings.*

**ONE SERVING: 297** CALORIES, **37G** PROTEIN, **10G** CARBOHYDRATE **8G** FAT (**1G** SATURATED), **260MG** CHOLESTEROL, **282MG** SODIUM, **0G** FIBER

## roasted asparagus

*½ pound fresh asparagus*
*2 teaspoons olive oil*
*Salt and freshly ground black pepper to taste*

Preheat the oven to 400 degrees. Cut or snap off the 1-inch fibrous stem on the asparagus and discard. Slice the remaining asparagus into 2-inch pieces (you should have about 2½ cups). Line a baking tray with foil and spoon the oil onto the foil. Sprinkle the oil with salt and pepper to taste. Add the asparagus and roll in oil, making sure all the spears are coated with the oil and seasonings. Spread the asparagus into a single layer and roast in the oven for 5 minutes. Roll the asparagus in the oil to recoat and roast 10 more minutes for thick spears, 5 more minutes for thin ones. Remove from the oven and serve with the shrimp.
*Makes 2 servings.*

**ONE SERVING: 55** CALORIES, **2G** PROTEIN, **3G** CARBOHYDRATE, **5G** FAT (**1G** SATURATED), **0MG** CHOLESTEROL, **3MG** SODIUM, **2G** FIBER

## helpful hints

- *To save roasting time, the asparagus can be cooked in a microwave oven on high: 3 minutes for thin asparagus and 5 minutes for thick spears.*
- *Buy shelled shrimp or ask for the shrimp to be shelled while you complete your shopping. Most stores will do this for a small fee that is well worth the time saved in shelling them yourself.*

## countdown

- *Preheat oven to 400 degrees.*
- *Start asparagus.*
- *Make shrimp.*
- *Make Italian greens.*

## shopping list

*TO BUY:*
*¾ pound large shrimp*
*1 small bottle dry red vermouth*
*1 small bunch fresh parsley*
*1 medium tomato*
*½ pound asparagus*
*1 bag washed, ready-to-eat, Italian-style salad*

*STAPLES:*
*Olive oil*
*No-sugar-added oil and vinegar dressing*
*Garlic*
*Hot pepper sauce*
*Salt*
*Black peppercorns*

# shrimp scampi with roasted asparagus and italian greens *continued*

## italian greens

*4 cups washed, ready-to-eat, Italian-style salad*

*2 tablespoons no-sugar-added oil and vinegar dressing*

*Salt and freshly ground black pepper to taste*

Place the salad in a small bowl and drizzle with the dressing. Season with salt and pepper to taste. Toss well and serve.

*Makes 2 servings.*

**ONE SERVING: 84** CALORIES, **1G** PROTEIN, **2G** CARBOHYDRATE, **8G** FAT (**1G** SATURATED), **0MG** CHOLESTEROL, **81MG** SODIUM, **0G** FIBER

# asian ginger salmon with sesame broccoli and yellow bean salad

*This is a very simple 15-minute dinner. It's a basic recipe that you can use as a blueprint to make other similar dinners. Boneless, skinless chicken breast can be used instead of salmon, cauliflower instead of broccoli, and green beans instead of yellow.*

## asian ginger salmon

*Olive oil spray*
*3/4 pound salmon fillet*
*Salt and freshly ground black pepper to taste*
*2 tablespoons low-salt soy sauce*
*2 tablespoons water*
*2 tablespoons chopped fresh ginger*

Heat a nonstick skillet on medium high, and spray with olive oil. Add the salmon and brown 2 minutes. Turn, salt and pepper the cooked side, then brown the second side for 2 minutes. Lower the heat and sauté for 5 minutes. Combine the soy sauce, water, and ginger in a small bowl. Remove the salmon from skillet, add the soy sauce mixture to the skillet, and cook several seconds. Divide the salmon between 2 plates and spoon the sauce over the salmon.
*Makes 2 servings.*

**ONE SERVING: 310** CALORIES, **43G** PROTEIN, **2G** CARBOHYDRATE, **12G** FAT (**3G** SATURATED), **120MG** CHOLESTEROL, **714MG** SODIUM, **0G** FIBER

## sesame broccoli

*1/4 pound broccoli florets (2 cups)*
*2 teaspoons olive oil*
*1/4 cup sesame seeds*
*Salt and freshly ground black pepper to taste*

Place the broccoli in a microwave-safe bowl and microwave on high for 5 minutes. Alternatively, bring a pot of water to a boil and add the broccoli. Boil 2 minutes, and then drain. Heat the oil in a nonstick skillet on medium high. Sauté the broccoli and sesame seeds 3 to 4 minutes, or until the sesame seeds are golden and the broccoli is bright green, but crisp. Season with salt and pepper to taste. Serve with the salmon.
*Makes 2 servings.*

**ONE SERVING: 158** CALORIES, **7G** PROTEIN, **6G** CARBOHYDRATE, **14G** FAT (**2G** SATURATED), **0MG** CHOLESTEROL, **79MG** SODIUM, **2G** FIBER

## helpful hints

- *Broccoli and beans can be microwaved at the same time for 3 minutes on high.*
- *To save washing an extra pan, prepare the salmon and cover with foil to keep warm. Use same skillet to sauté the broccoli.*
- *A washed, ready-to-eat salad can be substituted for one of the vegetables.*
- *To chop fresh ginger quickly, cut it into small cubes and press through a garlic press with large holes. If using a press with small holes, just capture the juice that is squeezed out; it will give enough flavor for the recipe.*

## countdown

- *Make salmon.*
- *Make broccoli.*
- *Make yellow beans.*

## shopping list

*TO BUY:*
*3/4 pound salmon fillet*
*1 small package sesame seeds*
*1/2 pound yellow wax beans*
*1/4 pound broccoli florets*
*1 small piece fresh ginger*

# asian ginger salmon with sesame broccoli and yellow bean salad *continued*

*STAPLES:*

*Olive oil*

*Olive oil spray*

*No-sugar-added olive oil and vinegar dressing*

*Low-salt soy sauce*

*Salt*

*Black peppercorns*

## yellow bean salad

*½ pound yellow wax beans, trimmed and cut in half (2 cups)*

*2 tablespoons no-sugar-added olive oil and vinegar dressing*

*Salt and freshly ground black pepper to taste*

Place the beans in a microwave-safe bowl and microwave on high for 3 minutes. Alternatively, bring a pot of water to a boil and add the beans. Boil for 2 minutes, and then drain. Toss the cooked beans with the salad dressing. Season with salt and pepper to taste and serve.

*Makes 2 servings.*

**ONE SERVING: 119** CALORIES, **2G** PROTEIN, **10G** CARBOHYDRATE, **9G** FAT (**1G** SATURATED), **0MG** CHOLESTEROL, **79MG** SODIUM, **2G** FIBER

# pan-glazed balsamic chicken with roasted squash and snow peas

*Balsamic vinegar makes a zesty glaze for chicken—and adds very few calories in the process. • Roasting or broiling intensifies the flavor of vegetables. The squash cooks in the oven while you prepare the other two dishes.*

## pan-glazed balsamic chicken

*Olive oil spray*
*3/4 pound boneless, skinless chicken breast*
*Salt and freshly ground black pepper to taste*
*1/2 cup good quality balsamic vinegar*
*1/4 cup pine nuts*
*1 tablespoon Dijon mustard*

Heat a medium-size nonstick skillet on medium high, and spray with olive oil. Brown the chicken for 3 minutes, turn, and cook for another 3 minutes. Remove from the heat and cover with a lid; let sit for 3 minutes. Remove the chicken to a plate, sprinkle with salt and pepper to taste, and cover with a plate or foil to keep warm. In the same skillet, add the vinegar and pine nuts. Let cook on medium high to reduce—about 30 seconds, or until about half the amount of liquid remains. Add the mustard and mix well to make a smooth glaze. Return the chicken to the skillet, turning to coat both sides with the glaze. Cook another minute, then divide between 2 plates to serve, and spoon any remaining glaze on top. *Makes 2 servings.*

**ONE SERVING: 378** CALORIES, **54G** PROTEIN, **4G** CARBOHYDRATE, **11G** FAT (**2G** SATURATED), **144MG** CHOLESTEROL, **306MG** SODIUM, **0G** FIBER

### helpful hint

- *To save cleaning time, sauté the chicken and remove to a plate. Cover with another plate or foil to keep warm. Use the same skillet to sauté the snow peas.*

### countdown

- *Preheat broiler.*
- *Start squash.*
- *Make chicken.*
- *Sauté snow peas.*

### shopping list

*TO BUY:*

*3/4 pound boneless, skinless chicken breast*
*1 small package pine nuts*
*1/2 pound fresh snow peas*
*1/2 pound small yellow squash*
*1 medium-size red bell pepper*

*STAPLES:*

*Olive oil*
*Olive oil spray*
*Balsamic vinegar*
*Dijon mustard*
*Garlic*
*Salt*
*Black peppercorns*

# pan-glazed balsamic chicken with roasted squash and snow peas *continued*

## roasted squash

*Olive oil spray*
*2 teaspoons olive oil*
*2 medium-size garlic cloves, crushed*
*1 tablespoon water*
*½ pound small yellow squash, cut into 1-inch slices (2 cups)*
*1 medium-size red bell pepper, cut into 1-inch pieces (2 cups)*
*Salt and freshly ground black pepper to taste*

Preheat the broiler. Line a baking sheet with foil and spray with olive oil. Place the foil-lined sheet under the broiler 5 inches from heat. Combine the olive oil with garlic and water in a small mixing bowl. Remove the baking sheet from the broiler and place the vegetables on the sheet. Spoon half of the olive oil mixture over the vegetables and toss well. Spread the vegetables out to form a single layer. Broil 10 minutes.Turn the vegetables over and spoon with the remaining olive oil mixture. Broil another 10 minutes. Vegetables should be cooked through, but not black. Sprinkle with salt and pepper to taste. Serve with the chicken.

*Makes 2 servings.*

**ONE SERVING: 104** CALORIES, **3G** PROTEIN, **11G** CARBOHYDRATE, **7G** FAT (**1G** SATURATED), **0MG** CHOLESTEROL, **4MG** SODIUM, **1G** FIBER

## snow peas

*2 teaspoons olive oil*
*½ pound snow peas, trimmed (about 2 cups)*
*Salt and freshly ground black pepper to taste*

Heat the olive oil in a nonstick skillet on medium high. Add the snow peas and sauté 2 minutes, tossing continuously. Season with salt and pepper to taste. Serve with the chicken.

*Makes 2 servings.*

**ONE SERVING: 66** CALORIES, **2G** PROTEIN, **5G** CARBOHYDRATE, **5G** FAT (**1G** SATURATED), **0MG** CHOLESTEROL, **3MG** SODIUM, **2G** FIBER

# salsa-smothered tex-mex meat loaf with sliced avocado

*This moist, well-seasoned meat loaf smothered in spicy salsa makes a great, homey meal. By forming the meat into small loaves instead of one large loaf, it takes only 20 minutes to cook, rather than the usual 45 minutes to an hour. The heat circulates more quickly around the loaves. The cooked loaves will keep a day in the refrigerator. If you have time, double the recipe and form 4 loaves. Save the other two for another quick meal.*

## salsa-smothered tex-mex meat loaf

*Olive oil spray*
*¼ cup thinly sliced red onion*
*1 cup thinly sliced mushrooms*
*10 ounces ground veal*
*2 egg whites*
*Salt and freshly ground black pepper to taste*
*1 large tomato, diced (1¼ cups)*
*½ cup chopped fresh cilantro*
*1 small jalapeño pepper seeded and chopped (1 tablespoon)*
*½ teaspoon ground cumin*
*1 tablespoon freshly squeezed lime juice*

Preheat the oven to 400 degrees. Line a baking tray with foil and spray with olive oil. Heat a nonstick skillet on medium high and spray with olive oil. Add the onion and mushrooms, and sauté 5 minutes. Combine the vegetables with the ground veal and egg whites in a medium-size mixing bowl. Add salt and pepper to taste. Place the meat directly on the foil-lined baking tray and shape into 2 loaves about 6 x 3-inches each. Bake 20 minutes. While the loaves bake, combine the diced tomato, cilantro, jalapeño, cumin, and lime juice in a small bowl. Season with salt and pepper to taste. Spoon the salsa over the baked meat loaves and serve on 2 plates with the avocado.

*Makes 2 servings.*

**ONE SERVING: 407** CALORIES, **45G** PROTEIN, **13G** CARBOHYDRATE **17G** FAT (**10G** SATURATED), **125MG** CHOLESTEROL, **164MG** SODIUM, **2G** FIBER

## sliced avocado

*½ small avocado, pitted, peeled, and sliced*
*1 tablespoon no-sugar-added oil and vinegar dressing*
*Salt and freshly ground black pepper to taste*

Arrange the avocado slices next to the meat loaves and drizzle with dressing. Season with salt and pepper to taste. Serve with the meat loaf.

*Makes 2 servings.*

**ONE SERVING: 114** CALORIES, **1G** PROTEIN, **3G** CARBOHYDRATE, **12G** FAT (**2G** SATURATED), **0MG** CHOLESTEROL, **43MG** SODIUM, **2G** FIBER

### helpful hints

- *Use the salsa recipe given or purchase a no–sugar-added version.*
- *Cilantro is used in both recipes. Chop all at one time and divide accordingly.*

### countdown

- *Preheat oven to 400 degrees.*
- *Make meat loaf.*
- *Prepare avocado.*

### shopping list

*TO BUY:*

*10 ounces ground veal*
*1 small avocado*
*1 small package sliced mushrooms (2 ounces needed)*
*2 limes*
*1 large tomato*
*1 small bunch cilantro*
*1 small jalapeño pepper*

*STAPLES:*

*Olive oil spray*
*Red onion*
*Eggs*
*No-sugar-added oil and vinegar dressing*
*Ground cumin*
*Salt*
*Black peppercorns*

# chicken marsala with roman spinach and radicchio salad

*The rich, smoky flavor of Sicily's Marsala wine makes a quick glaze for this chicken. To help cook the chicken faster, I flatten the chicken breast to about 1/2 inch thick. This also enlarges the surface area available to absorb the glaze.*

### helpful hints

- *To save cleaning a second skillet, use the same one to cook the chicken and spinach.*
- *Buy an inexpensive Marsala wine for this recipe. It also goes well with veal, pork, and turkey.*

### countdown

- *Make salad and set aside.*
- *Make chicken.*
- *Make spinach.*

### shopping list

*TO BUY:*

*1 small carton heavy whipping cream*

*10 ounces boneless, skinless chicken breast*

*1 bottle medium-dry Marsala wine*

*1 small head radicchio lettuce*

*1 small bunch radishes*

*1 bag washed, ready-to-eat fresh spinach (10 ounces needed)*

*STAPLES:*

*Olive oil*

*No-sugar-added oil and vinegar dressing*

*Garlic*

*Salt*

*Black peppercorns*

## chicken marsala

*10 ounces boneless, skinless chicken breasts*

*2 teaspoons olive oil*

*Salt and freshly ground black pepper to taste*

*1/2 cup medium-dry Marsala wine*

*1 tablespoon heavy whipping cream*

Remove all visible fat from the chicken. Pound with the palm of your hand to flatten to about 1/2 inch thick. Heat the oil in a nonstick skillet on medium high. Brown the chicken, about 2 minutes on each side. Season each cooked side with salt and pepper to taste. Add the Marsala wine to pan and continue to cook for 2 to 3 minutes. Remove the chicken to 2 plates. Continue to simmer the sauce for about 1 minute to reduce. Add the cream, and season with salt and pepper to taste. Spoon the sauce over the chicken, and cover with foil to keep warm before serving.

*Makes 2 servings.*

**ONE SERVING: 394** CALORIES, **45G** PROTEIN, **7G** CARBOHYDRATE, **14G** FAT (**4G** SATURATED), **131MG** CHOLESTEROL, **113MG** SODIUM, **0G** FIBER

## roman spinach

*8 cups fresh washed, ready-to-eat fresh spinach (10 ounces)*

*2 teaspoons olive oil*

*4 medium-size garlic cloves, crushed*

*Salt and freshly ground black pepper to taste*

Place the spinach in a large saucepan (do not add water). Cover and cook 5 minutes, tossing once or twice, then drain. Alternatively, place in a microwave-safe bowl and microwave on high for 5 minutes. Heat the olive oil in the same saucepan on medium, and add the garlic. Stir for about 30 seconds. Return the spinach to the pan. Season with salt and pepper to taste. Serve with the chicken.

*Makes 2 servings.*

**ONE SERVING: 97** CALORIES, **7G** PROTEIN, **10G** CARBOHYDRATE, **5G** FAT (**1G** SATURATED), **0MG** CHOLESTEROL, **172MG** SODIUM, **7G** FIBER

# chicken marsala with roman spinach and radicchio salad *continued*

## radicchio salad

*1 small head radicchio, torn into bite-size pieces (3 cups)*
*12 radishes*
*1 tablespoon no-sugar-added oil and vinegar dressing*
*Salt and freshly ground black pepper to taste*

Divide the radicchio leaves between 2 plates, and grate the radishes on top. Alternatively, grate the radishes in a food processor fitted with a grating blade. Spoon the dressing over the salad and season with salt and pepper to taste before serving.

*Makes 2 servings.*

**ONE SERVING: 103** CALORIES, **1G** PROTEIN, **6G** CARBOHYDRATE, **9G** FAT (**1G** SATURATED), **0MG** CHOLESTEROL, **96MG** SODIUM, **1G** FIBER

# sirloin burger and fresh slaw

## helpful hints

- *If pressed for time, use a store-bought coleslaw instead of the recipe given. Ask for the nutritional analysis of store-bought coleslaw, as some prepared versions have added sugar.*
- *To determine the weight of each slice of cheese, divide the package weight by the number of slices. With most brands, 1 slice equals 3/4 ounce.*

## countdown

- *Make coleslaw.*
- *Make burger.*

## shopping list

*TO BUY:*

*1 package reduced-fat cheddar cheese (1 1/2 ounces needed)*

*1/2 pound ground lean sirloin*

*1 bag presliced coleslaw mix*

*2 medium tomatoes*

*STAPLES:*

*Red onion*

*Olive oil spray*

*Mayonnaise made with soybean or olive oil*

*Dijon mustard*

*Distilled white vinegar*

*Sugar substitute*

*Salt*

*Black peppercorns*

*In the mood for a burger? Here's a quick one made with lean sirloin and accompanied by slaw. Sliced, ready-to-use cabbage for coleslaw can be found in the produce section of the supermarkets, making homemade coleslaw a breeze.*

## sirloin burger

*1/4 cup chopped red onion*

*1/2 pound ground lean sirloin*

*Salt and freshly ground black pepper to taste*

*Olive oil spray*

*2 slices reduced-fat cheddar cheese (1 1/2 ounces)*

*4 teaspoons Dijon mustard*

Combine the onion and ground sirloin in a medium-size bowl. Season with salt and pepper to taste. Form into 2 patties. Set a medium-size nonstick skillet over medium-high heat and spray with olive oil. Cook the sirloin burgers for 5 minutes. Turn and top each burger with a slice of cheese. Continue cooking for 3 more minutes. Top the cheese with mustard and serve.

*Makes 2 servings.*

**ONE SERVING: 338** CALORIES, **46G** PROTEIN, **2G** CARBOHYDRATE, **17G** FAT (**8G** SATURATED), **117MG** CHOLESTEROL, **496MG** SODIUM, **0G** FIBER

## fresh slaw

*2 tablespoons mayonnaise made with soybean or olive oil*

*2 tablespoons distilled white vinegar*

*4 teaspoons Dijon mustard*

*2 (.035-ounce) envelopes sugar substitute*

*Salt and freshly ground black pepper to taste*

*4 slices red onion (1/2 cup)*

*4 cups presliced coleslaw mix*

*2 medium tomatoes, sliced*

Combine the mayonnaise, vinegar, mustard, and sugar substitute in a medium-size bowl. Season with salt and pepper to taste. Add the onion and coleslaw mix, and toss well. Add more salt and pepper, if needed. Divide between 2 plates, and arrange the tomato slices on the side.

*Makes 2 servings.*

**ONE SERVING: 191** CALORIES, **5G** PROTEIN, **18G** CARBOHYDRATE, **12G** FAT (**2G** SATURATED), **5MG** CHOLESTEROL, **355MG** SODIUM, **2G** FIBER

# pacific rim pork with ginger-garlic stir-fry vegetables and pickled daikon radish salad

*Spicy, Pacific Rim flavors add zest to this easy-to-prepare dinner. • The pickled vegetable salad makes a great snack. Make extra and store in a plastic bag. Serve it on its own, or add to chicken or tuna salads. Daikon radish is a white, Oriental radish with a sweet, fresh flavor.*

## pacific rim pork

*3/4 pound pork tenderloin, visible fat removed*

*For Marinade:*

*1/4 cup low-salt soy sauce*
*1/4 cup distilled white vinegar*
*4 medium-size garlic cloves, crushed*
*4 teaspoons Dijon mustard*
*2 teaspoons ground ginger*
*Dash of freshly ground black pepper*

Preheat the broiler and place the rack on the top rung of the oven. Line a baking sheet with foil. Cut the tenderloin almost in half lengthwise and open like a book. Do not cut all of the way through. Combine the marinade ingredients in a small bowl. Add the pork and let marinate for 20 minutes. Remove from the marinade and place the pork on the foil-lined baking sheet. Broil 5 minutes, turn, and broil 3 more minutes. The pork is done when a meat thermometer inserted in the center registers 160 degrees. Slice and serve with the salad and vegetables.

*Makes 2 servings.*

**ONE SERVING: 293** CALORIES, **50G** PROTEIN, **2G** CARBOHYDRATE, **8G** FAT (**3G** SATURATED), **159MG** CHOLESTEROL, **478MG** SODIUM, **0G** FIBER

## pickled daikon radish salad

*1 cup water*
*1/2 cup plus 2 tablespoons distilled white vinegar*
*8 (.035-ounce) envelopes sugar substitute*
*1 teaspoon crushed red pepper*
*1 teaspoon salt*
*1 medium cucumber, peeled and sliced*
*2 cups Daikon (white) radish, peeled and sliced*
*2 tablespoons yellow onion, chopped*

Mix the water, vinegar, sugar substitute, crushed red pepper, and salt together in a medium-size bowl. Add the cucumber, radish, and onion and marinate 15 minutes. Drain and serve.

*Makes 2 servings.*

**ONE SERVING: 34** CALORIES, **1G** PROTEIN, **9G** CARBOHYDRATE, **0G** FAT (**0G** SATURATED), **0MG** CHOLESTEROL, **276MG** SODIUM, **1G** FIBER

## helpful hints

- *Red radishes can be substituted for the daikon radish.*
- *To keep from having to look back at the recipe as you stir-fry the ingredients, line them up on a cutting board or plate in the order of use so you know which ingredient comes next.*
- *For crisp, not steamed, stir-fried vegetables, start with a very hot wok or skillet. Let the vegetables sit a minute before tossing to allow the wok to regain its heat.*

## countdown

- *Preheat broiler.*
- *Marinate pork.*
- *Make pickled daikon radish salad.*
- *Prepare stir-fry vegetable ingredients.*
- *Broil pork.*
- *While pork cooks, make stir-fry vegetables.*

## shopping list

*TO BUY:*

*3/4 pound pork tenderloin*
*1 small jar ground ginger*
*1 bottle sesame oil*
*1 small head Chinese lettuce (napa cabbage)*
*1 package fresh bean sprouts*
*1 jar crushed red pepper*
*1 medium cucumber*
*1 Daikon (white) radish*

# pacific rim pork with ginger-garlic stir-fry vegetables and pickled daikon *continued*

*STAPLES:*

*Garlic*

*Yellow onion*

*Dijon mustard*

*Low-salt soy sauce*

*Distilled white vinegar*

*Sugar substitute*

*Salt*

*Black peppercorns*

## ginger-garlic stir-fry vegetables

*2 teaspoons sesame oil*

*2 teaspoons ground ginger*

*4 cups Chinese lettuce (napa cabbage), washed and sliced*

*2 cups fresh bean sprouts*

*4 medium-size garlic cloves, crushed*

Heat a wok or nonstick skillet on high. Add the oil. When the oil begins to smoke, add the ginger, lettuce, bean sprouts, and garlic. Stir-fry for 6 minutes and then serve.

*Makes 2 servings.*

**ONE SERVING: 92** CALORIES, **4G** PROTEIN, **10G** CARBOHYDRATE, **5G** FAT (**1G** SATURATED), **0MG** CHOLESTEROL, **13MG** SODIUM, **2G** FIBER

# veal scallopini with garlic greens and saffron cauliflower

*In this dish, romaine and radicchio leaves are just wilted in a skillet and flavored with garlic to form a crunchy, colorful topping for the veal scallops. • Veal scallops take only a few minutes to cook. The secret to keeping them juicy is to brown them in a hot skillet for 1 minute on each side. Then remove them to a plate and cover to keep warm. Boneless, skinless chicken breasts can be substituted, though they will need to cook longer. • Saffron is the stigmas from a saffron crocus. This spice is pricey because it is harvested by hand. Fortunately, a little goes a long way.*

## veal scallopini with garlic greens

*Olive oil spray*
*3/4 pound veal scallops*
*Salt and freshly ground black pepper to taste*
*4 medium-size garlic cloves, crushed*
*4 cups romaine and radicchio leaves torn into bite-size pieces*

Set a medium-size nonstick skillet over high heat and spray with olive oil. Brown the veal for 1 minute on each side. Salt and pepper the cooked sides and remove to 2 plates. Add the garlic and greens to the skillet. Toss 1 minute, or until the greens just start to wilt. Season with salt and pepper to taste. Serve the greens over the veal scallops.

*Makes 2 servings.*

**ONE SERVING: 398** CALORIES, **46G** PROTEIN, **3G** CARBOHYDRATE, **20G** FAT (**12G** SATURATED), **150MG** CHOLESTEROL, **114MG** SODIUM, **0G** FIBER

## saffron cauliflower

*1/2 pound cauliflower florets (4 cups)*
*4 teaspoons olive oil*
*1/4 teaspoon saffron strands*
*Salt and freshly ground black pepper to taste*

Place the cauliflower in a vegetable steamer set over boiling water. Steam 6 to 7 minutes, or until tender. Alternatively, place in a microwave-safe dish—do not add water—and microwave on high for 5 minutes. Spoon the olive oil into a large serving bowl and add the saffron. Microwave on high for 10 seconds. Add the cauliflower to the oil, season with salt and pepper to taste, and toss well before serving.

*Makes 2 servings.*

**ONE SERVING: 130** CALORIES, **4G** PROTEIN, **10G** CARBOHYDRATE, **9G** FAT (**1G** SATURATED), **0MG** CHOLESTEROL, **60MG** SODIUM, **5G** FIBER

## helpful hints

- *Turmeric or bijol can be used instead of the saffron.*
- *Buy cauliflower already cut into florets.*
- *Washed, ready-to-eat salad can be used. Make sure the leaves are firm. Mesclun or field greens will be too soft to work in this recipe.*

## countdown

- *Make cauliflower, cover to keep warm.*
- *Prepare veal and garlic greens.*

## shopping list

*TO BUY:*

*3/4 pound veal scallops*
*1 small package saffron strands*
*1/2 pound cauliflower florets*
*1 small head romaine lettuce*
*1 small head radicchio lettuce*

*STAPLES:*

*Olive oil*
*Olive oil spray*
*Garlic*
*Salt*
*Black peppercorns*

# southern comfort pecan-crusted grouper with vegetable creole

*Pecan-flavored grouper and vegetable creole are updated versions of Southern comfort foods. To cook fish fast, preheat the baking tray in the oven. The hot tray will help to cook the fish on the underside without having to turn the fish.*

## helpful hints

- *For an extra fiery bite, add another 1/8 teaspoon cayenne pepper to the grouper recipe.*
- *Vegetable creole keeps well. Make extra and save for another dinner.*
- *To save cleaning time, make the grouper and creole in the same skillet.*
- *Any type of firm, non-oily fish fillet can be used.*

## countdown

- *Preheat oven to 400 degrees.*
- *Make grouper.*
- *Make vegetable creole.*

## shopping list

*TO BUY:*

*3/4 pound grouper fillet*
*1 small package pecan pieces (2 ounces needed)*
*1 can no-sugar-added diced tomatoes (16 ounces needed)*
*1 medium-size green bell pepper*
*1 zucchini*

*STAPLES:*

*Eggs*
*Yellow onion*
*Garlic*
*Worcestershire sauce*
*Olive oil*
*Olive oil spray*
*Sugar substitute*
*Cayenne pepper*
*Salt*
*Black peppercorns*

## southern comfort pecan-crusted grouper

*1/4 teaspoon salt*
*1/4 teaspoon freshly ground black pepper*
*1/4 teaspoon cayenne pepper*
*2 egg whites, lightly beaten*
*1/2 cup finely chopped pecans (2 ounces)*
*3/4 pound grouper fillet*
*2 teaspoons olive oil*
*Olive oil spray*

Preheat the oven to 400 degrees. Line a baking sheet with foil and place in oven to heat. Combine the salt, black pepper, and cayenne on a plate. Line up the spice mixture, the beaten egg whites, and the pecans in a row on the countertop for easy coating of the grouper. First, roll the grouper in the spice mixture, coating both sides. Next, dip the grouper into the egg whites, and then roll in the pecans.

Heat the olive oil in a nonstick skillet on medium high. When the oil is hot, brown the grouper for 2 minutes. Turn and brown other side for 1 minute. Remove the baking tray from the oven and spray with olive oil. Place the grouper on the tray and return the tray to the oven for 5 minutes to finish cooking. Serve with the creole.
*Makes 2 servings.*

**ONE SERVING: 399** CALORIES, **39G** PROTEIN, **4G** CARBOHYDRATE, **26G** FAT (**3G** SATURATED), **62MG** CHOLESTEROL, **412MG** SODIUM, **3G** FIBER

## vegetable creole

*2 teaspoons olive oil*
*1/2 cup sliced yellow onion*
*1 medium-size green bell pepper, sliced, (1 cup)*
*1 zucchini, sliced (2 cups)*
*4 medium-size garlic cloves, crushed*
*2 cups canned no-sugar-added, diced tomatoes*
*1 tablespoon Worcestershire sauce*
*2 (.035-ounce) envelopes sugar substitute*

Heat the olive oil in a nonstick skillet on medium high. Add the onion, bell pepper, zucchini, and garlic and sauté for 5 minutes. Lower the heat to medium. Add the tomatoes, Worcestershire sauce, and sugar substitute. Cover with a lid, and cook for 5 minutes. Serve hot with the grouper.
*Makes 2 servings.*

**ONE SERVING: 156** CALORIES, **6G** PROTEIN, **22G** CARBOHYDRATE, **5G** FAT (**1G** SATURATED), **0MG** CHOLESTEROL, **378MG** SODIUM, **7G** FIBER

# sausage-pepper sauté with marinated artichoke salad

*This is a 15-minute meal. I keep low-fat turkey sausage links in my freezer for emergency meals and use whatever is in my vegetable drawer to go with it—bell peppers, celery, mushrooms, broccoli, or cauliflower. A jar of marinated artichokes or hearts of palm from the pantry can be made into an instant salad to complete a great, quick meal. Use this recipe as a base and create your own sausage meal.*

## sausage-pepper sauté

- *Olive oil spray*
- *4 low-fat turkey sausage links (3/4 pound), cut into 1-inch slices*
- *1 medium-size red bell pepper, sliced (2 cups)*
- *2 medium-size garlic cloves, crushed*
- *Salt and freshly ground black pepper to taste*
- *1/2 cup fresh basil leaves, torn into small pieces*

Set a medium-size nonstick skillet over medium-high heat and spray with olive oil. Add the sausage, bell pepper, and garlic, and sauté 10 minutes. Season with salt and pepper to taste. Sprinkle with the basil and serve.

*Makes 2 servings.*

**ONE SERVING: 344** CALORIES, **30G** PROTEIN, **14G** CARBOHYDRATE **18G** FAT (**5G** SATURATED), **90MG** CHOLESTEROL, **1084MG** SODIUM, **0G** FIBER

## marinated artichoke salad

- *2 (6-ounce) jars marinated artichoke hearts, drained*
- *2 cups washed, ready-to-eat, Italian-style salad*
- *2 tablespoons no-sugar-added oil and vinegar dressing*
- *Salt and freshly ground black pepper to taste*

Cut the artichoke hearts in half. Place the salad in a small bowl and toss with the dressing. Season with salt and pepper to taste. Place the artichoke hearts on top, and serve.

*Makes 2 servings.*

**ONE SERVING: 229** CALORIES, **3G** PROTEIN, **13G** CARBOHYDRATE, **17G** FAT (**1G** SATURATED), **0MG** CHOLESTEROL, **618MG** SODIUM, **3G** FIBER

### helpful hints

- *Most supermarkets carry marinated artichoke hearts in a jar or can.*
- *Low-fat turkey sausage links come in mild, medium, and hot. The heat is up to you. To determine the weight of each sausage, divide the package weight by the number of sausages.*

### countdown

- *Make sausage and peppers.*
- *Make artichoke salad.*

### shopping list

*TO BUY:*

- *1 package low-fat turkey sausage links (3/4 pound needed)*
- *2 jars marinated artichoke hearts (12 ounces needed)*
- *1 medium-size red bell pepper*
- *1 bag washed, ready-to-eat, Italian-style salad*
- *1 small bunch basil*

*STAPLES:*

- *Olive oil spray*
- *No-sugar-added oil and vinegar dressing*
- *Garlic*
- *Salt*
- *Black peppercorns*

# snapper veracruz with zucchini parmesan and italian greens

*This is a great meal for those evenings you need to get a tasty dinner on the table in 15 minutes. Fresh fish is the original fast food. Simply cover the fish with salsa, broil, and serve.*

## helpful hints

- *Any type of salsa can be used—just make sure it does not have sugar added.*
- *Any type of thin fish fillet, such as sole or flounder, can be used.*
- *Buy good quality Parmesan cheese and ask the grocer to grate it for you or chop it in the food processor yourself. Freeze extra for quick use later—simply spoon out what you need and leave the rest frozen.*
- *For optimum taste, make sure the dried oregano is less than 6 months old.*

## countdown

- *Preheat oven to 400 degrees.*
- *Make fish.*
- *While fish bakes, make zucchini.*
- *Make salad.*

## shopping list

*TO BUY:*

*3/4 pound snapper fillet*
*1 jar no-sugar-added tomato salsa*
*1 bag washed, ready-to-eat, Italian-style salad*
*1/2 pound zucchini*

*STAPLES:*

*Olive oil*
*Olive oil spray*
*No-sugar-added oil and vinegar dressing*
*Parmesan cheese*
*Dried oregano*
*Salt*
*Black peppercorns*

## snapper veracruz

*Olive oil spray*
*3/4 pound snapper fillet*
*Salt and freshly ground black pepper to taste*
*1 cup no-sugar-added tomato salsa*

Preheat the oven to 400 degrees. Line a baking sheet with foil and spray with olive oil. Place the fish on the baking sheet, spray with olive oil, and season with salt and pepper to taste. Bake 10 minutes. Spoon the salsa over the fish and bake 5 more minutes before serving.

*Makes 2 servings.*

**ONE SERVING: 244** CALORIES, **39G** PROTEIN, **10G** CARBOHYDRATE, **4G** FAT (**1G** SATURATED), **62MG** CHOLESTEROL, **872MG** SODIUM, **4G** FIBER

## zucchini parmesan

*1/2 pound zucchini, sliced (2 cups)*
*4 teaspoons olive oil*
*Salt and freshly ground black pepper to taste*
*2 tablespoons freshly grated Parmesan cheese*

Place the zucchini in a microwave-safe bowl and heat on high for 5 minutes. Alternatively, bring a medium saucepan of water to a boil, and add the zucchini. Boil for 3 minutes and drain. Toss with the olive oil, and season with salt and pepper to taste. Sprinkle with Parmesan cheese, and serve.

*Makes 2 servings.*

**ONE SERVING: 123** CALORIES, **4G** PROTEIN, **4G** CARBOHYDRATE, **11G** FAT (**2G** SATURATED), **4MG** CHOLESTEROL, **110MG** SODIUM, **1G** FIBER

## italian greens

*2 tablespoons no-sugar-added oil and vinegar dressing*
*2 teaspoons dried oregano*
*4 cups washed, ready-to-eat, Italian-style salad*

Spoon the dressing into a salad bowl and stir in the oregano. Add the salad, toss well, and serve.

*Makes 2 servings.*

**ONE SERVING: 88** CALORIES, **1G** PROTEIN, **3G** CARBOHYDRATE, **9G** FAT (**1G** SATURATED), **0MG** CHOLESTEROL, **81MG** SODIUM, **1G** FIBER

# rosemary-roasted pork with a fennel gratin and brussels sprouts

*Northern Italy inspired this roasted pork dinner. The secret to roasting the pork in only 15 minutes is to butterfly it by cutting it in half lengthwise. • Pecorino cheese is an alternative to using Parmesan cheese, but with a sharper flavor. It's made from sheep's milk and the most popular kinds are hard and perfect for grating. • Fennel has a pale green bulb and stalk with feathery leaves. Both the base and stem can be eaten raw or cooked. It has a slight anise or licorice flavor when raw that becomes even milder when cooked.*

## rosemary-roasted pork

*Olive oil spray*
*3/4 pound pork tenderloin*
*2 teaspoons olive oil*
*2 tablespoons chopped fresh rosemary or 2 teaspoons dried*
*Salt and freshly ground black pepper to taste*

Preheat the oven to 400 degrees. Line a baking tray with foil, spray with olive oil, and place in the oven to heat. Remove all visible fat from the pork and cut the loin nearly in half lengthwise. Open the pork and lay flat like a book. Pound it flat with the palm of your hand or with the bottom of a skillet. Rub the pork with olive oil and sprinkle with rosemary on both sides. Place the pork on the hot baking tray. Roast 15 minutes. Remove from the oven, cover with foil, and let the meat rest for 5 minutes. Season with salt and pepper to taste. Slice and serve.
*Makes 2 servings.*

**ONE SERVING: 345** CALORIES, **49G** PROTEIN, **0G** CARBOHYDRATE, **15G** FAT (**4G** SATURATED), **159MG** CHOLESTEROL, **115MG** SODIUM, **0G** FIBER

## helpful hints

- *Parmesan cheese can be used instead of pecorino cheese.*
- *A quick way to chop fresh rosemary is to snip it right from the stem with scissors.*
- *Celery can be substituted for the fennel in the recipe.*

## countdown

- *Preheat oven to 400 degrees.*
- *Start pork.*
- *Make fennel.*
- *Steam Brussels sprouts.*

## shopping list

*TO BUY:*

*1 small piece pecorino cheese*
*3/4 pound pork tenderloin*
*1 small bunch fresh rosemary or 1 jar dried*
*1 medium bulb fennel*
*1/4 pound Brussels sprouts*

*STAPLES:*

*Olive oil spray*
*Olive oil*
*Salt*
*Black peppercorns*

# rosemary-roasted pork with a fennel gratin and brussels sprouts *continued*

## fennel gratin

*4 teaspoons olive oil*

*½ medium bulb fennel, stalks and leaves removed, thinly sliced (2 cups)*

*Salt and freshly ground black pepper to taste*

*2 tablespoons grated pecorino cheese*

Heat the olive oil in a nonstick skillet on medium high. Add the fennel and toss in the oil. Cover with a lid and cook 2 minutes. (Or, place in a microwave-safe bowl, add the oil, and toss to coat. Cover, and microwave on high for 8 minutes.) Season with salt and pepper to taste and toss well. Sprinkle with the cheese and place in the oven with the pork for 5 minutes, or until the cheese starts to melt. Use the same baking tray as the pork to save clean-up time. Serve with the pork.

*Makes 2 servings.*

**ONE SERVING: 135** CALORIES, **2G** PROTEIN, **0G** CARBOHYDRATE, **11G** FAT (**2G** SATURATED), **4MG** CHOLESTEROL, **106MG** SODIUM, **0G** FIBER

## brussels sprouts

*¼ pound Brussels sprouts, damaged outer leaves removed and sprouts halved (2 cups)*

*2 teaspoons olive oil*

*Salt and freshly ground black pepper to taste*

Place the Brussels sprouts in the basket of a vegetable steamer. Place over boiling water and steam for 6 or 7 minutes. Alternatively, microwave on high for 5 minutes. Transfer the cooked Brussels sprouts to a serving bowl. Add the olive oil, and season with salt and pepper to taste. Toss well before serving.

*Makes 2 servings.*

**ONE SERVING: 60** CALORIES, **1G** PROTEIN, **4G** CARBOHYDRATE, **5G** FAT (**1G** SATURATED), **0MG** CHOLESTEROL, **12MG** SODIUM, **1G** FIBER

# chicken with fresh herbs, pan-roasted asparagus, and baby turnips

*This fresh herb stuffing gives a fragrant flavor to the chicken and keeps it moist during cooking. The stuffing, a combination of chopped fresh tarragon, scallions, and mushrooms, is so simple, it really only takes minutes to make. The herbs and mushrooms can be chopped in a food processor to save even more time. • Small, baby turnips are sweet and need only a little sautéing to bring out their flavors and keep their crunchy texture.*

## chicken with fresh herbs

- *2 (6-ounce) boneless, skinless chicken breasts*
- *2 tablespoons fresh tarragon or 2 teaspoons dried*
- *2 scallions, sliced*
- *2 medium-size button mushrooms*
- *2 tablespoons non-fat plain yogurt*
- *Salt and freshly ground black pepper to taste*
- *Olive oil spray*

Holding the chicken breast flat with the palm of your hand, make a horizontal slit in each breast. It should be deep enough to form a pocket the length of the chicken breast. In a food processor or by hand, chop the tarragon, scallions, and mushrooms together. Add the yogurt and blend well. Season with salt and pepper to taste. Salt and pepper the inside slits of the chicken. Spoon the herb stuffing into the slit. Gently press the chicken breast together to close the slits. Set a medium-size nonstick skillet over medium-high heat, and spray with olive oil. Brown the chicken breasts for 2 minutes on each side, seasoning each cooked side with salt and pepper. Lower the heat to medium, cover with a lid, and cook 6 more minutes. Serve hot. *Makes 2 servings.*

**ONE SERVING: 309** CALORIES, **55G** PROTEIN, **2G** CARBOHYDRATE, **10G** FAT (**2G** SATURATED), **144MG** CHOLESTEROL, **138MG** SODIUM, **0G** FIBER

### helpful hint

- *Dried tarragon can be substituted for fresh. Make sure the dried leaves are green. If they have started to turn brown, it's time to buy a new jar.*

### countdown

- *Prepare all ingredients.*
- *Start chicken.*
- *While chicken cooks, make asparagus and turnips.*

### shopping list

*TO BUY:*

- *1 small container non-fat plain yogurt*
- *2 (6-ounce) boneless, skinless chicken breasts*
- *1/2 pound fresh asparagus*
- *1/2 baby turnips*
- *1 small bunch fresh tarragon or 1 jar dried*
- *1 small package button mushrooms*
- *1 small bunch scallions (2 needed)*

*STAPLES:*

- *Olive oil*
- *Olive oil spray*
- *Garlic*
- *Salt*
- *Black peppercorns*

## chicken with fresh herbs, pan-roasted asparagus and baby turnips *continued*

# pan-roasted asparagus and baby turnips

*½ pound fresh asparagus*

*4 teaspoons olive oil*

*½ pound baby turnips, peeled and cut into 1-inch cubes (about 2 cups)*

*1 medium-size garlic clove, crushed*

*Salt and freshly ground black pepper to taste*

Cut or snap off the 1-inch fibrous stem on the asparagus and discard. Slice the remaining asparagus into 2-inch pieces (you should have about 2½ cups). Heat the olive oil in a medium-size nonstick skillet on medium high, and add the turnips. Sauté 5 minutes, turning to make sure all sides are browned. Add the asparagus and garlic and continue to sauté 5 minutes for thin asparagus or 10 minutes for thick. Season with salt and pepper to taste. Serve with the chicken.

*Makes 2 servings.*

**ONE SERVING: 134** CALORIES, **3G** PROTEIN, **12G** CARBOHYDRATE, **9G** FAT (**1G** SATURATED), **0MG** CHOLESTEROL, **90MG** SODIUM, **5G** FIBER

# steak au poivre with french green beans and hearts of palm salad

*Here's a meal that's perfect for those evenings when you want something a little special. • Steak au Poivre is a very simple, very French dish. This recipe calls for cracked or coarsely broken black peppercorns. This product is available in the spice section of the supermarket. • Hearts of palm are the tender heart of the Sabal palm tree. They are available in cans or jars at the supermarket. • I've called for heavy whipping cream in this recipe because it is easy to find in the market. Crème fraîche, however, is available in some supermarkets and adds a tangy flavor and creamy texture to the sauce. Use it instead of the heavy cream if at all possible. • Brandy is the generic name for cognac or Armagnac. You can buy a generic brandy in small splits at many markets and most liquor stores.*

## steak au poivre (black pepper steak)

- *2 (5 ounce) beef tenderloin steaks*
- *1 tablespoon cracked black pepper*
- *4 teaspoons canola oil*
- *Salt to taste*
- *2 tablespoons cognac or brandy*
- *1 tablespoon heavy whipping cream*

Cover the steaks with the cracked pepper, pressing it into the meat with the palm of your hand. Heat the oil in a nonstick skillet on medium high. Brown the steaks for 4 minutes. If the steaks are browning too quickly, reduce the heat to medium. Turn and salt the cooked sides to taste. Brown the second side for 2 minutes, or until a meat thermometer registers 140 degrees. Remove the steaks to 2 plates. Add the cognac to the hot pan, scraping up the brown bits as it cooks. Add the cream and mix well. Taste for salt and adjust the seasoning if necessary. Spoon the sauce on top of the steaks and serve.

*Makes 2 servings.*

**ONE SERVING: 376** CALORIES, **30G** PROTEIN, **2G** CARBOHYDRATE, **24G** FAT (**8G** SATURATED), **98MG** CHOLESTEROL, **81MG** SODIUM, **0G** FIBER

## helpful hints

- *If pressed for time, use a bottled, no-sugar-added oil and vinegar dressing instead of the recipe provided here.*
- *Strip, flank, or skirt can be substituted instead of the beef tenderloin steak.*
- *Any type of lettuce leaves can be used instead of red lettuce.*
- *Regular green beans can be used instead of small green beans. Cut large ones in half.*
- *To save cleaning an extra skillet, prepare the steaks and green beans in the same skillet.*

## countdown

- *Make the hearts of palm salad.*
- *Blanch the green beans.*
- *Make the steak.*
- *Sauté the green beans.*

# steak au poivre with french green beans and hearts of palm salad *continued*

## shopping list

*TO BUY:*

*1 small carton heavy whipping cream*

*2 (5-ounce) beef tenderloin steaks*

*1 jar cracked black pepper*

*1 small bottle brandy, preferably cognac*

*1 jar or can hearts of palm (10 ounces needed)*

*1/2 pound small green beans (haricots verts)*

*1 small head red lettuce*

*STAPLES:*

*Garlic*

*Canola oil*

*Red wine vinegar*

*Dijon mustard*

*Salt*

*Black peppercorns*

## french green beans

*1/2 pound small green beans (haricots verts), trimmed (2 cups)*

*4 teaspoons canola oil*

*2 medium-size garlic cloves, crushed*

*Salt and freshly ground black pepper to taste*

Bring a medium saucepan full of water to a boil. Add the beans. As soon as the water comes back to a boil, drain the beans. Return the beans to the pan and fill the pan with ice water to stop the cooking. Drain the beans. In the same saucepan, heat the oil on high. Add the beans and garlic, and sauté 2 or 3 minutes until the beans are crisp. Season with salt and pepper to taste and serve on the plates with the steak.

*Makes 2 servings.*

**ONE SERVING: 88** CALORIES, **3G** PROTEIN, **11G** CARBOHYDRATE, **5G** FAT (**1G** SATURATED), **0MG** CHOLESTEROL, **4MG** SODIUM, **2G** FIBER

## hearts of palm salad

*1 tablespoon red wine vinegar*

*4 teaspoons Dijon mustard*

*Salt and freshly ground black pepper to taste*

*2 teaspoons canola oil*

*2 cups hearts of palm, drained and cut into 1/2-inch slices (10 ounces)*

*Several red lettuce leaves*

In a salad bowl, whisk the vinegar and mustard together until smooth. Season with salt and pepper to taste. Whisk in the oil, and adjust for seasoning as necessary. Add the hearts of palm to the dressing. Toss well. Place the lettuce on 2 small plates, spoon the hearts of palm on top, and serve.

*Makes 2 servings.*

**ONE SERVING: 100** CALORIES, **5G** PROTEIN, **9G** CARBOHYDRATE, **6G** FAT (**1G** SATURATED), **0MG** CHOLESTEROL, **868MG** SODIUM, **4G** FIBER

# which carbs

## introduction

When I teach classes, I find that this is the most important section. My students are afraid to start reintroducing carbs for fear they will negate all of the benefits they've achieved. Regaining lost weight can happen right here.

The question that keeps coming up at every class is, "How do I start to add carbohydrates to my meals?" Two things usually happen at this point. You're losing weight and feel good, so you stay on the Quick Start phase until you get bored or have a special event. Or, you think, "Great, I've lost weight! Now I can have the foods I love and forget about the carb restrictions." But neither solution leads to a healthy lifestyle of low-carb eating.

This section shows you how to start bringing carbs back into your life without gaining weight. I have carefully chosen these recipes to reincorporate high-fiber, low simple sugar carbohydrates. The most important addition is high-fiber cereal in the morning.

As with the other sections, I have organized the menus into a meal-at-a-glance chart with some easy and quick meals to accommodate busy mid-week schedules and some more elaborate recipes suited to a more relaxed weekend pace. They are arranged to give variety throughout the day and over the course of the week. The meals are ordered in the chapter in the same sequence, so just follow the meals in the order given in the chart for a complete two-week plan.

## breakfast

You can choose from a variety of breakfasts to fit your taste. Quick ideas like Microwave Cheddar Scramble with Bran Cereal and the Dijon Ham and Cheddar Grill with Cinnamon Oatmeal can be completed in less than 5 minutes. You can also enjoy Pecan Ham Roll-Ups or Shrimp, Red Pepper, and Tomato Frittata with Berry and Banana Yogurt Bran Cup.

## lunch

Chicken Salad Amandine and a quick Salad Niçoise with Citrus from the French Riviera are two of the tempting choices during this phase.

## dinner

Neapolitan Steak Pizzaiola with Parmesan Linguine and Italian Greens, Five-Spiced Chicken Legs with Garlic Bean Sprouts and Rice, and

Whisky Pork Chops with Rosemary Lentils and Red Beet Salad are some of the meals that have been carefully planned to slowly reintroduce carbohydrates.

During the Which Carb 14-day meal plan, you will consume an average of 75 to 85 grams of carbohydrate per day. Carbohydrates percentage is based on carbohydrates less fiber consumed—the normal way of calculating carbohydrate consumption. The balance of these meals is 23 percent of calories from carbohydrates, 38 percent of calories from lean protein, 27 percent of calories from monounsaturated fat, and 8 percent of calories from saturated fat.

# which carbs 14-day menu plan

| week 1 | breakfast | lunch | dinner |
|---|---|---|---|
| sunday | Sausage, Mushroom, and Onion Egg Pizzetta with Bran Cereal . . . . . . .92 | Nuevo Tex-Mex Layered Salad . . . .107 | Thai Peanut-Rub Pork with Stir-Fry Broccoli Noodles . . . . . . . .122 |
| monday | Arugula and Ham Scramble with Oatmeal . . . . . . . . .93 | Smoked Whitefish Salad . . . . . . . . . .108 | Pesto Chicken with Steamed Artichokes and Fresh Figs . . . . . . .123 |
| tuesday | Turkey and Cottage Cheese Plate with Pecan Oatmeal . . . . . . . . .94 | Salad Niçoise with Citrus . . . . . . .109 | Grilled Scallops Parmigiana with Lemon-Pepper Zucchini and Fresh Kiwi-Berry Jumble . .125 |
| wednesday | Dijon Ham and Cheddar Grill with Cinnamon Oatmeal . . . . . . . . .95 | Chicken Salad Amandine . . . . . . .110 | Herbed Veal Cutlets with Spaghetti and Parmesan Spinach . . . . . . . . .127 |
| thursday | Omelette aux Fines Herbes with Bran Cereal . . . . . . .96 | Roast Turkey Sandwich with Greek Sadziki Sauce and Pistachios . . . .111 | Garlic Shrimp Stir-Fry with Chinese Cabbage and Bean Sprouts . . . . .128 |
| friday | Smoked Turkey Roll-Ups with Spiced Oatmeal . . . . . . . . .97 | California Chef's Salad . . . . . . . . . .112 | Sole Amandine with Baby Limas and Grilled Tomatoes . . . . . . . .130 |
| saturday | Shrimp, Red Pepper, and Tomato Frittata with Berry and Banana Yogurt Bran Cup . . . . . . . . .98 | Citrus, Turkey, and Salsa Salad with Plum Plate . . . . . . .113 | Smothered Steak with Caramelized Onions and Hearts of Palm Salad . . . . . .131 |

| week 2 | breakfast | lunch | dinner |
| --- | --- | --- | --- |
| sunday | Asian Omelette with Bran Cereal . . . . . . . .99 | Jamaican Jerk Chicken Salad with Hearts of Palm . . . .114 | Whisky Pork Chops with Rosemary Lentils and Red Beet Salad . . . . . . . .133 |
| monday | Grilled Tuna–Stuffed Sweet Peppers and Bran Cereal . . .100 | Delicatessen Salad with Cucumber and Coleslaw . . . . . . . . .115 | Seared Sesame Tuna and Stir-Fry Bok Choy with Shiitake Noodles . . .135 |
| tuesday | Pecan Ham Roll-Ups with Cinnamon Oatmeal . . . . . . . . .101 | Country Bacon and Egg Salad with Fresh Berries . . . . . . .116 | Chicken Provençal with Endive and Watercress Salad . . . . . . . . . .137 |
| wednesday | Microwave Cheddar Scramble with Bran Cereal . . . . . . . . . . .102 | Balsamic and Dill Salmon Salad with Raspberries . . . . . .117 | Mussels Marinière with Mesclun Salad . . . .139 |
| thursday | Cheese and Roasted Red Pepper–Stuffed Endive with Bran Cereal . . .103 | Hollywood Cobb Salad . . . . . . . . . .118 | Spicy Vietnamese Stir-Fry Crab with Asian Vegetables . . . . . . .140 |
| friday | Spanish Omelette and Bran Cereal . . . . . .104 | South Beach Black Bean and Salsa Wraps . .119 | Neapolitan Steak Pizzaiola with Parmesan Linguine and Italian Greens . . . . . . . . .142 |
| saturday | Raspberry-Red Smoothie with Toasted Walnut Oatmeal . . . . . . . .105 | Wild Greens with Chili Chicken . . . . . . . . . .120 | Five-Spiced Chicken Legs with Garlic Bean Sprouts and Rice . . . . . . . .144 |

# which carb breakfasts

# sausage, mushroom, and onion egg pizzetta with bran cereal

## helpful hints

- *Sliced mushrooms can be found in the produce section of the supermarket.*
- *To determine the weight of each slice of cheese, divide the package weight by the number of slices. With most brands, 1 slice equals 3/4 ounce.*
- *There are several types of low-fat turkey sausage links available in the supermarkets. To determine the weight of each sausage, divide the package weight by the number of sausages.*

## countdown

- *Preheat broiler.*
- *Make egg pizza base.*
- *Complete pizza.*

## shopping list

*TO BUY:*

*1 small package reduced-fat mozzarella cheese (3 ounces needed)*

*1 package low-fat turkey sausage links (6 ounces needed)*

*1 can or jar low-fat, no-sugar-added tomato sauce (4 ounces needed)*

*1 small package button mushrooms (6 mushrooms needed)*

*STAPLES:*

*Red onion*
*Olive oil spray*
*Egg substitute*
*High-fiber, no-sugar-added bran cereal*
*Skim milk*
*Black peppercorns*

*Sausage, mushrooms, onion, and tomato sauce form the topping for an egg pizza base. This is a fun breakfast that takes about 15 minutes to make. It's great for a weekday or weekend treat, breakfast, lunch, or dinner.*

## sausage, mushroom, and onion egg pizzetta

*2 cups egg substitute*
*Freshly ground black pepper*
*Olive oil spray*
*1/2 cup low-fat, no-sugar-added tomato sauce*
*2 small low-fat turkey sausage links, cut into 1-inch slices (6 ounces)*
*6 button mushrooms, sliced (1 cup)*
*1 tablespoon diced red onion*
*4 slices reduced-fat mozzarella cheese (3 ounces)*

Preheat the broiler. Season the egg substitute with pepper to taste. Set a small (8-inch) skillet over medium-high heat. Spray with olive oil and pour in half the egg substitute. Swirl in the pan to make a thin layer. Let cook 2 minutes, turn over for 1 minute, and remove from the heat. Spread the tomato sauce on top. Add the sausage, mushrooms, onion, and mozzarella cheese. Place under the broiler about 10 inches from the heat. Broil 10 minutes. Carefully slide onto a plate and serve. Repeat for the second serving.

*Makes 2 servings.*

## bran cereal

*1 cup high-fiber, no-sugar-added bran cereal*
*1 cup skim milk*

Divide between 2 cereal bowls.

*Makes 2 servings.*

TOTAL BREAKFAST **ONE SERVING: 387** CALORIES, **38G** PROTEIN, **39G** CARBOHYDRATE, **13G** FAT (**5G** SATURATED), **55MG** CHOLESTEROL, **1189MG** SODIUM, **15G** FIBER

# arugula and ham scramble with oatmeal

*Ham blends well with savory arugula in this simple-to-make scrambled egg dish.*

## arugula and ham scramble

- *1 cup egg substitute*
- *2 cups arugula, coarsely chopped or sliced*
- *Freshly ground black pepper to taste*
- *2 teaspoons olive oil*
- *½ pound sliced lean ham, cubed (about 8 slices)*

Combine the egg substitute and arugula, seasoning with pepper to taste. Heat the oil in a medium-size nonstick skillet on medium high. Add the ham and sauté for 2 minutes. Add the arugula and egg mixture; scramble for 1 minute, or until the egg is cooked to desired doneness. Serve.

*Makes 2 servings.*

## oatmeal

- *1 cup oatmeal*
- *2 cups water*
- *1 cup skim milk*
- *2 (.035-ounce) envelopes sugar substitute (optional)*

To prepare in the microwave, combine the oatmeal and water in a microwave-safe bowl. Microwave on high for 4 minutes. Stir in the milk and sugar substitute, divide between 2 bowls, and serve warm.

Alternatively, to prepare on the stovetop, combine the oatmeal and water in a small saucepan over medium-high heat, and bring to a boil. Reduce the heat to medium, and cook about 5 more minutes, stirring occasionally. Stir in the milk and sugar substitute, divide between 2 bowls, and serve warm.

*Makes 2 servings.*

TOTAL BREAKFAST **ONE SERVING: 427** CALORIES, **41G** PROTEIN, **42G** CARBOHYDRATE, **11G** FAT (**2G** SATURATED), **54MG** CHOLESTEROL, **1274MG** SODIUM, **4G** FIBER

## helpful hints

- *To quickly wash arugula, place it in a bowl of cold water, and then lift it out of the bowl. The sand will be left behind.*
- *To quickly chop or slice the arugula for this dish, place the leaves on top of each other and slice them at one time.*
- *Use spinach if arugula is unavailable.*

## countdown

- *Prepare all ingredients.*
- *Make eggs.*
- *Make oatmeal.*

## shopping list

*TO BUY:*

*½ pound sliced lean ham*
*1 small bunch arugula*

*STAPLES:*

*Egg substitute*
*Olive oil*
*Oatmeal*
*Skim milk*
*Sugar substitute*
*Black peppercorns*

# turkey and cottage cheese plate with pecan oatmeal

## helpful hints

- *Other types of fresh herbs such as dill, parsley, or basil can be used in place of chives.*
- *Toasting pecans can be tricky, as they burn quickly. Watch them carefully.*

## countdown

- *Make turkey.*
- *Make oatmeal.*

## shopping list

*TO BUY:*

*1 small carton low-fat cottage cheese (8 ounces needed)*

*1/2 pound sliced roast turkey breast*

*1 package pecan pieces (1 ounce needed)*

*1 jar freeze-dried chives*

*STAPLES:*

*Oatmeal*

*Skim milk*

*Sugar substitute*

*This breakfast is ideal when you're on the go, and it takes only a few minutes to put together. The addition of a few pecans to the oatmeal gives it a crunchy texture and nutty flavor.*

## turkey and cottage cheese plate

*1 cup low-fat cottage cheese*
*2 tablespoons freeze-dried chives*
*1/2 pound sliced roast turkey breast*

Combine the cottage cheese and chives in a small bowl. Place the turkey slices on 2 plates and spoon the cottage cheese mixture on the slices. Fold the turkey slices in half and serve.

*Makes 2 servings.*

## pecan oatmeal

*1 cup oatmeal*
*2 cups water*
*1/4 cup pecan pieces (1 ounce)*
*1 cup skim milk*
*2 (.035-ounce) envelopes sugar substitute (optional)*

To prepare in the microwave, combine the oatmeal and water in a microwave-safe bowl. Microwave on high for 4 minutes. Alternatively, to prepare on the stovetop, combine the oatmeal and water in a small saucepan over medium-high heat, and bring to a boil. Reduce the heat to medium, and cook about 5 more minutes, stirring occasionally.

Place the pecans on a foil-lined tray and toast in a toaster oven or under the broiler for 1 minute, or until golden. Stir the milk, sugar substitute, and toasted pecans into the oatmeal. Divide between 2 bowls and serve.

*Makes 2 servings.*

TOTAL BREAKFAST **ONE SERVING: 473** CALORIES, **40G** PROTEIN, **40G** CARBOHYDRATE, **17G** FAT (**4G** SATURATED), **52MG** CHOLESTEROL, **439MG** SODIUM, **5G** FIBER

# dijon ham and cheddar grill with cinnamon oatmeal

*For those mornings when you don't feel like eggs, try this quick cheese and ham melt. If you like spicy food, adjust the amount of cayenne accordingly.*

## dijon ham and cheddar grill

- *½ pound sliced lean smoked ham (about 8 slices)*
- *4 slices sliced reduced-fat, aged cheddar cheese (3 ounces)*
- *2 tablespoons Dijon mustard*
- *Pinch cayenne pepper*
- *1 medium tomato, cut into ½-inch slices*

Line a baking tray with foil. Place the ham on foil and cheese on top. Spread the cheese with mustard and sprinkle with cayenne. Place in a toaster oven or under broiler for 4 minutes, or until the cheese melts. Place the tomato slices on 2 plates with the ham and cheese to serve.

*Makes 2 servings.*

## cinnamon oatmeal

- *1 cup oatmeal*
- *2 cups water*
- *1 cup skim milk*
- *½ teaspoon ground cinnamon*
- *2 (.035-ounce) envelopes sugar substitute (optional)*

To prepare in the microwave, combine the oatmeal and water in a microwave-safe bowl. Microwave on high for 4 minutes. Stir in the milk, cinnamon, and sugar substitute, divide between 2 bowls, and serve warm.

Alternatively, to prepare on the stovetop, combine the oatmeal and water in a small saucepan over medium-high heat, and bring to a boil. Reduce the heat to medium, and cook about 5 more minutes, stirring occasionally. Stir in the milk, cinnamon, and sugar substitute, divide between 2 bowls, and serve warm.

*Makes 2 servings.*

TOTAL BREAKFAST **ONE SERVING: 484** CALORIES, **40G** PROTEIN, **43G** CARBOHYDRATE, **16G** FAT (**8G** SATURATED), **84MG** CHOLESTEROL, **1773MG** SODIUM, **4G** FIBER

### helpful hints

- *To determine the weight of each slice of cheese or ham, divide the package weight by the number of slices.*
- *No-sugar-added instant oatmeal can be used.*

### countdown

- *Preheat broiler or toaster oven.*
- *Make cheese and ham melt.*
- *Make oatmeal.*

### shopping list

*TO BUY:*

- *1 package sliced reduced-fat, aged cheddar cheese (3 ounces needed)*
- *½ pound sliced lean smoked ham*
- *1 medium tomato*

*STAPLES:*

- *Oatmeal*
- *Skim milk*
- *Ground cinnamon*
- *Dijon mustard*
- *Cayenne pepper*
- *Sugar substitute*

# omelette aux fines herbes with bran cereal

## helpful hints

- *To determine the weight of each slice of cheese, divide the package weight by the number of slices. With most brands, 1 slice equals 3/4 ounce.*
- *Make sure the dried chives and tarragon are less than 6 months old.*
- *Parsley, chives, and tarragon can be chopped together in a food processor or mini chop.*

## countdown

- *Prepare all ingredients.*
- *Make omelette.*
- *Assemble bran cereal.*

## shopping list

*TO BUY:*

*1 small package sliced reduced-fat Swiss cheese (1 1/2 ounces needed)*
*1 jar freeze-dried chives*
*1 large bunch fresh parsley*

*STAPLES:*

*Eggs*
*Skim milk*
*High-fiber, no-sugar-added bran cereal*
*Olive oil*
*Dried tarragon*
*Salt*
*Black peppercorns*

*Omelette aux Fines Herbes is on almost every French bistro menu. This is a quick version of this very French breakfast. I use freeze-dried chives and dried tarragon chopped with fresh parsley to speed up preparation. The secret here is chopping the dried herbs with the fresh parsley. The moisture from the parsley helps to release the juices from the dried herbs.*

## omelette aux fines herbes

*1 tablespoon freeze-dried chives*
*1/2 tablespoon dried tarragon*
*1 cup fresh parsley leaves*
*2 eggs*
*6 egg whites*
*Salt and freshly ground black pepper to taste*
*2 teaspoons olive oil*
*2 slices reduced-fat Swiss cheese (1 1/2 ounces)*

Chop the chives, tarragon, and parsley together. Whisk the eggs and egg whites together in a medium-size bowl. Stir in the herbs and add salt and pepper to taste. Heat the oil in a medium-size nonstick skillet on medium high. Pour in the egg mixture and let set 1 minute. Cover with a lid, and cook 2 to 3 minutes more, or until the egg is almost set. Turn the omelette over, place the cheese slices on top, and cover. Cook 1 more minute. Slide a knife under the omelette and fold in half. Cut the folded omelette in half, and serve on 2 plates.
*Makes 2 servings.*

## bran cereal

*1 cup skim milk*
*1 cup high-fiber, no-sugar-added bran cereal*

Divide the milk and cereal between 2 bowls.
*Makes 2 servings.*

TOTAL BREAKFAST **ONE SERVING: 343** CALORIES, **33G** PROTEIN, **36G** CARBOHYDRATE, **15G** FAT (**4G** SATURATED), **226MG** CHOLESTEROL, **488MG** SODIUM, **13G** FIBER

# smoked turkey roll-ups with spiced oatmeal

*Turkey slices filled with nutty-flavored arugula and alfalfa sprouts provide a quick-grab breakfast. The roll-ups can be made the night before and eaten on the run.*

## smoked turkey roll-ups

*½ pound sliced lean smoked turkey breast*
*2 tablespoons mayonnaise made with olive or soybean oil*
*Several arugula leaves*
*2 cups alfalfa sprouts*

Place the turkey slices on a countertop or plate. Spread the turkey with mayonnaise. Top with arugula leaves and sprouts. Roll up, divide between 2 plates, and serve.

*Makes 2 servings.*

## spiced oatmeal

*1 cup oatmeal*
*2 cups water*
*2 (.035-ounce) envelopes sugar substitute (optional)*
*½ teaspoon ground nutmeg*
*1 cup skim milk*

To prepare in the microwave, combine the oatmeal and water in a microwave-safe bowl. Microwave on high for 4 minutes. Stir in the sugar substitute and nutmeg. Stir in the milk, divide between 2 bowls, and serve warm.

Alternatively, to prepare on the stovetop, combine the oatmeal and water in a small saucepan over medium-high heat, and bring to a boil. Reduce the heat to medium, and cook about 5 more minutes, stirring occasionally. Stir in the sugar substitute and nutmeg. Stir in the milk, divide between 2 bowls, and serve warm.

*Makes 2 servings.*

TOTAL BREAKFAST **ONE SERVING: 484** CALORIES, **43G** PROTEIN, **36G** CARBOHYDRATE, **18G** FAT (**3G** SATURATED), **87MG** CHOLESTEROL, **218MG** SODIUM, **5G** FIBER

## helpful hints

- *Fresh basil or parsley can be substituted for the arugula.*
- *Any type of sprout can be used.*

## countdown

- *Make turkey roll-ups.*
- *Make oatmeal.*

## shopping list

*TO BUY:*

*½ pound sliced lean smoked turkey breast*
*1 small bunch arugula*
*1 container alfalfa sprouts*

*STAPLES:*

*Mayonnaise made with olive or soybean oil*
*Oatmeal*
*Skim milk*
*Ground nutmeg*
*Sugar substitute*

# shrimp, red pepper, and tomato frittata with berry and banana yogurt bran cup

*This is an unusual frittata topped with sliced tomatoes and melted cheese.*

## shrimp, red pepper, and tomato frittata

*2 whole eggs*
*6 egg whites*
*Salt and freshly ground black pepper to taste*
*2 teaspoons olive oil*
*1 medium-size red bell pepper, sliced (2 cups)*
*1/2 pound cooked shrimp, cut in half crosswise*
*1 medium tomato, sliced*
*1/4 cup shredded, reduced-fat cheddar cheese (1 ounce)*

Preheat the oven to 400 degrees. Lightly beat the whole eggs and egg whites together in a medium-size bowl, and season with salt and pepper to taste.

Heat the oil in a medium-size nonstick skillet on medium. Add the bell pepper and sauté for 3 minutes. Add the shrimp and pour the egg mixture into the skillet, swirling in the pan to cover the bell pepper. Let set for 1 minute. Place the tomato slices on top and sprinkle with the cheese.

Place in the oven for 5 minutes, or until the eggs are set to the desired consistency. Divide the frittata between 2 plates and serve.

*Makes 2 servings.*

## berry and banana yogurt bran cup

*1 cup light strawberry-banana flavored yogurt*
*1 cup high-fiber, no-sugar-added bran cereal*

Divide the yogurt between 2 bowls and sprinkle with the bran.

*Makes 2 servings.*

TOTAL BREAKFAST **ONE SERVING: 467** CALORIES, **53G** PROTEIN, **41G** CARBOHYDRATE, **17G** FAT (**5G** SATURATED), **399MG** CHOLESTEROL, **716MG** SODIUM, **13G** FIBER

### helpful hints

- *Use skillet with an ovenproof handle, and be careful of the hot handle when skillet is removed from the oven.*
- *Buy cooked shrimp in the seafood department, or look for good quality, large, frozen cooked shrimp.*
- *To determine the weight of each slice of cheese, divide the package weight by the number of slices. With most brands, 1 slice equals 3/4 ounce.*

### countdown

- *Preheat oven to 400 degrees.*
- *Make frittata.*
- *Assemble bran cup.*

### shopping list

*TO BUY:*

*1 package shredded, reduced-fat cheddar cheese (1 ounce needed)*
*1 carton light strawberry-banana flavored yogurt*
*1/2 pound cooked shrimp*
*1 medium-size red bell pepper*
*1 medium tomato*

*STAPLES:*

*Eggs*
*Olive oil*
*High-fiber, no-sugar-added bran cereal*
*Salt*
*Black peppercorns*

# asian omelette with bran cereal

*Crisp water chestnuts and bean sprouts give an Oriental flavor to this omelette. It's adapted from the popular Chinese dish, Egg Foo Yong.*

## asian omelette

*2 teaspoons olive oil*
*½ cup fresh bean sprouts*
*½ cup sliced water chestnuts*
*Freshly ground black pepper to taste*
*1 cup egg substitute*
*¼ pound sliced lean ham, chopped (about 4 slices)*

Heat the oil in a nonstick skillet on medium high. Add the bean sprouts and water chestnuts, and sauté for 1 minute. Season the egg substitute with pepper to taste, and pour into the skillet, swirling to cover the vegetables. Let set 1 minute. Sprinkle the ham on top, cover, and cook 2 to 3 minutes longer, or until the egg sets to desired consistency. Cut the omelette in half, slide out of the skillet, and serve.

*Makes 2 servings.*

## bran cereal

*1 cup skim milk*
*1 cup high-fiber, no-sugar-added bran cereal*

Divide the milk and cereal between 2 bowls.

*Makes 2 servings.*

TOTAL BREAKFAST **ONE SERVING: 369** CALORIES, **42G** PROTEIN, **44G** CARBOHYDRATE, **8G** FAT (**1G** SATURATED), **28MG** CHOLESTEROL, **1146MG** SODIUM, **15G** FIBER

## helpful hint

- *To save time, buy sliced water chestnuts.*

## countdown

- *Make omelette.*
- *Assemble cereal.*

## shopping list

*TO BUY:*

*¼ pound sliced lean ham*
*1 small can sliced water chestnuts*
*1 small package fresh bean sprouts*

*STAPLES:*

*Egg substitute*
*Olive oil*
*Skim milk*
*High-fiber, no-sugar-added bran cereal*
*Black peppercorns*

# grilled tuna–stuffed sweet peppers and bran cereal

*This popular combination of tuna salad and melted cheese works well for breakfast.*

## helpful hint

- *Any reduced-fat blend of Mexican cheeses can be substituted for Monterey jack cheese.*

## countdown

- *Preheat broiler.*
- *Make tuna melt.*
- *Assemble cereal.*

## shopping list

*TO BUY:*

*1 package sliced reduced-fat Monterey Jack cheese (3 ounces needed)*

*1 (6-ounce) can tuna packed in water*

*1 small bunch fresh basil*

*2 small red bell peppers*

*STAPLES:*

*Mayonnaise made from soybean or olive oil*

*High-fiber, no-sugar-added bran cereal*

*Skim milk*

*Salt*

*Black peppercorns*

## grilled tuna–stuffed sweet peppers

*1 (6-ounce) can tuna packed in water, drained and rinsed (1 cup)*

*2 tablespoons mayonnaise made from soybean or olive oil*

*6 to 8 fresh basil leaves, torn into bite-size pieces (about 4 tablespoons)*

*Salt and freshly ground black pepper to taste*

*2 small red bell peppers, seeded and halved*

*4 slices reduced-fat Monterey Jack cheese (3 ounces)*

Preheat the broiler. Line a baking tray with foil. In a small bowl, flake the tuna with a fork. Stir in the mayonnaise and basil; season with salt and pepper to taste. Spoon the tuna salad into the bell pepper halves, and top with the cheese. Broil 2 minutes, or until cheese has melted. Divide between 2 plates and serve.

*Makes 2 servings.*

## bran cereal

*1 cup skim milk*

*1 cup high-fiber, no-sugar-added bran cereal*

Divide the milk and cereal between 2 bowls.

*Makes 2 servings.*

TOTAL BREAKFAST **ONE SERVING: 455** CALORIES, **43G** PROTEIN, **39G** CARBOHYDRATE, **21G** FAT (**6G** SATURATED), **60MG** CHOLESTEROL, **957MG** SODIUM, **13G** FIBER

# pecan ham roll-ups with cinnamon oatmeal

*Cream cheese and pecans make a quick filling for sliced ham. These can be made a day ahead and used for a quick-take breakfast.*

## pecan ham roll-ups

*1/4 cup reduced-fat cream cheese*
*2 tablespoons skim milk*
*6 pecans, chopped (2 tablespoons)*
*1/2 pound sliced lean ham (about 8 slices)*

Blend the cream cheese, milk, and pecans in a food processor. Or, chop the pecans by hand and combine with the cream cheese and milk. Lay the ham slices on the countertop or plate, and spread with the cream cheese mixture. Roll up, divide between 2 plates, and serve.

*Makes 2 servings.*

## cinnamon oatmeal

*1 cup oatmeal*
*2 cups water*
*1 cup skim milk*
*1/2 teaspoon ground cinnamon*
*2 (.035-ounce) envelopes sugar substitute (optional)*

To prepare in the microwave, combine the oatmeal and water in a microwave-safe bowl. Microwave on high for 4 minutes. Stir in the milk, cinnamon, and sugar substitute, divide between 2 bowls, and serve warm.

Alternatively, to prepare on the stovetop, combine the oatmeal and water in a small saucepan over medium-high heat, and bring to a boil. Reduce the heat to medium, and cook about 5 more minutes, stirring occasionally. Stir in the milk, cinnamon, and sugar substitute. Divide between 2 bowls, and serve warm.

*Makes 2 servings.*

TOTAL BREAKFAST **ONE SERVING: 449** CALORIES, **32G** PROTEIN, **42G** CARBOHYDRATE, **18G** FAT (**6G** SATURATED), **76MG** CHOLESTEROL, **1169MG** SODIUM, **5G** FIBER

## helpful hints

- *To determine the weight of each slice of ham, divide the package weight by the number of slices. With most brands, 1 slice equals 3/4 ounce.*
- *Warm water can be used instead of skim milk to soften the cream cheese.*

## countdown

- *Make ham roll-ups.*
- *Make oatmeal.*

## shopping list

*TO BUY:*

*1/4 cup reduced-fat cream cheese*
*1/2 pound sliced lean ham*
*1 small package pecan pieces (1/2 ounce needed)*

*STAPLES:*

*Oatmeal*
*Skim milk*
*Ground cinnamon*
*Sugar substitute*

# microwave cheddar scramble with bran cereal

## helpful hint

- *To determine the weight of each slice of cheese, divide the package weight by the number of slices. With most brands, 1 slice equals 3/4 ounce.*

## countdown

- *Make eggs.*
- *Assemble cereal.*

## shopping list

*TO BUY:*

*1 small package sliced reduced-fat cheddar cheese (3 ounces needed)*

*STAPLES:*

*Egg substitute*

*Skim milk*

*High-fiber, no-sugar-added bran cereal*

*Black peppercorns*

*This is a breakfast you can make on the run. The eggs take 1 1/2 minutes to cook and, best of all, there's no skillet to wash.*

## microwave cheddar scramble

*2 cups egg substitute, divided*

*4 slices reduced-fat cheddar cheese, divided (3 ounces)*

*Freshly ground black pepper to taste*

Combine 1 cup of the egg substitute with 2 slices of the cheese in a microwave-safe bowl. Season with pepper to taste. Microwave on high for 1 1/2 minutes. Stir, and then heat another 30 seconds. Repeat for the second serving. Serve hot.

*Makes 2 servings.*

## bran cereal

*1 cup skim milk*

*1 cup high-fiber, no-sugar-added bran cereal*

Divide the milk and cereal between 2 bowls.

*Makes 2 servings.*

TOTAL BREAKFAST **ONE SERVING: 358** CALORIES, **41G** PROTEIN, **35G** CARBOHYDRATE, **10G** FAT (**6G** SATURATED), **32MG** CHOLESTEROL, **998MG** SODIUM, **13G** FIBER

# cheese and roasted red pepper–stuffed endive with bran cereal

*This is a quick breakfast that you can put together in minutes. In fact, it's also a good snack. Keep the mixture in the refrigerator and use it as a dip or spread with other vegetables.*

## cheese and roasted red pepper–stuffed endive

- *2 cups low-fat cottage cheese*
- *¼ cup low-fat cream cheese (2 ounces)*
- *2 cups canned, roasted red bell peppers, drained and diced*
- *1 cup chopped purple basil*
- *Salt and freshly ground black pepper to taste*
- *2 large heads Belgian endive*

Combine the cottage cheese, cream cheese, roasted red pepper, and purple basil by hand in a medium-size bowl or in a food processor. Season with salt and pepper to taste. Remove any damaged outer leaves from the endive, break off leaves, and divide between 2 plates. Spoon the filling onto the wide end of each leaf and serve.

*Makes 2 servings.*

## bran cereal

- *1 cup skim milk*
- *1 cup high-fiber, no-sugar-added bran cereal*

Divide the milk and cereal between 2 bowls.

*Makes 2 servings.*

TOTAL BREAKFAST **ONE SERVING: 394** CALORIES, **36G** PROTEIN, **47G** CARBOHYDRATE, **11G** FAT (**8G** SATURATED), **44MG** CHOLESTEROL, **1005MG** SODIUM, **13G** FIBER

## helpful hints

- *Buy a large Belgian endive if available. The leaves will hold more filling.*
- *Be sure to drain the roasted red bell peppers to make a drier filling.*
- *Regular green basil can be substituted for purple basil.*

## countdown

- *Make stuffed endive*
- *Assemble cereal.*

## shopping list

*TO BUY:*

- *1 small package low-fat cream cheese*
- *1 carton low-fat cottage cheese (1 pound needed)*
- *1 small can or jar roasted red bell peppers*
- *1 small bunch purple basil*
- *2 large Belgian endives*

*STAPLES:*

- *Skim milk*
- *High-fiber, no-sugar-added bran cereal*
- *Salt*
- *Black peppercorns*

# spanish omelette and bran cereal

## helpful hint

- *Use a skillet with an ovenproof handle, but be careful with the hot handle when removing from the oven.*

## countdown

- *Preheat broiler.*
- *Make omelette.*
- *Assemble cereal.*

## shopping list

*TO BUY:*

*1/4 pound sliced turkey breast*

*1 small bunch scallions (8 scallions needed)*

*1 medium tomato*

*STAPLES:*

*Eggs*

*Skim milk*

*Olive oil*

*High-fiber, no-sugar-added bran cereal*

*Salt*

*Black peppercorns*

*This zesty breakfast classic is updated here to make a quick meal. You can add chiles, garlic, and bell peppers for variety and additional spice. Just use this recipe as a guideline.*

## spanish omelette

*2 whole eggs*

*4 egg whites*

*1/2 pound sliced turkey breast, chopped*

*8 scallions, sliced (1 cup)*

*Salt and freshly ground black pepper to taste*

*2 teaspoons olive oil*

*1 medium tomato, cubed*

Preheat the broiler. Whisk the whole eggs and egg whites together in a medium-size mixing bowl. Stir in the turkey and scallions, and season with salt and pepper to taste. Heat the oil in a medium-size nonstick skillet on medium high. Add the tomato, and sauté for 3 minutes. Add the egg mixture, swirling to cover the tomato. Let set 1 minute, and then place under the broiler for 5 minutes. Divide the omelette in half, slide out of the skillet, and serve on 2 plates. *Makes 2 servings.*

## bran cereal

*1 cup skim milk*

*1 cup high-fiber, no-sugar-added bran cereal*

Divide the milk and cereal between 2 bowls. *Makes 2 servings.*

TOTAL BREAKFAST **ONE SERVING: 465** CALORIES, **54G** PROTEIN, **39G** CARBOHYDRATE, **16G** FAT (**4G** SATURATED), **295MG** CHOLESTEROL, **455MG** SODIUM, **13G** FIBER

# raspberry-red smoothie with toasted walnut oatmeal

*When I did the research for an article I wrote about smoothies, I was astounded at their high carbohydrate content. But the cool, smooth, frozen drinks are so good that I decided to create one that was quick, easy, delicious—and good for us too. My family proclaimed this one a winner. • Use a microwave to make the oatmeal, and this breakfast will take only 10 minutes to make.*

## raspberry-red smoothie

*1 cup fresh or frozen raspberries*
*½ cup light raspberry-flavored yogurt*
*2 teaspoons vanilla extract*
*2 (.035-ounce) envelopes sugar substitute*
*2 cups ice cubes*

Place the raspberries, yogurt, vanilla extract, and sugar substitute in a blender. Blend until smooth. Add the ice cubes, and blend until thick. Pour into 2 glasses and serve cold.

*Makes 2 servings.*

## toasted walnut oatmeal

*1 cup oatmeal*
*2 cups water*
*¼ cup walnuts*
*1 cup skim milk*
*2 (.035-ounce) envelopes sugar substitute (optional)*

To prepare in the microwave, combine the oatmeal and water in a microwave-safe bowl. Microwave on high for 4 minutes. Alternatively, to prepare on the stovetop, combine the oatmeal and water in a small saucepan over medium-high heat, and bring to a boil. Reduce the heat to medium, and cook about 5 more minutes, stirring occasionally.

Place the walnuts on a foil-lined tray and toast in toaster oven or under broiler for 1 minute, or until lightly toasted. Stir the milk, sugar substitute, and toasted walnuts into the oatmeal. Divide between 2 bowls and serve warm.

*Makes 2 servings.*

## smoked turkey breast

*6 ounces sliced smoked turkey breast, cubed*
*Several lettuce leaves*

Place lettuce on 2 plates with the turkey cubes on top, and serve.

*Makes 2 servings.*

TOTAL BREAKFAST **ONE SERVING: 492** CALORIES, **38G** PROTEIN, **49G** CARBOHYDRATE, **16G** FAT (**2G** SATURATED), **63MG** CHOLESTEROL, **149MG** SODIUM, **8G** FIBER

## helpful hints

- *If using frozen raspberries, make sure they are not packed in syrup.*
- *Any type of lettuce can be used.*
- *No-sugar-added, instant oatmeal can be used.*
- *Toasting walnuts can be tricky, as they burn quickly. Watch them carefully.*

## countdown

- *Make smoothie.*
- *Make oatmeal.*
- *Assemble turkey.*

## shopping list

*TO BUY:*

*1 carton light raspberry-flavored yogurt*
*6 ounces sliced smoked turkey breast*
*1 small package walnuts (1 ounce needed)*
*1 small container fresh or frozen raspberries*
*1 small head lettuce*

*STAPLES:*

*Vanilla extract*
*Oatmeal*
*Skim milk*
*Sugar substitute*

# which carb lunches

# nuevo tex-mex layered salad

*This is a very pretty salad that will impress company. Arrange the salad in a large glass bowl so that the layers of colors show through. The salad can be made several hours in advance. Keep covered and refrigerated, and add the dressing just before serving.*

## nuevo tex-mex layered salad

*1 medium tomato, divided*
*1/4 cup chopped red onion*
*1 jalapeño pepper, seeded and chopped*
*1/2 teaspoon ground cumin*
*Salt and freshly ground black pepper to taste*
*2/3 cup canned black beans, rinsed and drained*
*4 cups iceberg lettuce, washed and shredded*
*1 medium-size green bell pepper, chopped (1 cup)*
*1/2 pound sliced smoked lean deli turkey breast, cut into 1/2-inch strips*
*1/4 cup no-sugar-added oil and vinegar dressing*

Chop half of the tomato; slice the remaining half. Combine the chopped tomato with the onion and jalapeño in a medium-size bowl. Stir in the ground cumin. (These steps can be done in a food processor or by hand.) Season with salt and pepper to taste. Gently stir in the black beans. Layer the lettuce, bell pepper, half the black bean mixture, and turkey in a medium glass bowl. Arrange the tomato slices on the turkey, and spoon the remaining black beans over the tomatoes. Pour the dressing over salad and serve. *Makes 2 servings.*

**ONE SERVING: 467** CALORIES, **41G** PROTEIN, **27G** CARBOHYDRATE **21G** FAT (**4G** SATURATED), **80MG** CHOLESTEROL, **238MG** SODIUM, **3G** FIBER

### helpful hint

- *Buy ready-to-eat, shredded lettuce in produce section of market.*

### countdown

- *Prepare ingredients.*
- *Make salad.*

### shopping list

*TO BUY:*

*1/2 pound sliced smoked lean deli turkey breast*
*1 small can black beans*
*1 medium tomato*
*1 jalapeño pepper*
*1 head iceberg lettuce*
*1 medium-size green bell pepper*

*STAPLES:*

*Red onion*
*No-sugar-added oil and vinegar dressing*
*Ground cumin*
*Salt*
*Black peppercorns*

# smoked whitefish salad

## helpful hints

- *If using fresh dill, simply snip the leaves with scissors.*
- *Make sure dried dill is less than 6 months old. It should be green, not brown or gray.*

## countdown

- *Prepare ingredients.*
- *Make salad.*

## shopping list

*TO BUY:*

*1 carton non-fat, plain yogurt*
*1/2 pound smoked white fish*
*1 bunch fresh dill or 1 jar dried*
*1 small bunch fresh scallions (4 scallions needed)*
*1 small head Boston lettuce*
*2 medium tomatoes*

*STAPLES:*

*Celery*
*Mayonnaise made with olive and soybean oil*
*Rye bread*
*Salt*
*Black peppercorns*

*Whitefish is a mild-flavored member of the salmon family. Its high fat content makes it perfect for smoking.*

## smoked whitefish salad

*2 tablespoons mayonnaise made with olive and soybean oil*
*2 tablespoons non-fat, plain yogurt*
*1/4 cup snipped fresh dill or 1 teaspoon dried*
*1/2 pound smoked whitefish, flaked*
*4 scallions, sliced (1/2 cup)*
*2 celery stalks, sliced (1 cup)*
*Salt and freshly ground black pepper to taste*
*Several Boston lettuce leaves*
*2 medium tomatoes, sliced*
*2 slices rye bread*

Combine the mayonnaise, yogurt, and dill in a medium-size bowl. Add the whitefish, scallions, and celery. Season with salt and pepper to taste. Toss well. Serve on 2 plates over the lettuce with sliced tomatoes and bread.

*Makes 2 servings.*

**ONE SERVING: 327** CALORIES, **34G** PROTEIN, **22G** CARBOHYDRATE **14G** FAT (**2G** SATURATED), **43MG** CHOLESTEROL, **1447MG** SODIUM, **4G** FIBER

# salad niçoise with citrus

*This quick salad from the French Riviera is filled with olives, tomatoes, asparagus, and tuna. You can add any other greens or leftover vegetables. These ingredients were chosen to give a variety of textures, colors, and flavors: crisp, pale green lettuce; ripe red tomatoes; soft, pink tuna; and dark, green asparagus. Use this recipe as a base and create your own version of this classic.*

## salad niçoise

*1/4 cup red wine vinegar*
*2 tablespoons Dijon mustard*
*1/4 cup diced red onion*
*2 tablespoons water*
*2 tablespoons olive oil*
*Salt and freshly ground black pepper to taste*
*2 (6-ounce) cans low-salt, solid white tuna packed in water, drained and rinsed*
*1/2 pound fresh asparagus*
*4 cups washed, ready-to-eat, field greens or French-style salad*
*2 medium tomatoes, cut into wedges*
*8 pitted black olives, quartered*

To prepare the vinaigrette dressing, whisk the vinegar and mustard together in a large bowl with the onion and water. Whisk in the oil to a smooth consistency. Season with salt and pepper to taste. Flake the tuna into the vinaigrette.

Cut or snap off the 1-inch fibrous stem on the asparagus and discard. Slice the remaining asparagus into 2-inch pieces (you should have about 2 1/2 cups). Bring a medium saucepan of water to a boil. Add the asparagus. As soon as the water comes back to a boil, drain the asparagus and refresh in cold water. (If using thick asparagus boil 5 minutes.)

To microwave the asparagus instead, place asparagus in a microwave-safe bowl and microwave on high for 4 minutes. Add the asparagus to the tuna mixture and toss gently. Divide the lettuce between 2 plates. Spoon the tuna-asparagus mixture over the lettuce. Arrange the tomato wedges around the plate, sprinkle the olives over the top, and serve.

*Makes 2 servings.*

**ONE SERVING: 424** CALORIES, **51G** PROTEIN, **14G** CARBOHYDRATE **20G** FAT (**2G** SATURATED), **75MG** CHOLESTEROL, **1283MG** SODIUM, **3G** FIBER

## citrus

*2 medium oranges*

Divide the oranges between 2 plates and serve.

*Makes 2 servings.*

**ONE SERVING: 62** CALORIES, **1G** PROTEIN, **15G** CARBOHYDRATE, **0G** FAT (**0G** SATURATED), **0MG** CHOLESTEROL, **0MG** SODIUM, **3G** FIBER

### helpful hint

- *Use the dressing recipe provided here or purchase a no-sugar-added oil and vinegar dressing and add diced red onion.*

### countdown

- *Make dressing.*
- *Blanch asparagus.*
- *Assemble salad.*

### shopping list

*TO BUY:*

*2 (6-ounce) cans low-salt, solid white tuna, packed in water*
*1 jar or can pitted black olives*
*1/2 pound fresh asparagus*
*1 bag washed, ready-to-eat field greens or French-style salad*
*2 medium tomatoes*
*2 medium oranges*

*STAPLES:*

*Red onion*
*Dijon mustard*
*Red wine vinegar*
*Olive oil*
*Salt*
*Black peppercorns*

# chicken salad amandine

## helpful hints

- *Make sure the bottle of dried tarragon is less than 6 months old. It should be a green color, not brown or gray. This freshness will make a marked difference in the flavor of the salad.*
- *Any type of lettuce can be used.*
- *Toasting almonds intensifies their flavor, but can be tricky. Watch them carefully, as they burn easily. This step can be omitted.*

## countdown

- *Toast almonds.*
- *Make salad.*

## shopping list

*TO BUY:*

*1 carton non-fat, plain yogurt*

*1/2 pound roast chicken breast*

*1 small package slivered almonds (1 ounce needed)*

*1 Golden Delicious apple*

*1 small head radicchio*

*STAPLES:*

*Celery*

*Mayonnaise made with olive or soybean oil*

*Dried tarragon*

*Salt*

*Black peppercorns*

*Almonds and apples add a crunchy texture and varied flavors to this chicken salad. Use leftover roasted chicken or store-bought rotisserie chicken for a fast meal.*

## chicken salad amandine

*2 tablespoons slivered almonds*

*2 tablespoons mayonnaise made with olive or soybean oil*

*1/4 cup non-fat, plain yogurt*

*4 teaspoons dried tarragon*

*Salt and freshly ground black pepper to taste*

*1/2 pound roast chicken breast, skin removed and cut into 1-inch pieces*

*2 celery stalks, sliced (1 cup)*

*1 Golden Delicious apple, cored and cut into 1/2-inch cubes (about 1 1/2 cups)*

*1 small head radicchio*

Place almonds on a foil-lined tray and toast in a toaster oven or under the broiler for 1 minute. Alternatively, toast in a nonstick skillet over medium heat for 1 minute, or until golden. Combine the mayonnaise, yogurt, and tarragon in a medium-size bowl. Season with salt and pepper to taste. Add the chicken, celery, toasted almonds, and apple. Toss well, and adjust seasonings if necessary. Carefully remove the leaves from the radicchio, making them into small cups. Spoon the chicken salad into the radicchio leaves. Serve on 2 plates.

*Makes 2 servings.*

**ONE SERVING: 457** CALORIES, **43G** PROTEIN, **24G** CARBOHYDRATE, **23G** FAT (**3G** SATURATED), **101MG** CHOLESTEROL, **282MG** SODIUM, **5G** FIBER

# roast turkey sandwich with greek sadziki sauce and pistachios

*The refreshing flavor of mint and cucumber mingle with roasted turkey in this grilled Middle Eastern sandwich. Sadziki is a yogurt sauce that can also be used as a vegetable dip. It takes only seconds to make in a food processor.*

## roast turkey sandwich with greek sadziki sauce

*1 medium cucumber, peeled and seeded (about 1½ cups)*
*½ cup non-fat, plain yogurt*
*2 medium-size garlic cloves, crushed*
*2 tablespoons chopped fresh mint*
*¼ cup chopped red onion*
*Salt and freshly ground black pepper to taste*
*2 slices whole wheat bread, toasted*
*½ pound sliced roast turkey breast, skin removed and meat cut into 1-inch pieces*
*2 cups washed, ready-to-eat, shredded lettuce*

Chop the cucumber in the bowl of a food processor and drain. Stir in the yogurt, garlic, mint, and onion into the food processor bowl with the drained cucumber. Season with salt and pepper to taste.

Place a slice of toasted bread on each plate. Top with roast turkey and shredded lettuce. Spoon a little sadziki sauce over the lettuce. Serve any extra lettuce and sauce on the side.

*Makes 2 servings.*

**ONE SERVING: 302** CALORIES, **40G** PROTEIN, **23** CARBOHYDRATE, **6** FAT (**1G** SATURATED), **81MG** CHOLESTEROL, **241MG** SODIUM, **6G** FIBER

## pistachios

*¼ cup shelled pistachio nuts*

Divide the pistachios between 2 plates and serve.

*Makes 2 servings.*

**ONE SERVING: 131** CALORIES,**5G** PROTEIN, **6G** CARBOHYDRATE, **11G** FAT (**1G** SATURATED), **0MG** CHOLESTEROL, **2MG** SODIUM, **0G** FIBER

### helpful hint

- *Ready-to-eat shredded lettuce can be found in the produce department of the market.*

### countdown

- *Make sadziki sauce.*
- *Make sandwich.*

### shopping list

*TO BUY:*

*1 carton non-fat plain yogurt*
*½ pound sliced roast turkey breast*
*1 small package pistachio nuts (1½ ounces needed)*
*1 medium cucumber*
*1 bunch fresh mint*
*1 bag washed, ready-to-eat, shredded lettuce*

*STAPLES:*

*Garlic*
*Red onion*
*Whole wheat bread*
*Salt*
*Black peppercorns*

# california chef's salad

## helpful hints

- *To quickly julienne meat, ask the deli to cut the meat in 1/2-inch slices. You can then easily cut the slices into 1/2-inch julienne strips.*
- *Any type of sprouts can be used.*
- *If making salad in advance, add the dressing just before serving.*
- *Any type of no-sugar-added dressing can be used instead of the dressing recipe given.*
- *You can double or triple the dressing recipe. Store covered in the refrigerator.*
- *To determine the weight of each slice of cheese, divide the package weight by the number of slices. With most brands, 1 slice equals 3/4 ounce.*

## countdown

- *Make dressing.*
- *Prepare ingredients.*
- *Assemble salad.*

## shopping list

*TO BUY:*

*1 small package sliced reduced-fat Swiss cheese (1 1/2 ounces needed)*

*2 ounces sliced smoked deli chicken breast*

*2 ounces sliced lean deli roast beef*

*2 ounces sliced lean deli ham*

*1 head romaine lettuce*

*2 small cucumbers*

*1 medium-size red bell pepper*

*1 container alfalfa sprouts*

*STAPLES:*

*Canola oil*

*Dijon mustard*

*Balsamic vinegar*

*Salt*

*Black pepper*

*Julienned slices of ham, turkey, roast beef, and cheese alongside an array of fresh vegetables are the basis for this very American favorite. There are probably as many versions as people who make it. Use whatever lean cold meats and vegetables you have on hand, referring to the proportions given in the recipe as a guideline. Traditionally, the ingredients in a Chef's Salad are cut in julienne strips (large match sticks). However, if you are pressed for time, you can slice them in a food processor fitted with a thick slicing blade.*

## california chef's salad

*1/4 cup balsamic vinegar*

*1 tablespoon Dijon mustard*

*2 tablespoons water*

*2 tablespoons canola oil*

*Salt and freshly ground black pepper to taste*

*8 large romaine lettuce leaves, washed, dried, and sliced*

*2 small cucumbers, peeled and julienned*

*1 medium-size red bell pepper, julienned (2 cups)*

*2 slices reduced-fat Swiss cheese, julienned (1 1/2 ounces)*

*2 ounces sliced smoked deli chicken breast, julienned (2/3 cup)*

*2 ounces sliced lean deli roast beef, julienned (1/2 cup)*

*2 ounces sliced lean deli ham, julienned (1/2 cup)*

*1 cup alfalfa sprouts*

Mix the vinegar and mustard together in a small bowl until smooth. Add the water and oil, blending well. Season with salt and pepper to taste. Divide the romaine leaves between 2 plates. Place the remaining ingredients on the leaves in pie-shaped segments, like the spokes of a wheel. Spoon the dressing over the top and serve.

*Makes 2 servings.*

**ONE SERVING: 400** CALORIES, **34G** PROTEIN, **19G** CARBOHYDRATE **22G** FAT (**5G** SATURATED), **71MG** CHOLESTEROL, **519MG** SODIUM, **2G** FIBER

# citrus, turkey, and salsa salad with plum plate

*The nutty flavor and creamy texture of ripe avocado blends well with sweet orange and smoky turkey in this quick salad—only 5 minutes from start to finish. • Ask the produce manager for a ripe avocado if you don't find one displayed. Sometimes they don't display ones that will ripen within a day. A quick way to help avocados ripen is to remove the stem, place the avocado in a paper bag, and leave in a warm spot. • Curly endive has a loose head with lacy, green-rimmed leaves that curl at the pointed tips.*

## citrus, turkey, and salsa salad

- *1/2 pound sliced lean smoked turkey breast, cut into 1-inch cubes (1 1/2 cups)*
- *1 ripe small avocado, pitted and cut into 1-inch cubes (1/2 cup)*
- *1 cup no-sugar-added tomato salsa*
- *2 small oranges, peeled and cut into 1-inch cubes (about 2 cups)*
- *1 cup alfalfa sprouts*
- *Salt and freshly ground black pepper to taste*
- *Several curly endive leaves*

Combine the turkey, avocado, and salsa in a medium-size bowl, tossing well. Gently stir in the orange cubes and sprouts. Season with salt and pepper to taste. Place the curly endive on 2 plates, spoon the turkey-avocado mixture on top, and serve. *Makes 2 servings.*

**ONE SERVING: 464** CALORIES, **40G** PROTEIN, **33G** CARBOHYDRATE **19G** FAT (**3G** SATURATED), **80MG** CHOLESTEROL, **850MG** SODIUM, **12G** FIBER

## plum plate

- *2 medium plums, halved and pitted*

Slice the plums. Divide between 2 plates and serve. *Makes 2 servings.*

**ONE SERVING: 36** CALORIES, **1G** PROTEIN, **9G** CARBOHYDRATE, **0G** FAT (**0G** SATURATED), **0MG** CHOLESTEROL, **0MG** SODIUM, **0.5G** FIBER

### helpful hint

- *Any type of lettuce can be used.*

### countdown

- *Prepare ingredients.*
- *Assemble salad.*

### shopping list

*TO BUY:*

- *1/2 pound sliced lean smoked turkey breast*
- *1 jar no-sugar-added tomato salsa (8 ounces needed)*
- *1 ripe small avocado*
- *2 small oranges*
- *1 container alfalfa sprouts*
- *1 small head curly endive*
- *2 medium plums*

*STAPLES:*

- *Salt*
- *Black peppercorns*

# jamaican jerk chicken salad with hearts of palm

## helpful hints

- *Use the jerk recipe provided or purchase a jerk seasoning or marinade. Make sure it does not have added sugar.*
- *Make sure the dried thyme is less than 6 months old.*
- *This jerk chicken will keep 1 to 2 days in the refrigerator. Double the recipe and save half for another lunch.*

## countdown

- *Prepare ingredients.*
- *Make chicken.*
- *While chicken cooks, arrange hearts of palm and lettuce on plate.*

## shopping list

*TO BUY:*

*3/4 pound boneless, skinless chicken breast*

*1 jar or can hearts of palm*

*1 small head romaine lettuce*

*2 medium tangerines*

*STAPLES:*

*Yellow onion*

*Dried thyme*

*Ground nutmeg*

*Olive oil spray*

*No-sugar-added oil and vinegar dressing*

*Sugar substitute*

*Salt*

*Black peppercorns*

*"Jerking" is an ancient Jamaican method for preserving and cooking meat. It's a long process that involves marinating the meat and then slowly cooking it over a pimento (allspice) wood fire. For this Jerk Chicken Salad, I adapted the flavors and inspiration of jerk cooking to create an exotic, quick meal.*

## jamaican jerk chicken salad with hearts of palm

*1 tablespoon chopped yellow onion*

*2 teaspoons dried thyme*

*Pinch of salt*

*1/2 teaspoon ground nutmeg*

*2 (.035-ounce) envelopes sugar substitute*

*1 teaspoon freshly ground black pepper*

*3/4 pound boneless, skinless chicken breast*

*Olive oil spray*

*1/2 small head romaine lettuce, torn into bite-size pieces*

*2 cups sliced hearts of palm*

*2 tablespoons no-sugar-added oil and vinegar dressing*

In a food processor or by hand, combine the onion, thyme, salt, nutmeg, sugar substitute, and black pepper together. The juice from the onion will bind the ingredients together. Remove any visible fat from the chicken breast and poke several holes in the meat with a knife or fork. Spoon the jerk seasoning over both sides of the chicken and let marinate for 15 minutes before cooking.

Set a nonstick skillet over medium heat and spray with olive oil. Sauté the chicken for 5 minutes, then turn and sauté 5 more minutes, or until a meat thermometer registers 160 degrees.

Divide the lettuce between 2 plates. Scatter the hearts of palm slices over the lettuce. Drizzle the dressing over the lettuce. Slice the chicken into strips and arrange on the lettuce to serve.

*Makes 2 servings.*

**ONE SERVING: 437** CALORIES, **60G** PROTEIN, **15G** CARBOHYDRATE **18G** FAT (**3G** SATURATED), **144MG** CHOLESTEROL, **981MG** SODIUM, **5G** FIBER

## tangerine

*2 medium tangerines*

Divide the tangerines between 2 plates and serve.

*Makes 2 servings.*

**ONE SERVING: 37** CALORIES, **1G** PROTEIN, **9G** CARBOHYDRATE, **0G** FAT (**0G** SATURATED), **0MG** CHOLESTEROL, **1MG** SODIUM, **0G** FIBER

# delicatessen salad with cucumber and coleslaw

*You can put together this salad plate in minutes with whatever you have in the refrigerator. Use the proportions in this recipe as a guideline for ordering similar dishes in restaurants.*

## delicatessen salad with cucumber and coleslaw

- *1/4 pound sliced smoked turkey breast*
- *1/4 pound sliced lean roast beef*
- *1/2 cup no-sugar-added deli coleslaw*
- *1 medium cucumber, peeled and sliced*
- *2 tablespoons mayonnaise made with olive or soybean oil*
- *2 tablespoons horseradish*

Arrange the meat slices with the coleslaw and cucumbers on 2 plates. Mix the mayonnaise and horseradish together and spoon over the meat to serve.

*Makes 2 servings.*

**ONE SERVING: 406** CALORIES, **34G** PROTEIN, **13G** CARBOHYDRATE **23G** FAT (**5G** SATURATED), **96MG** CHOLESTEROL, **305MG** SODIUM, **2** FIBER

## cantaloupe

- *1/2 cantaloupe, cubed (2 cups)*

Divide the cantaloupe between 2 dessert bowls and serve.

*Makes 2 servings.*

**ONE SERVING: 39** CALORIES, **1G** PROTEIN, **9G** CARBOHYDRATE, **0G** FAT (**0G** SATURATED), **0MG** CHOLESTEROL, **10MG** SODIUM, **1G** FIBER

### helpful hints

- *Any type of lean deli meats can be used.*
- *Any type of vegetables can be used.*
- *Fresh cantaloupe cubes can be found in the produce department of most supermarkets or at a salad bar.*
- *Ask for the nutritional analysis of store-bought coleslaw, as some prepared versions have added sugar.*

### countdown

- *Prepare the ingredients.*
- *Assemble plate.*

### shopping list

*TO BUY:*

- *1/4 pound sliced smoked turkey breast*
- *1/4 pound sliced lean roast beef*
- *1 container no-sugar-added deli coleslaw (3 1/2 ounces needed)*
- *1 jar horseradish*
- *1 medium cucumber*
- *1 cantaloupe or cut cantaloupe cubes*

*STAPLES:*

- *Mayonnaise made with olive or soybean oil*

# country bacon and egg salad with fresh berries

## helpful hints

- *You can make the egg salad in a food processor or mini chop. Be careful to pulse the blades and watch that it does not become too finely chopped or mushy.*
- *There are several brands of lean Canadian bacon available. Look for the one with the lowest fat content.*

## countdown

- *Preheat toaster oven or broiler.*
- *Make hard-boiled eggs.*
- *Make egg salad.*

## shopping list

*TO BUY:*

*1/2 pound sliced lean Canadian bacon*
*1 bunch flat leaf parsley*
*1 head romaine*
*2 medium tomatoes*
*1 container fresh strawberries*

*STAPLES:*

*Celery*
*Eggs*
*Mayonnaise made with olive or soybean oil*
*Dijon mustard*
*Red onion*
*Salt*
*Black peppercorns*

*Egg salad can be bought in a deli or made from scratch. It is usually available on lunch menus as well. Whichever one you have, use this recipe as a portion guideline. This one is made with 2 whole eggs and 6 egg whites to produce a light, tasty result.*

## country bacon and egg salad

*8 eggs (only 2 yolks are used)*
*1/2 pound sliced lean Canadian bacon*
*2 tablespoons mayonnaise made with olive or soybean oil*
*2 tablespoons Dijon mustard*
*2 tablespoons warm water*
*2 tablespoons diced red onion*
*1/4 cup chopped fresh flat leaf parsley*
*2 celery stalks, diced (1 cup)*
*Salt and freshly ground black pepper to taste*
*Several romaine leaves, torn into bite-size pieces*
*2 medium tomatoes, quartered*

Preheat the toaster oven or broiler. Place the eggs in a medium saucepan and cover with cold water. Set over medium-high heat and bring to a boil. Reduce the heat to low and gently simmer for 12 minutes. Drain the hot water and fill the pan with cold water. When the eggs are cool to the touch, peel, cut in half, and discard 6 of the yolks. Mash the remaining 2 whole eggs and 6 egg whites with a fork.

Meanwhile, place the Canadian bacon in one layer on a foil-lined tray and toast in toaster oven or under a broiler until brown. Combine the mayonnaise, mustard, water, onion, and parsley in a bowl. Stir in the eggs and celery, mixing well. Season with salt and pepper to taste. Place the lettuce and tomatoes on 2 plates. Spoon the egg salad on top of the lettuce. Cut the browned bacon into bite-size pieces and sprinkle over the egg salad. Serve.

*Makes 2 servings.*

**ONE SERVING: 411** CALORIES, **41G** PROTEIN, **17G** CARBOHYDRATE, **21G** FAT (**4G** SATURATED), **270MG** CHOLESTEROL, **1743MG** SODIUM, **1G** FIBER

## fresh berries

*2 cups fresh strawberries*

Divide the strawberries between 2 dessert bowls and serve.

*Makes 2 servings.*

**ONE SERVING: 45** CALORIES, **1G** PROTEIN, **11G** CARBOHYDRATE, **1G** FAT (**0G** SATURATED), **0MG** CHOLESTEROL, **2MG** SODIUM, **3** FIBER

# balsamic and dill salmon salad with raspberries

*Fresh salmon mixed with cucumber and dill makes a richly-flavored, yet light, salmon salad. If you have time, double the recipe and save half for another lunch.*

## balsamic and dill salmon salad

*2 tablespoons mayonnaise made with olive or soybean oil*
*4 teaspoons balsamic vinegar*
*¼ cup fresh dill or 2 teaspoons dried*
*1 medium cucumber, seeded and diced (about 1½ cups)*
*Olive oil spray*
*½ pound salmon fillet*
*Salt and freshly ground black pepper to taste*
*2 medium-size green bell peppers, halved and seeded*

Combine the mayonnaise, balsamic vinegar, dill, and cucumber in a small bowl. Set a nonstick skillet over medium-high heat and spray with olive oil. Add the salmon and sauté for 3 minutes. Turn and sauté 2 more minutes. Flake the salmon into the mayonnaise mixture with a fork. Season with salt and pepper to taste, and gently mix. Spoon the mixture into the bell pepper halves and serve.

*Makes 2 servings.*

**ONE SERVING: 364** CALORIES, **31G** PROTEIN, **13G** CARBOHYDRATE, **20G** FAT (**4G** SATURATED), **85MG** CHOLESTEROL, **159MG** SODIUM, **1G** FIBER

## raspberries

*2 cups fresh raspberries*

Divide the raspberries between 2 dessert bowls and serve.

*Makes 2 servings.*

**ONE SERVING: 61** CALORIES, **1G** PROTEIN, **14G** CARBOHYDRATE, **1G** FAT (**0G** SATURATED), **0MG** CHOLESTEROL, **0MG** SODIUM, **6G** FIBER

### helpful hints

- *This can be made with any type of leftover fish.*
- *Make sure the bottle of dried dill is less than 6 months old. For optimum flavor, the dill should be a green color, not brown or gray.*

### countdown

- *Sauté salmon.*
- *Make salad.*

### shopping list

*TO BUY:*

*½ pound salmon fillet*
*1 medium cucumber*
*1 small bunch fresh dill or 1 jar dried*
*2 medium-size green bell peppers*
*1 container fresh raspberries*

*STAPLES:*

*Olive oil spray*
*Mayonnaise made with olive or soybean oil*
*Balsamic vinegar*
*Salt*
*Black peppercorns*

# hollywood cobb salad

## helpful hints

- *Ask the deli to cut the chicken breast into 1-inch-thick slices to make it easier to cut into cubes.*
- *A hard-boiled egg can be substituted for the avocado.*
- *To speed the ripening of an avocado, remove the stem and store it in a paper bag in a warm spot.*

## countdown

- *Make dressing.*
- *Prepare ingredients.*
- *Assemble salad.*

## shopping list

*TO BUY:*

*1/2 pound sliced skinless deli chicken breast*
*1 jar freeze-dried chives*
*1 head iceberg lettuce*
*1 small head chicory lettuce*
*2 medium tomatoes*
*1 small avocado*
*2 medium peaches*

*STAPLES:*

*No-sugar-added oil and vinegar dressing*

*Roasted chicken breast, avocado, and lettuce were key ingredients in Robert Cobb's first Cobb salad he served at the Brown Derby restaurant at Hollywood and Vine in the 1930s. It was so popular among the Hollywood moguls that it has become a favorite on restaurant menus throughout the States.*

## hollywood cobb salad

*2 cups finely sliced iceberg lettuce*
*1 cup finely sliced chicory or curly endive*
*2 medium tomatoes, cut into large dice (2 cups)*
*1/2 pound sliced skinless deli chicken breast, cut into 1-inch cubes (2 cups)*
*1/2 small ripe avocado, pitted, peeled, and cubed (1/2 cup)*
*2 tablespoons freeze-dried chives*
*2 tablespoons no-sugar-added oil and vinegar dressing*

Arrange the iceberg and chicory lettuce in 2 shallow bowls or on 2 plates. Arrange the tomatoes, chicken, and avocado in rows over lettuce. Sprinkle with the chives, drizzle with dressing, and serve.
*Makes 2 servings.*

**ONE SERVING: 378** CALORIES, **40G** PROTEIN, **11** CARBOHYDRATE, **21G** FAT (**4G** SATURATED), **96MG** CHOLESTEROL, **183MG** SODIUM, **3G** FIBER

## peaches

*2 medium peaches*

Divide the peaches between 2 plates and serve.
*Makes 2 servings.*

**ONE SERVING: 37** CALORIES, **1G** PROTEIN, **10G** CARBOHYDRATE, **0G** FAT (**0G** SATURATED), **0MG** CHOLESTEROL, **0MG** SODIUM, **1G** FIBER

# south beach black bean and salsa wraps

*With the help of prepared black bean pâté and deli turkey breast, you can assemble this lunch in 5 minutes. It can be made the night before and stored in the refrigerator until needed for lunch. You can use these wraps as hors d'oeuvres or take them along as a meal for picnics, boating trips, or tailgate parties.*

## south beach black bean and salsa wraps

- *12 large romaine leaves, washed and patted dry*
- *12 squares foil, parchment paper, or wax paper (11 x 4 inches)*
- *1/4 cup prepared no-sugar-added black bean pâté*
- *1/2 cup shredded, reduced-fat Monterey Jack cheese (2 ounces)*
- *1/2 pound sliced turkey breast*
- *1 cup no-sugar-added tomato salsa*

Remove 1 inch of the thick stem from each lettuce leaf and crush the remaining stem so that the leaf lies flat. Place the squares of foil on the countertop. Place one leaf on each square. Spread the pâté on each leaf and sprinkle with cheese. Top with a layer of turkey. Roll the lettuce up lengthwise like a cigar. Wrap the foil tightly around the lettuce to hold it in place. Cut in half crosswise, and serve on 2 plates with the salsa on the side.

*Makes 2 servings.*

**ONE SERVING: 349** CALORIES, **15G** PROTEIN, **17G** CARBOHYDRATE **5G** FAT (**3G** SATURATED), **10MG** CHOLESTEROL, **1070MG** SODIUM, **5G** FIBER

## yogurt

- *1 cup light fruit-flavored yogurt*

Divide the yogurt between 2 dessert bowls and serve.

*Makes 2 servings.*

**ONE SERVING: 50** CALORIES, **32G** PROTEIN, **0G** CARBOHYDRATE, **4G** FAT (**1G** SATURATED), **80MG** CHOLESTEROL, **72MG** SODIUM, **0G** FIBER

### helpful hints

- *Look for romaine lettuce with large leaves.*
- *Black bean pâté is usually located with the dips in the snack section of the supermarket.*

### countdown

- *Prepare ingredients.*
- *Assemble wraps.*

### shopping list

*TO BUY:*

- *1 carton light fruit-flavored yogurt*
- *1 package shredded, reduced-fat Monterey Jack cheese (2 ounces needed)*
- *1/2 pound sliced turkey breast*
- *1 jar no-sugar-added black bean pâté*
- *1 jar no-sugar-added tomato salsa (4 ounces needed)*
- *1 head romaine lettuce*

# wild greens with chili chicken

## helpful hints

- *Chop onion, garlic, and spices together in a food processor or mini chop to make a quick marinade.*
- *If pressed for time, use a bottled, no-sugar-added dressing and add scallions to it.*

## countdown

- *Preheat broiler.*
- *While chicken marinates, prepare greens and make dressing.*

## shopping list

*TO BUY:*

*1/2 pound boneless, skinless chicken breast*
*1 small head romaine lettuce*
*2 medium tomatoes*
*2 lemons*
*1 small bunch scallions (4 scallions needed)*

*STAPLES:*

*Red onion*
*Garlic*
*Olive oil*
*Ground cumin*
*Chili powder*
*Dijon mustard*
*Salt*
*Black peppercorns*

*This broiled Chili Chicken is full of hot, spicy, Southwestern flavors, and tastes delicious served over a cool bed of lettuce with the Green Onion Dressing.*

## wild greens with chili chicken

*1/2 cup chopped red onion*
*2 medium-size garlic cloves, crushed*
*1 tablespoon chili powder*
*1 teaspoon ground cumin*
*Pinch salt*
*Pinch freshly ground black pepper*
*1/2 pound boneless, skinless chicken breasts*
*1/4 cup freshly squeezed lemon juice (2 medium lemons)*
*2 tablespoons Dijon mustard*
*4 teaspoons olive oil*
*1 tablespoon water*
*4 scallions, sliced (1/2 cup)*
*1/2 small head Romaine lettuce, torn into bite-size pieces (about 4 cups)*
*2 medium tomatoes, cut into wedges*

Preheat the broiler. Combine the onion, garlic, chili powder, cumin, salt, and pepper in a small bowl by hand or with a food processor or mini chop. Remove any visible fat from the chicken and poke several holes in the meat with a knife or fork. Place in a bowl and spread the marinade evenly over the chicken. Let marinate 15 minutes, turning once. Cover a baking tray with foil. Place the chicken on the tray and broil 4 to 5 inches from heat for 5 minutes. Turn and broil another 5 minutes. Remove from the oven and let cool. When cool, slice into strips.

Whisk the lemon juice and mustard together in a small bowl. Whisk in the oil, and then water. Stir in the scallions. Place the lettuce on 2 plates. Top with the tomatoes and chicken strips. Drizzle the dressing over the salad or serve on the side.

*Makes 2 servings.*

**ONE SERVING: 367** CALORIES, **41G** PROTEIN, **18G** CARBOHYDRATE, **16G** FAT (**3G** SATURATED), **96MG** CHOLESTEROL, **603MG** SODIUM, **1G** FIBER

# which carb dinners

# thai peanut-rub pork with stir-fry broccoli noodles

*This blend of spices and peanuts rubbed into the pork forms a well-seasoned crust. Rubs are a quick way to add flavor to meats and a great alternative to marinades, since you don't have to wait for the meat to absorb the marinade flavors. These Thai spices are fun, easy to use, and provide a different way to spice up pork tenderloin.*

## helpful hints

- *If rice vinegar is unavailable, substitute 1 tablespoon water mixed with distilled white vinegar.*
- *Chop the cilantro for both recipes at one time and divide accordingly.*
- *To keep from looking back at the recipe as you stir-fry the ingredients, line them up on a cutting board or plate in the order of use.*
- *For crisp, not steamed, stir-fried vegetables, start with a very hot wok. Let the vegetables sit a minute before tossing to allow the wok to regain its heat.*

## countdown

- *Preheat broiler*
- *Make pork dish.*
- *While pork broils, make broccoli noodles.*

## shopping list

*TO BUY:*

*10 ounces pork tenderloin*
*1 small package dry roasted, unsalted peanuts (1 ounce needed)*
*1 box whole wheat fettuccini (2 ounces needed)*
*1 small bottle oyster sauce*
*1 small bottle rice vinegar*
*1 small bunch fresh cilantro*
*1 package broccoli florets (1/4 pound needed)*

*STAPLES:*

*Garlic*
*Olive oil spray*
*Garlic powder*
*Ground coriander*
*Sugar substitute*
*Cayenne pepper*

## thai peanut-rub pork

*Olive oil spray*
*20 dry-roasted, unsalted peanuts (2 tablespoons ground)*
*1/4 cup fresh cilantro*
*1 1/2 teaspoons garlic powder*
*1 tablespoon ground coriander*
*2 (.035-ounce) envelopes sugar substitute*
*Pinch of cayenne pepper*
*10 ounces pork tenderloin*

Preheat the broiler. Line a baking tray with foil, and spray with olive oil. Chop the peanuts and cilantro in a food processor. Add the garlic powder, coriander, sugar substitute, and cayenne, pulsing to incorporate. Alternatively, chop and mix by hand. Remove any visible fat from the pork. Rub the mixture on both sides of the pork, pressing the mixture onto the meat and making sure all the sides are coated. Place on baking tray and broil 8 inches from heat for 7 minutes; turn and broil another 8 minutes. The pork is done when a meat thermometer registers 160 degrees. Remove the loin to a plate and cover with foil to keep warm. Slice before serving.
*Makes 2 servings.*

**ONE SERVING: 333** CALORIES, **45**G PROTEIN, **6G** CARBOHYDRATE, **15G** FAT (**4G** SATURATED), **133MG** CHOLESTEROL, **137MG** SODIUM, **1G** FIBER

## stir-fry broccoli noodles

*2 ounces whole wheat fettuccini (1/2 cup)*
*1/4 pound broccoli florets (2 cups)*
*2 tablespoons oyster sauce*
*2 tablespoons rice vinegar*
*Olive oil spray*
*4 medium-size garlic cloves, crushed*
*1/4 cup chopped fresh cilantro*

Bring a large saucepan of water to a boil and add the fettuccine. Boil 8 minutes. Add the broccoli and continue to boil for 2 minutes. Drain and set aside. Combine the oyster sauce and vinegar in a small bowl; set aside. Spray a wok or skillet with olive oil and heat on high. When hot, add the fettuccini, broccoli, and garlic. Stir-fry for 2 minutes, then push the ingredients to the sides of the pan, leaving a well in the center. Add the oyster sauce mixture and toss well. Spoon onto plates and sprinkle with chopped cilantro.
*Makes 2 servings.*

**ONE SERVING: 208** CALORIES, **10G** PROTEIN, **37G** CARBOHYDRATE, **3G** FAT (**1G** SATURATED), **0MG** CHOLESTEROL, **491MG** SODIUM, **6G** FIBER

# pesto chicken with steamed artichokes and fresh figs

*Pesto is a flavorful Italian sauce filled with garlic, basil, pine nuts, parsley, and olive oil. It's most widely used as a luscious dressing for pasta. Typically, pesto is not cooked. In this recipe, the sauce is added to the cooked chicken for a minute just before serving. The sauce is warmed by the chicken, while still preserving the fresh basil and parsley flavors. • Steaming or boiling artichokes takes about 45 minutes. To cut the time in half, cut the artichokes in half and cook them in about 2 inches of water for 20 minutes. The artichokes can also be cooked in a microwave, as described in this recipe. • Artichokes may be served hot or cold. To eat, pull off the outer petals one at a time. Dip the base of each petal into the sauce; pull the petal through your teeth to remove the soft, pulpy portion of petal, then discard. For this recipe, the fuzzy section near the base, called the choke, will be removed. The bottom, or heart, of the artichoke is entirely edible. Many think it's the best part. Cut it into small pieces and dip in the sauce.*

## pesto chicken

*2 ounces whole wheat fettuccini (1/2 cup)*
*Salt and freshly ground black pepper to taste*
*3/4 quarter pound boneless, skinless chicken breast*
*1/4 cup store-bought pesto*

Bring a large saucepan of water to a boil. Add the fettuccini and boil 8 minutes, or according to package instructions. Do not overcook. Drain, leaving about 3 tablespoons pasta water on the pasta. Divide between 2 dinner plates, and season with salt and pepper to taste.

Remove all visible fat from the chicken and pound the breast flat with the palm of your hand or a heavy skillet to about 1/2 inch thick. Set a nonstick skillet over medium-high heat and add the chicken. Brown 2 minutes on each side, seasoning the cooked sides with salt and pepper. Lower the heat to medium and sauté another minute. Spoon the pesto over the chicken. Remove the pan from the heat. Cover, and let sit for 1 minute. Divide the chicken and spoon over the pasta to serve.

*Makes 2 servings.*

**ONE SERVING: 427** CALORIES, **57G** PROTEIN, **6G** CARBOHYDRATE, **20G** FAT (**5G** SATURATED), **154MG** CHOLESTEROL, **416MG** SODIUM, **2G** FIBER

## helpful hints

- *Pesto can be found in the refrigerated case in the supermarket. There are also shelf-stable jars of pesto that are very good.*
- *Artichokes are not available all year round. Asparagus or broccoli can be steamed or microwaved and served with this dressing instead.*
- *Fresh figs are not available all year round. Plums, apricots, or pears can be substituted.*

## countdown

- *Start artichokes.*
- *Make pasta.*
- *Make chicken.*

## shopping list

*TO BUY:*

*3/4 pound boneless, skinless chicken breast*
*1 small container pesto*
*1 box whole wheat fettuccini (2 ounces needed)*
*2 medium artichokes*
*4 medium figs*

*STAPLES:*

*No-sugar-added oil and vinegar dressing*
*Salt*
*Black peppercorns*

# pesto chicken with steamed artichokes and fresh figs *continued*

## steamed artichokes

*2 medium artichokes*

*2 tablespoons no-sugar-added oil and vinegar dressing*

Cut the stem off the artichokes as close to base as possible. Cut off the top quarter and prickly points of visible leaves. Slice the artichokes in half from top to stem. Scrape out the fuzzy chokes with a spoon. Remove the small inner leaves (they're usually purple) and discard. Fill a large nonstick skillet with 1 inch of water, place the artichokes cut-side down, and bring to a boil. Cover and let boil 20 minutes. Check after the first 10 minutes, and add more water if needed.

Alternatively, to cook artichokes in the microwave, set the artichokes in a deep, microwave-safe bowl. Add ½ cup water, cover the bowl with plastic wrap, and microwave for 7 to 8 minutes on high, giving the bowl a quarter turn halfway through cooking time. Let stand 5 minutes.

The artichokes are done when a petal pulls off easily. Remove the cooked artichokes from the pan and place on 2 plates. Place the dressing in 2 small bowls on the side, and use as dipping sauce for the artichoke leaves and hearts.

*Makes 2 servings.*

**ONE SERVING: 181** CALORIES, **6G** PROTEIN, **25G** CARBOHYDRATE, **9G** FAT (**1G** SATURATED), **0MG** CHOLESTEROL, **233MG** SODIUM, **0G** FIBER

## fresh figs

*4 medium figs*

Divide the figs between 2 plates and serve.

*Makes 2 servings.*

**ONE SERVING: 74** CALORIES, **1G** PROTEIN, **19G** CARBOHYDRATE, **0.5G** FAT (**0G** SATURATED), **0MG** CHOLESTEROL, **0MG** SODIUM, **3G** FIBER

# grilled scallops parmigiana with lemon-pepper zucchini and fresh kiwi-berry jumble

*Sweet, juicy scallops are easy to cook. The secret to this meal is buying fresh, good quality scallops. • These baked Parmesan scallops take only 15 minutes to make. The zucchini can be cooked while the scallops bake, so the whole meal can be prepared in 15 to 20 minutes. • Scallops are readily available. You can use any type for this recipe. If you buy small bay scallops, then bake for only 10 minutes.*

## grilled scallops parmigiana

- *3/4 pound large scallops, rinsed*
- *1/4 cup white wine*
- *2 teaspoons olive oil*
- *4 cups washed, ready-to-eat fresh spinach*
- *1/4 cup freshly grated Parmesan cheese*
- *Salt and freshly ground black pepper to taste*

Preheat the oven to 350 degrees. Place the scallops in a small baking dish just large enough to hold the scallops in one layer. Add the wine, tossing to coat the scallops. Bake for 15 minutes. While the scallops are baking, heat the oil in a medium-size nonstick skillet on medium high. Add the spinach. Sauté 2 to 3 minutes, or until wilted. Spoon onto 2 dinner plates. Remove the scallops from the oven and turn on broiler. When the broiler is hot, sprinkle Parmesan cheese over the scallops and place under broiler for 1 minute, or until golden. Watch them carefully, as they will brown very quickly. Season with salt and pepper to taste. Spoon over the spinach and serve. *Makes 2 servings.*

**ONE SERVING: 286** CALORIES, **37G** PROTEIN, **9G** CARBOHYDRATE, **10G** FAT (**3G** SATURATED), **63MG** CHOLESTEROL, **573MG** SODIUM, **4G** FIBER

## lemon-pepper zucchini

- *2 teaspoons olive oil*
- *1/2 pound zucchini, sliced (about 2 cups)*
- *2 tablespoons freshly squeezed lemon juice (1 lemon)*
- *1/4 teaspoon freshly ground black pepper*
- *Salt to taste*

In the skillet used for the spinach, heat the oil on medium high. Add the zucchini, and sauté for 5 minutes. Toss with the lemon juice and pepper. Season with salt to taste. Serve with the scallops. *Makes 2 servings.*

**ONE SERVING: 62** CALORIES, **2G** PROTEIN, **5G** CARBOHYDRATE, **5G** FAT (**1G** SATURATED), **0MG** CHOLESTEROL, **4MG** SODIUM, **1G** FIBER

### helpful hints

- *Buy good quality Parmesan cheese and ask the grocer to grate it for you or chop it in the food processor yourself. Freeze extra for quick use later—simply spoon out what you need and leave the rest frozen.*
- *Any type of berries can be used.*
- *To save cleaning an extra skillet, use the same one to cook both the spinach and zucchini.*
- *Both the spinach and zucchini can be cooked in a microwave oven. Place in separate microwave-safe bowls and microwave the spinach on high for 2 to 3 minutes and the zucchini on high for 3 to 4 minutes. Place the spinach on a plate as a bed for the scallops. Toss the zucchini with olive oil and lemon juice; season with salt and pepper to taste.*

### countdown

- *Preheat oven to 350 degrees.*
- *Start scallops.*
- *Make spinach.*
- *Make zucchini.*
- *Complete scallops.*

# grilled scallops parmigiana with lemon-pepper zucchini and fresh kiwi-berry jumble *continued*

## shopping list

*TO BUY:*

*3/4 pound large scallops*
*1 small bottle dry white wine*
*1 bag washed, ready-to-eat fresh spinach*
*1/2 pound zucchini*
*2 lemons*
*2 kiwis*
*1 package fresh raspberries*

*STAPLES:*

*Olive oil*
*Parmesan cheese*
*Salt*
*Black peppercorns*

## fresh kiwi-berry jumble

*2 kiwis, peeled and cubed*
*1 cup raspberries*

Combine the kiwi cubes and the raspberries. Spoon into 2 dessert bowls and serve.

*Makes 2 servings.*

**ONE SERVING: 77** CALORIES, **1G** PROTEIN, **18G** CARBOHYDRATE, **1G** FAT (**0G** SATURATED), **0MG** CHOLESTEROL, **4MG** SODIUM, **3G** FIBER

# herbed veal cutlets with spaghetti and parmesan spinach

*This quick meal takes only 15 minutes to make. The light breading adds flavor and keeps the veal moist.*

## herbed veal cutlets

*½ pound veal cutlets*
*Salt and freshly ground black pepper to taste*
*1 tablespoon fresh oregano or 2 teaspoons dried*
*¼ cup plain bread crumbs, whole wheat if possible*
*2 egg whites, lightly beaten*
*2 teaspoons olive oil*

Sprinkle both sides of the veal cutlets with a little salt and pepper. Combine the oregano with the bread crumbs on a plate. Dredge the veal in the bread crumb mixture, coating well. Next, dip the veal into the egg whites. Dredge the veal in the bread crumbs again. Heat the oil in a nonstick skillet on medium high. Sauté the veal 1 minute, then turn and sauté for 2 more minutes. Season with salt and pepper to taste. Serve on 2 plates with the spaghetti and spinach.
*Makes 2 servings.*

**ONE SERVING: 314** CALORIES, **34G** PROTEIN, **3G** CARBOHYDRATE, **17G** FAT (**8G** SATURATED), **100MG** CHOLESTEROL, **155MG** SODIUM, **0G** FIBER

## spaghetti

*2 ounces thin whole wheat spaghetti (½ cup)*
*½ cup no-sugar-added pasta sauce*

Bring a large saucepan filled with water to a boil. Add the spaghetti and boil 5 minutes, or according to package instructions. Do not overcook. Drain, leaving about 3 tablespoons of water in the pan. Return the spaghetti to the pan and add the sauce. Toss well and serve with the veal.
*Makes 2 servings.*

**ONE SERVING: 163** CALORIES, **8G** PROTEIN, **29G** CARBOHYDRATE, **1G** FAT (**1G** SATURATED), **0MG** CHOLESTEROL, **208MG** SODIUM, **5G** FIBER

## parmesan spinach

*8 cups washed, ready-to-eat fresh spinach*
*2 tablespoons freshly grated Parmesan cheese*
*Salt and freshly ground black pepper to taste*

Place the spinach in a microwave-safe bowl and microwave on high for 6 minutes. Alternatively, place the spinach in a saucepan over medium heat. Do not add water: the spinach will release enough of its own liquid to cook. Cover and cook until the spinach is wilted, about 5 minutes. Watch to make sure it does not burn. Add the Parmesan cheese to the cooked spinach. Season with salt and pepper to taste.
*Makes 2 servings.*

**ONE SERVING: 74** CALORIES, **9G** PROTEIN, **8G** CARBOHYDRATE, **3G** FAT (**1G** SATURATED), **4MG** CHOLESTEROL, **278MG** SODIUM, **7G** FIBER

## helpful hints

- *Buy good quality Parmesan cheese and ask the grocer to grate it for you or chop it in the food processor yourself. Freeze extra for quick use later—simply spoon out what you need and leave the rest frozen.*
- *Any type of whole wheat pasta can be used.*

## countdown

- *Prepare all ingredients.*
- *Make pasta.*
- *Make veal.*
- *Make spinach.*

## shopping list

*TO BUY:*

*½ pound veal cutlets*
*1 small package plain bread crumbs, whole wheat if possible*
*1 box thin whole wheat spaghetti (2 ounces needed)*
*1 jar no-sugar-added pasta sauce (8 ounces needed)*
*1 small bunch fresh oregano or 1 jar dried*
*1 bag washed, ready-to-eat fresh spinach*

*STAPLES:*

*Olive oil*
*Eggs*
*Parmesan cheese*
*Salt*
*Black peppercorns*

# garlic shrimp stir-fry with chinese cabbage and bean sprouts

## helpful hints

- *Buy shelled shrimp or ask for the shrimp to be shelled for you while you complete your shopping. Most stores will do this for a small fee—well worth the time saved in shelling them yourself.*
- *Sliced, washed, and ready-to-eat cabbage is available in the supermarket. This can be used instead of the Chinese cabbage, but should be microwaved for 1 minute first.*
- *To chop fresh ginger quickly, cut it into small cubes and press through a garlic press with large holes. If using a press with small holes, just capture the juice that is squeezed out; it will give enough flavor for the recipe.*
- *If rice vinegar is unavailable, substitute 1 tablespoon water mixed with 1 tablespoon distilled white vinegar.*
- *To keep from having to look back at the recipe as you stir-fry the ingredients, line them up on a cutting board or plate in the order of use so you know which ingredient comes next.*
- *For crisp, not steamed, stir-fried vegetables, start with a very hot wok or skillet. Let the vegetables sit a minute before tossing to allow the wok to regain its heat.*

*Garlic, cashew nuts, and sesame oil flavor this quick shrimp dinner. The cooking time for this dinner is about 8 minutes. Use the helpful hint suggestions for quick preparation of the ingredients to make this a complete 15-minute meal.*

## garlic shrimp stir-fry

*2 tablespoons low-salt soy sauce*
*2 tablespoons rice vinegar*
*2 tablespoons chopped fresh ginger*
*6 medium-size garlic cloves, crushed*
*Several drops hot pepper sauce*
*4 teaspoons sesame oil*
*2 slices yellow onion*
*½ medium-size red bell pepper, sliced (1 cup)*
*¾ pound medium shrimp, shelled and deveined*
*½ pound fresh snow peas, trimmed (2 cups)*
*2 tablespoons cashews*

Combine the soy sauce, rice vinegar, ginger, garlic, and hot sauce in a small bowl. Make sure all ingredients are prepped and ready for cooking.

Heat the sesame oil in a wok or skillet on high. When the oil is smoking, add the onion and bell pepper. Stir-fry 3 minutes. Add the shrimp and snow peas, and stir-fry 2 minutes. Add the cashews and sauce, and continue to stir-fry, tossing continuously for 2 minutes. Add salt to taste. Divide between 2 plates and serve.

*Makes 2 servings.*

**ONE SERVING: 411** CALORIES, **41G** PROTEIN, **21G** CARBOHYDRATE **18G** FAT (**3G** SATURATED), **260MG** CHOLESTEROL, **944MG** SODIUM, **2G** FIBER

# garlic shrimp stir-fry with chinese cabbage and bean sprouts *continued*

## chinese cabbage and bean sprouts

- *1 cup thinly sliced Chinese cabbage (napa cabbage)*
- *1 cup fresh bean sprouts*
- *2 tablespoons low-carbohydrate miso dressing*

Place the cabbage and bean sprouts in a small bowl and toss with dressing. Serve with the stir-fry. *Makes 2 servings.*

**ONE SERVING: 73** CALORIES, **5G** PROTEIN, **8G** CARBOHYDRATE, **3G** FAT (**0.5G** SATURATED), **0MG** CHOLESTEROL, **321MG** SODIUM, **1G** FIBER

### countdown

- *Prepare ingredients.*
- *Make cabbage and bean sprouts.*
- *Make shrimp stir-fry.*

### shopping list

*TO BUY:*

- *¾ pound medium shrimp*
- *1 small package cashew nuts (1 ounce needed)*
- *1 small bottle sesame oil*
- *1 small bottle low-carbohydrate miso dressing*
- *1 small bottle rice vinegar*
- *1 medium-size red bell pepper*
- *1 small piece fresh ginger*
- *½ pound fresh snow peas*
- *1 small head Chinese cabbage (Napa cabbage)*
- *1 small package fresh bean sprouts*

*STAPLES:*

- *Yellow onion*
- *Garlic*
- *Hot pepper sauce*
- *Low-salt soy sauce*

# sole amandine with baby limas and grilled tomatoes

*Sole Amandine, a French classic, appears on menus at French restaurants from the most elegant to simple brasseries. Dressed up or down, lemon juice and almonds are all the fillet of sole needs to give it a wonderful flavor. • This quick dinner takes only 10 minutes to make. It's a perfect mid-week meal when you're on the run.*

## helpful hints

- *Any type of non-oily fish fillet can be used.*
- *To save washing another skillet, use the same skillet for the fish and lima beans.*

## countdown

- *Preheat broiler or toaster oven.*
- *Make fish.*
- *Make lima beans.*
- *Make salad.*

## shopping list

*TO BUY:*

*¾ pound sole fillet*
*1 small package slivered almonds (1 ounce needed)*
*1 small package frozen baby lima beans*
*1 lemon*
*1 small bunch parsley (optional)*
*2 medium tomatoes*

*STAPLES:*

*Olive oil*
*Salt*
*Black peppercorns*

## sole amandine

*¾ pound sole fillet*
*4 teaspoons olive oil*
*Salt and freshly ground black pepper to taste*
*2 tablespoons slivered almonds*
*2 tablespoons freshly squeezed lemon juice (1 lemon)*
*2 tablespoons freshly chopped parsley (optional)*

Rinse the sole and pat dry with a paper towel. Heat the oil in a medium-size nonstick skillet on medium high. Sauté the fish for 2 minutes on each side. Remove to 2 plates, season with salt and pepper to taste, and cover with foil to keep warm. Add the almonds to the same skillet and sauté until slightly golden, about 1 minute. Sprinkle the fish with lemon juice, almonds, and parsley, and serve. *Makes 2 servings.*

**ONE SERVING: 264** CALORIES, **28G** PROTEIN, **4G** CARBOHYDRATE, **17G** FAT (**2G** SATURATED), **60MG** CHOLESTEROL, **98MG** SODIUM, **1G** FIBER

## baby limas

*2 cups frozen baby lima beans*
*2 teaspoons olive oil*
*Salt and freshly ground black pepper to taste*

Defrost the lima beans. Bring a small pot of water to a boil. Add the beans, cook 1 minute, and drain. Alternatively, place in a microwave-safe dish and heat on high for 2 minutes. Add the oil to the same skillet used for the fish and heat on high. Sauté the beans for 1 minute. Add salt and pepper to taste. *Makes 2 servings.*

**ONE SERVING: 154** CALORIES, **7G** PROTEIN, **21G** CARBOHYDRATE, **5G** FAT (**1G** SATURATED), **0MG** CHOLESTEROL, **3MG** SODIUM, **4G** FIBER

## grilled tomatoes

*2 medium tomatoes, halved*
*Salt and freshly ground black pepper to taste*

Preheat the broiler or toaster oven. Season the tomato halves with salt and pepper to taste. Grill for 4 minutes, and serve with the fish and lima beans. *Makes 2 servings.*

**ONE SERVING: 25** CALORIES, **2G** PROTEIN, **5G** CARBOHYDRATE, **0G** FAT (**0G** SATURATED), **0MG** CHOLESTEROL, **10MG** SODIUM, **0G** FIBER

# smothered steak with caramelized onions and hearts of palm salad

*Caramelized onions, mushrooms, and garlic are perfect toppings for steak. There's no reason to shy away from enjoying a steak if you pick one of the lean cuts now available. For speed, this steak is broiled. If you have time, grill the steak or cook it on a stove-top grill for extra flavor.*

## smothered steak with caramelized onions

*10 ounces strip steak, visible fat removed*
*Olive oil spray*
*1 cup sliced red onion*
*½ cup fat-free, low-salt chicken broth*
*4 medium-size garlic cloves, crushed*
*½ pound portobello mushrooms, sliced (3 cups)*
*Salt and freshly ground black pepper to taste*

Line a baking tray with foil and place under the broiler. Spray the steak with oil on both sides and set aside. Heat a small nonstick skillet on medium high and add the onion. Sauté 1 minute. Add the chicken broth, cover with a lid, and cook on high for 3 minutes. Uncover and cook another minute, or until all of the liquid has evaporated. Add the garlic and mushrooms, and sauté for 2 minutes. Season with salt and pepper to taste. Remove the hot baking tray from the broiler and place steak on tray. Broil 4 minutes for a 1-inch thick steak, 2 minutes for a thinner one. Turn the steak, and salt and pepper the cooked side. Broil another 4 minutes for thicker steak, 2 minutes for a thinner one. Transfer the steak to 2 plates, smother with the onion and mushrooms, and serve. *Makes 2 servings.*

**ONE SERVING: 365** CALORIES, **53G** PROTEIN, **10G** CARBOHYDRATE **14G** FAT (**6G** SATURATED), **127MG** CHOLESTEROL, **237MG** SODIUM, **0G** FIBER

## hearts of palm salad

*Several red lettuce leaves, washed and torn into bite-size pieces*
*½ cup canned or jarred hearts of palm, drained and sliced thinly*
*2 tablespoons no-sugar added oil and vinegar dressing*

Place lettuce on 2 plates and top with the hearts of palm. Drizzle with salad dressing and serve. *Makes 2 servings.*

**ONE SERVING: 90** CALORIES, **1G** PROTEIN, **3G** CARBOHYDRATE, **9G** FAT (**1G** SATURATED), **0MG** CHOLESTEROL, **234MG** SODIUM, **1G** FIBER

### helpful hints

- *Beef fillet, sirloin, round, skirt, or flank steak can also be used.*
- *Fresh pineapple cubes are available in the produce sections of most supermarkets.*
- *Any type of lettuce can be used.*
- *If pressed for time, omit the Pineapple Kabobs and serve 1 cup of pineapple cubes per person.*

### countdown

- *Preheat broiler.*
- *Make steak.*
- *Make salad.*
- *Assemble pineapple.*

### shopping list

*TO BUY:*

*10 ounces strip steak*
*1 can or jar hearts of palm*
*½ pound portobello mushrooms*
*1 small head red lettuce leaves*
*1 package fresh pineapple cubes*

# smothered steak with caramelized onions and hearts of palm salad *continued*

*STAPLES:*

*Garlic*
*Red onion*
*Olive oil spray*
*No-sugar-added oil and vinegar dressing*
*Fat-free, low-salt chicken broth*
*Ground cinnamon*
*Sugar substitute*
*Salt*
*Black peppercorns*

## pineapple kabobs

*1 tablespoon ground cinnamon*
*2 (.035-ounce) envelopes sugar substitute*
*2 cups pineapple cubes*
*2 skewers*

Line a baking tray with foil. Mix the cinnamon and sugar substitute together in a medium-size bowl. Toss the pineapple cubes in the mixture, making sure all sides are coated. Thread the cubes onto 2 skewers and place on the baking tray. Broil 6 to 7 inches from the heat for 5 minutes. Turn the skewers over and broil an additional 3 minutes. Serve warm.

*Makes 2 servings.*

**ONE SERVING: 86** CALORIES, **1G** PROTEIN, **23G** CARBOHYDRATE, **1G** FAT (**0G** SATURATED), **0MG** CHOLESTEROL, **3MG** SODIUM, **2G** FIBER

# whisky pork chops with rosemary lentils and red beet salad

*Whisky lends an intriguing flavor to this simple French pork dish. This is a hearty meal and takes about 30 to 40 minutes to make from start to finish.*

## whisky pork chops

- *2 teaspoons olive oil*
- *2 (5-ounce) boneless, center loin pork chops, visible fat removed*
- *½ cup whisky*
- *½ cup fat-free, low-salt chicken broth*
- *2 tablespoons Dijon mustard*
- *Salt and freshly ground black pepper to taste*

Heat the oil in a medium-size nonstick skillet on medium high. Add the pork chops, and brown for 2 minutes on both sides. Pour off excess fat. Add the whisky and flambé: If cooking over gas, warm the whisky in the pan for a few seconds and then tip the pan to let the flame ignite the liquid. Immediately remove from the heat and let the flame burn down. If you cook with electric heat, then throw a lighted match into the warmed whisky. Be sure to remove the match before serving.

Stir in the broth, cover, and lower the heat. Cook on low for 3 minutes, or until the chops are cooked through and a meat thermometer registers 160 degrees. Remove the chops to a plate and cover with foil to keep warm. Add the mustard and blend in with the sauce. Cook 1 to 2 minutes to reduce and slightly thicken. Season with salt and pepper to taste. Remove the chops to 2 plates, spoon the sauce over chops, and serve.

*Makes 2 servings.*

**ONE SERVING: 448** CALORIES, **42G** PROTEIN, **1G** CARBOHYDRATE, **12G** FAT (**3G** SATURATED), **133MG** CHOLESTEROL, **596MG** SODIUM, **0G** FIBER

### helpful hints

- *Lentils don't need to be soaked and will cook in about 20 minutes. Start them first so that they will be ready by the time the pork is finished.*
- *For safety's sake when flambéing, keep pan lid nearby to snuff out the flame, if necessary.*
- *Whisky can be bought in small splits at most liquor stores.*

### countdown

- *Start lentils.*
- *Preheat broiler.*
- *Make pork chops.*
- *Assemble salad.*
- *Make cinnamon grapefruit.*

### shopping list

*TO BUY:*

- *2 (5-ounce) boneless, center loin pork chops*
- *1 small bottle whisky*
- *1 can or jar sliced beets*
- *1 small package dried lentils*
- *1 small bunch fresh parsley*
- *1 small bunch fresh rosemary or 1 jar dried*
- *1 grapefruit*

# whisky pork chops with rosemary lentils and red beet salad *continued*

*STAPLES:*

- *Yellow onion*
- *Garlic*
- *Olive oil*
- *Distilled white vinegar*
- *Fat free, low-salt chicken broth*
- *Dijon mustard*
- *Ground cinnamon*
- *Sugar substitute*
- *Salt*
- *Black peppercorns*

## rosemary lentils

- *1 cup fat-free, low-salt chicken broth*
- *1 cup water*
- *½ cup dried lentils*
- *½ cup diced yellow onion*
- *2 teaspoons fresh rosemary (1 teaspoon dried)*
- *2 medium-size garlic cloves, crushed*
- *Salt and freshly ground black pepper to taste*
- *¼ cup chopped fresh parsley*

Bring the broth and water to a rolling boil in a medium-size pot. Add the lentils, onion, rosemary, and garlic slowly, so that the water does not stop boiling. Reduce the heat to medium, cover with a lid, and simmer 20 minutes. Remove the lid and continue to cook on high heat, until any remaining liquid has been absorbed. Season with salt and pepper to taste. Sprinkle with fresh parsley and serve with the pork.
*Makes 2 servings.*

**ONE SERVING: 85** CALORIES, **7G** PROTEIN, **15G** CARBOHYDRATE, **0.5G** FAT (**0G** SATURATED), **0MG** CHOLESTEROL, **285MG** SODIUM, **2G** FIBER

## red beet salad

- *2 cups sliced canned beets*
- *2 tablespoons distilled white vinegar*
- *2 (.035-ounce) envelopes sugar substitute*

Place beets on 2 salad plates. Combine the vinegar and sugar substitute, spoon over the beets, and serve.
*Makes 2 servings.*

**ONE SERVING: 58** CALORIES, **2G** PROTEIN, **15G** CARBOHYDRATE, **0G** FAT (**0G** SATURATED), **0MG** CHOLESTEROL, **84MG** SODIUM, **0G** FIBER

## cinnamon grapefruit

- *1 grapefruit*
- *½ teaspoon cinnamon*
- *2 (.035-ounce) envelopes sugar substitute*

Preheat the broiler. Line a baking tray with foil or use a small oven-to-table dish. Peel the grapefruit over a bowl to catch the juice. With a serrated knife, cut the grapefruit into ½-inch slices (as you would slice a tomato). Place in a single layer in the dish. Sprinkle with the cinnamon and broil for 3 minutes. Mix the sugar substitute into the grapefruit juice, and spoon over the broiled grapefruit before serving.
*Makes 2 servings.*

**ONE SERVING: 40** CALORIES, **1G** PROTEIN, **11G** CARBOHYDRATE, **0G** FAT (**0G** SATURATED), **0MG** CHOLESTEROL, **0MG** SODIUM, **1G** FIBER

# seared sesame tuna and stir-fry bok choy with shiitake noodles

*Seared tuna with black and white sesame seeds is a popular favorite in many restaurants that you can make at home in minutes. Taste can vary considerably among the species of tuna. The yellowfin and blackfin tuna are more delicately flavored and particularly worth looking for. Black sesame seeds are available in some supermarkets. You can use either all white sesame seeds or a combination of both.*

## seared sesame tuna

*10 ounces fresh tuna steak*
*3 tablespoons sesame seeds*
*4 teaspoons olive oil*
*Salt and freshly ground black pepper to taste*

Rinse the tuna and pat dry with a paper towel. Spoon the sesame seeds over both sides of the tuna, pressing the seeds into the fish with the back of a spoon. Heat the oil in a wok or nonstick skillet on high. When the oil begins to smoke, add the tuna. Brown for 1 minute, then turn. Brown another minute, then lower the heat to medium high. Cook another 3 to 4 minutes. Season with salt and pepper to taste. The tuna should be seared outside and just barely warm inside. Immediately remove from the pan to slow the cooking process. Cut the tuna in half, divide between 2 plates, and serve.

*Makes 2 servings.*

**ONE SERVING: 353** CALORIES, **36G** PROTEIN, **1G** CARBOHYDRATE, **23G** FAT (**4G** SATURATED), **53MG** CHOLESTEROL, **60MG** SODIUM, **0G** FIBER

## helpful hints

- *To chop fresh ginger quickly, cut it into small cubes and press through a garlic press with large holes. If using a press with small holes, just capture the juice that is squeezed out; it will give enough flavor for the recipe.*
- *To save clean-up time, cook the tuna first, then remove and stir-fry the bok choy and pasta in the same wok.*
- *To keep from having to look back at the recipe as you stir-fry the ingredients, line them up on a cutting board or plate in the order of use so you know which ingredient comes next.*
- *For crisp, not steamed, stir-fried vegetables, start with a very hot wok or skillet. Let the vegetables sit a minute before tossing to allow the wok to regain its heat.*

# seared sesame tuna and stir-fry bok choy with shiitake noodles *continued*

## countdown

- *Prepare all ingredients.*
- *Boil pasta.*
- *Make tuna in wok and remove.*
- *Stir-fry bok choy and pasta.*

## shopping list

*TO BUY:*

*10 ounces fresh tuna steak*

*1 small jar sesame seeds (white, black, or combination)*

*1 box whole wheat thin spaghetti (2 ounces needed)*

*1 small bottle dry sherry*

*1 small bok choy (1/4 pound needed)*

*1 container shiitake mushrooms (1/4 pound needed)*

*1 small bunch scallions (4 scallions needed)*

*2-inch piece fresh ginger*

*STAPLES:*

*Garlic*

*Olive oil*

*Low-sodium soy sauce*

*Salt*

*Black peppercorns*

# stir-fry bok choy with shiitake noodles

*2 ounces whole wheat thin spaghetti (1/2 cup)*

*2 tablespoons low-sodium soy sauce*

*2 tablespoons dry sherry*

*2 tablespoons water*

*4 medium-size garlic cloves, crushed*

*2-inch piece fresh ginger, peeled and chopped (2 tablespoons)*

*2 teaspoons olive oil*

*1/4 pound bok choy, sliced (2 cups)*

*1/4 pound shiitake mushrooms, sliced (2 cups)*

*4 scallions, sliced (1/2 cup)*

*Salt and freshly ground black pepper to taste*

Bring a large saucepan filled with water to a boil. Add the spaghetti and boil 5 minutes or according to package instructions. Do not overcook. Drain.

Combine the soy sauce, sherry, water, garlic, and ginger in a small bowl. Make sure all ingredients are prepped and ready for the wok. Heat the oil until smoking in the same wok or skillet used for tuna. Add the spaghetti, bok choy, and mushrooms. Stir-fry 2 minutes. Draw to the sides of the wok, leaving a well in the middle. Add the sauce and toss with vegetables for 2 minutes. Add the scallions, and season with salt and pepper to taste. Toss well. Spoon onto plates with the tuna.

*Makes 2 servings.*

**ONE SERVING: 273** CALORIES, **10G** PROTEIN, **38G** CARBOHYDRATE, **6G** FAT (**1G** SATURATED), **0MG** CHOLESTEROL, **629G** SODIUM, **6G** FIBER

# chicken provençal with endive and watercress salad

*The mild, warm climate and bright sun of the South of France nurture the colorful array of Provençal ingredients. Ripe tomatoes, garlic, olives, and fresh herbs delicately spice the cuisine of this region. Memories of meals we had in Provence inspired this dinner. • Anchovies are used as a base for the chicken sauce. They practically melt to nothing when sautéed, yet give the sauce a rich flavor. Be sure to rinse them well before use to remove most of the salt.*

## chicken provençal

*3/4 pound boneless, skinless chicken breast*
*1/2 medium-size red onion, diced (1 cup)*
*4 anchovy fillets packed in olive oil, rinsed*
*4 medium plum tomatoes, diced (1 1/2 cups)*
*2 medium-size garlic cloves, crushed*
*2 tablespoons fresh thyme leaves or 2 teaspoons dried*
*1 teaspoon balsamic vinegar*
*2 teaspoons olive oil*
*8 pitted black olives, halved*
*Freshly ground black pepper to taste*

Remove any visible fat from the chicken. Set a nonstick skillet over medium-high heat. Add the chicken, onion, and anchovies. Brown the chicken for 2 minutes on each side. While chicken browns, mash the anchovies with the back of your cooking spoon. Lower the heat and add the tomatoes, garlic, and thyme. Cover and simmer for 5 minutes. Divide the chicken between 2 plates. Stir the sauce and add the vinegar, oil, and black olives. Season with pepper to taste. Spoon the sauce over the chicken.
*Makes 2 servings.*

**ONE SERVING: 416** CALORIES, **62G** PROTEIN, **31G** CARBOHYDRATE **16G** FAT (**3G** SATURATED), **144MG** CHOLESTEROL, **585MG** SODIUM, **2G** FIBER

## brown rice

*1/2 cup brown rice*
*Salt and freshly ground black pepper to taste*

Rinse the rice and place in a large saucepan. Fill with water and bring to a boil. Boil 30 minutes. Drain, and add salt and pepper to taste. Divide between 2 plates and place the chicken and sauce on top.
*Makes 2 servings.*

**ONE SERVING: 85** CALORIES, **3G** PROTEIN, **18G** CARBOHYDRATE, **1G** FAT (**0G** SATURATED), **0MG** CHOLESTEROL, **0MG** SODIUM, **1G** FIBER

## helpful hints

- *Fresh thyme gives the dish a sweet flavor, though dried can be used.*
- *If using dried spices, make sure the bottle is less than 6 months old.*
- *Any type of tomatoes can be substituted for plum tomatoes.*
- *The quickest way to wash watercress is to place it head first into a bowl of water. Leave for a minute, then lift out and shake dry, leaving dirt and grit behind.*
- *To give chicken a crisp texture, make sure the skillet is very hot before browning.*
- *I call for regular brown rice instead of quick-cooking brown rice because it contains more nutrients. If you're really pressed for time, the quick-cooking brown rice works fine.*
- *I like to cook my rice like pasta, using a pot of boiling water that's large enough for the rice to roll freely. Use the method given here or follow the directions on the package of rice.*

# chicken provençal with endive and watercress salad *continued*

## countdown

- *Make rice.*
- *Make chicken.*
- *Make salad.*

## shopping list

*TO BUY:*

*3/4 pound boneless, skinless chicken breast*

*1 container pitted black olives*

*1 small package brown rice*

*1 tin anchovy fillets packed in olive oil*

*4 medium plum tomatoes*

*1 bunch fresh thyme or 1 jar dried*

*2 small heads Belgian endive*

*1 small bunch watercress*

*STAPLES:*

*Red onion*

*Garlic*

*Olive oil*

*Balsamic vinegar*

*No-sugar-added oil and vinegar dressing*

*Salt*

*Black peppercorns*

# endive and watercress salad

*2 small heads Belgian endive*

*1 small bunch fresh watercress, stemmed and washed*

*2 tablespoons no-sugar-added oil and vinegar dressing*

*Salt and freshly ground black pepper to taste*

Wipe the endives with a damp paper towel. Remove 1 inch from the bases. Cut the leaves crosswise into 1-inch slices. Place in a small bowl. Break the watercress into smaller pieces and add to the bowl. Drizzle dressing over the top, season with salt and pepper to taste, and serve.

*Makes 2 servings.*

**ONE SERVING: 87** CALORIES, **1G** PROTEIN, **2G** CARBOHYDRATE, **9G** FAT (**2G** SATURATED), **0MG** CHOLESTEROL, **101MG** SODIUM, **0G** FIBER

# mussels marinière with mesclun salad

*Imagine eating on the quay in Deauville, France, watching the fishing boats come in, breathing the fresh sea air, and drinking a glass of chilled white wine. What a treat! Moules à la Marinière or Mussels in White Wine is a French dish normally enjoyed in these quaint surroundings. If you can't go to France, prepare this dish for a satisfying experience. It takes less than 15 minutes to prepare, never mind the fabulous taste!. • Store mussels in the refrigerator. When ready for use, carefully scrub them with a vegetable brush under cold water. Scrape off the beard or thin hairs along the shell. Their shells should be tightly closed or snap shut when tapped. Discard any that do not close. • First serve the mussels in large soup bowls. Then serve the reduced broth in the same bowls.*

## mussels marinière

- *2 teaspoons olive oil*
- *½ cup sliced yellow onion*
- *2 celery stalks, sliced (1 cup)*
- *2 medium carrots, sliced (1 cup)*
- *½ cup dry white wine*
- *Freshly ground black pepper to taste*
- *2 pounds mussels*
- *¼ cup fresh parsley, chopped*
- *2 slices multigrain bread*

Heat the oil in a large saucepan on medium high. Sauté the onion, celery, and carrots until they start to cook, but not color, about 5 minutes. Add the wine and freshly ground pepper to taste. Add the mussels and cover tightly with a lid. Bring to a boil, and let boil about 3 more minutes. The wine will boil up over the mussels causing them to open. As soon as they open, remove the pan from the heat. Do not over cook.

Lift the mussels out of the pan with a slotted spoon and divide between 2 large soup bowls. Discard any mussels that do not open. Do not try to force open any mussels that do not open. Sprinkle with parsley and serve. Meanwhile, bring the liquid to a boil and reduce rapidly by half. Ladle out the reduced broth to serve with all of the vegetables, leaving ¼ inch of the broth in the pan—it may have some sand from the mussels in it. Serve with bread to dip in the broth. *Makes 2 servings.*

**ONE SERVING: 374** CALORIES, **33G** PROTEIN, **31G** CARBOHYDRATE **11G** FAT (**1G** SATURATED), **64MG** CHOLESTEROL, **861MG** SODIUM, **5G** FIBER

## mesclun salad

- *4 cups washed, ready-to-eat mesclun salad or field greens*
- *2 tablespoons no-sugar-added oil and vinegar dressing*

Place salad in a salad bowl and toss with the dressing. *Makes 2 servings.*

**ONE SERVING: 84** CALORIES, **1G** PROTEIN, **2G** CARBOHYDRATE, **8G** FAT (**1G** SATURATED), **0MG** CHOLESTEROL, **81MG** SODIUM, **0G** FIBER

### helpful hint

- *The onion, celery, and carrots can be sautéed ahead of time. Cook the mussels in wine just before serving.*

### countdown

- *Prepare ingredients.*
- *Cook vegetables.*
- *Add mussels.*

### shopping list

*TO BUY:*

- *2 pounds mussels*
- *1 small bottle dry white wine*
- *1 small bunch fresh parsley*
- *1 bag washed, ready-to-eat mesclun salad or field greens*

*STAPLES:*

- *Celery*
- *Yellow onion*
- *Carrots*
- *Olive oil*
- *No-sugar-added oil and vinegar dressing*
- *Multigrain bread*
- *Black peppercorns*

# spicy vietnamese stir-fry crab with asian vegetables

## helpful hints

- *Canned or frozen crab—backfin, lump meat, or claw meat can be used.*
- *Buy tomato paste in a tube. You can use a small amount, and store the rest in the refrigerator until needed again.*
- *Use a food processor to chop the shallots and peanuts.*
- *To chop fresh ginger quickly, cut it into small cubes and press through a garlic press with large holes. If using a press with small holes, just capture the juice that is squeezed out; it will give enough flavor for the recipe.*
- *If using ground ginger instead of fresh, add it into sauce.*
- *To keep from having to look back at the recipe as you stir-fry the ingredients, line them up on a cutting board or plate in the order of use so you know which ingredient comes next.*
- *For crisp, not steamed, stir-fried vegetables, start with a very hot wok or skillet. Let the vegetables sit a minute before tossing to allow the wok to regain its heat.*
- *Any type of berries can be used.*
- *Any flavor of light yogurt can be used.*
- *Be careful toasting the pecans, as they burn easily.*

*Oriental spices give this crab a zesty tang. Vietnamese cuisine benefits from the country's long relationship with France. This dish is normally made with whole crab claws in the shell. I have simplified the shopping and cooking by using canned or frozen crab. • This entire meal is made in a wok. A nonstick skillet can also be used and still achieve a good result. • Shallots are part of the onion family. They are small, tear-drop shaped, and milder than onions. Red onion can be substituted. • Lemon grass has long, thin, green-gray leaves with a scallion-like base. Slice the end off the bulb and cut slices up to the woody part of the stem. Grated lemon rind can be substituted.*

## spicy vietnamese stir-fry crab with asian vegetables

*2 (6½-ounce) cans backfin lump crabmeat, drained*
*¼ cup tomato paste*
*½ teaspoon hot pepper sauce*
*½ cup water*
*2 (.035-ounce) envelopes sugar substitute*
*4 teaspoons canola oil*
*¼ cup chopped shallots*
*2 medium-size garlic cloves, crushed*
*2 tablespoons chopped fresh ginger or 2 teaspoons ground ginger*
*4 stalks lemon grass, sliced, or grated lemon rind from 2 lemons*
*½ pound fresh bean sprouts (3 cups)*
*½ pound snow peas, trimmed (2 cups)*
*2 tablespoons unsalted, roasted peanuts, chopped*

Flake the crabmeat with a fork into a medium-size bowl, looking carefully for any shell or cartilage that might remain. Combine the tomato paste, hot pepper sauce, water, and sugar substitute in a small bowl; set aside. Make sure all ingredients are prepped and ready for stir-frying. Heat the oil in a wok or skillet on high until smoking. Add the shallots, garlic, ginger, and lemon grass, and stir-fry 2 minutes. Add the bean sprouts and snow peas. Stir-fry 2 minutes. Add the crab and stir-fry 3 more minutes.

Push the ingredients to sides of pan leaving a well in the center. Add the sauce, and toss with ingredients for an additional minute. Remove to 2 plates, sprinkle with peanuts, and serve. *Makes 1 serving.*

**ONE SERVING: 493** CALORIES, **52G** PROTEIN, **25G** CARBOHYDRATE, **23G** FAT (**3G** SATURATED), **144MG** CHOLESTEROL, **694MG** SODIUM, **4G** FIBER

# spicy vietnamese stir-fry crab with asian vegetables *continued*

## red raspberry parfait

*2/3 cup fresh raspberries*
*2 (.035-ounce) envelopes sugar substitute (optional)*
*1 cup light, white chocolate–strawberry yogurt*
*6 pecan pieces, toasted (1 tablespoon)*

Purée the raspberries in a food processor and blend in the sugar substitute. Scoop half the yogurt into 2 bowls or parfait glasses. Pour in half the sauce; top with the remaining yogurt. Pour the remaining sauce over the yogurt, and top with the toasted pecans.

Refrigerate until ready to serve.

*Makes 2 servings.*

**ONE SERVING: 110** CALORIES, **5G** PROTEIN, **15G** CARBOHYDRATE, **4G** FAT (**0.5G** SATURATED), **3MG** CHOLESTEROL, **58MG** SODIUM, **2G** FIBER

### countdown

- *Prepare all ingredients and line up on a plate or cutting board in order of use.*
- *Stir-fry crab dish.*
- *Prepare parfait.*

### shopping list

*TO BUY:*

*1 carton light white chocolate–strawberry flavored yogurt*
*2 (6 1/2-ounce) cans backfin lump crabmeat*
*1 small can or tube tomato paste*
*1 small package roasted peanuts (1 ounce needed)*
*1 small package pecans (1/2 ounce needed)*
*2 large shallots*
*1 small piece fresh ginger or 1 jar ground ginger*
*1 small bunch lemon grass (4 stalks needed)*
*1/2 pound fresh bean sprouts*
*1/2 pound snow peas*
*1 container fresh raspberries*

*STAPLES:*

*Garlic*
*Canola oil*
*Hot pepper sauce*
*Sugar substitute*

# neapolitan steak pizzaiola with parmesan linguine and italian greens

*The Italian city of Naples claims pizza as its symbol. The same earthy flavors they use in their popular Italian sauce go with steak. Here is a quick version of the zesty, tomato-based sauce that can be made in 20 minutes for a great, quick, mid-week supper.*

## helpful hints

- *Make sure the dried oregano is less than 6 months old.*
- *Any type of washed, ready-to-eat salad can be used.*
- *Buy good quality Parmesan cheese and ask the grocer to grate it for you or chop it in the food processor yourself. Freeze extra for quick use later—simply spoon out what you need and leave the rest frozen.*

## countdown

- *Begin boiling water for pasta.*
- *Make salad.*
- *Make steak.*
- *Make pasta.*

## neapolitan steak pizzaiola

*½ pound flank or skirt steak, visible fat removed*
*1 cup no-sugar-added canned, peeled plum tomatoes*
*¼ cup diced yellow onion*
*2 medium-size garlic cloves, crushed*
*2 teaspoons dried oregano*
*1 teaspoon balsamic vinegar*
*2 teaspoons olive oil*
*8 pitted black olives, halved*
*2 (.035-ounce) envelopes sugar substitute*
*Salt and freshly ground black pepper to taste*

Set a medium-size nonstick skillet over medium-high heat. Brown the steak for 2 minutes on each side. Lower the heat and cook 3 to 4 more minutes. Remove the steak to a plate and cover with foil or another plate to keep warm. Lower the heat and add the tomatoes, onion, garlic, and oregano. Cover and simmer 5 minutes. Stir in the vinegar, oil, black olives, and sugar substitute. Season with salt and pepper to taste. Remove from the heat, slice the steak, and serve with the sauce on top.

*Makes 2 servings.*

**ONE SERVING: 336** CALORIES, **42G** PROTEIN, **10G** CARBOHYDRATE **16G** FAT (**6G** SATURATED), **101MG** CHOLESTEROL, **240MG** SODIUM, **4G** FIBER

## parmesan linguine

*2 ounces whole wheat linguine or spaghetti (½ cup)*
*2 teaspoons olive oil*
*Salt and freshly ground black pepper to taste*
*2 tablespoons freshly grated Parmesan cheese*

Bring a large saucepan filled with water to boil. Add the pasta, and cook 8 minutes, or according to package instructions. Do not overcook. Drain, leaving 3 tablespoons of water on the pasta, and toss with oil. Season with salt and pepper to taste, and sprinkle with Parmesan cheese. Serve with the steak.

*Makes 2 servings.*

**ONE SERVING: 208** CALORIES, **9G** PROTEIN, **26G** CARBOHYDRATE, **6G** FAT (**2G** SATURATED), **4MG** CHOLESTEROL, **113MG** SODIUM, **5G** FIBER

# neapolitan steak pizzaiola with parmesan linguine and italian greens *continued*

## italian greens

*4 cups washed, ready-to-eat, Italian-style salad*
*4 teaspoons balsamic vinegar*
*Salt and freshly ground black pepper to taste*

Place the salad in a bowl and sprinkle with balsamic vinegar. Add salt and pepper to taste and toss before serving.

*Makes 2 servings.*

**ONE SERVING: 10** CALORIES, **1G** PROTEIN, **2G** CARBOHYDRATE, **0G** FAT (**0G** SATURATED), **0MG** CHOLESTEROL, **6MG** SODIUM, **0** FIBER

## shopping list

*TO BUY:*

*½ pound flank or skirt steak, visible fat removed*
*1 box whole wheat linguine or spaghetti (2 ounces needed)*
*1 container pitted black olives*
*1 can no-sugar-added, peeled plum tomatoes (8 ounces needed)*
*1 bag washed, ready-to-eat, Italian-style salad*

*STAPLES:*

*Yellow onion*
*Garlic*
*Olive oil*
*Balsamic vinegar*
*Parmesan cheese*
*Dried oregano*
*Sugar substitute*
*Salt*
*Black peppercorns*

# five-spiced chicken legs with garlic bean sprouts and rice

## helpful hints

- *To save clean-up time, use the same wok or skillet for the chicken and the rice with bean sprouts.*
- *Chinese 5-spice powder can be found in the spice section of the supermarket.*
- *Distilled white vinegar diluted with a little water can be used instead of rice vinegar.*
- *To keep from having to look back at the recipe as you stir-fry the ingredients, line them up on a cutting board or plate in the order of use so you know which ingredient comes next.*
- *For crisp, not steamed, stir-fried vegetables, start with a very hot wok or skillet. Let the vegetables sit a minute before tossing to allow the wok to regain its heat.*

## countdown

- *Start rice.*
- *Place chicken on to cook.*
- *Complete Bean Sprouts and Rice.*

*Aromatic flavors of Chinese 5-spice powder make this dish a winner. It takes a little longer to cook this dish—about 30 minutes—but the flavor is worth the time. The powder usually consists of cinnamon, cloves, fennel seed, star anise, and Szechwan peppercorns. • Boneless, skinless chicken legs and thighs are now available in the supermarkets. With the skin removed, the fat content is greatly reduced. Their richer-flavored meat make a nice alternative to boneless, skinless chicken breasts. • This dish tastes great the second day. Make extra for another quick meal.*

## five-spiced chicken legs

*½ cup fat-free, low-salt chicken broth*
*¼ cup rice vinegar*
*1 teaspoon Chinese 5-spice powder*
*6 large garlic cloves*
*2 tablespoons low-salt soy sauce*
*½ cup water*
*2 teaspoons sesame oil*
*10 ounces boneless, skinless chicken legs or thighs, visible fat removed*
*¼ pound broccoli florets (2 cups)*
*½ pound sliced button mushrooms (3 cups)*

Combine the chicken broth, vinegar, Chinese 5-spice, whole garlic cloves, soy sauce, and water in a small bowl. Make sure all ingredients are prepped and ready for stir-frying. Heat the oil in a wok or skillet on high until smoking. Brown the chicken on all sides, about 2 minutes. Add the chicken broth mixture, and reduce the heat to medium low. Simmer gently for 15 minutes, turning the chicken several times. The liquid should be just at the bubbling stage. Add the broccoli and mushrooms, and continue cooking for 5 minutes. The sauce will boil down to a glaze as the chicken cooks. Remove the garlic cloves. Spoon the completed dish into a bowl and cover with foil to keep warm. *Makes 2 servings.*

**ONE SERVING: 419** CALORIES, **45G** PROTEIN, **13G** CARBOHYDRATE **20G** FAT (**4G** SATURATED), **130MG** CHOLESTEROL, **897MG** SODIUM, **1G** FIBER

# five-spiced chicken legs with garlic bean sprouts and rice *continued*

## garlic bean sprouts and rice

*1/2 cup brown rice*

*Salt and freshly ground black pepper to taste*

*2 teaspoons sesame oil*

*2 cups fresh bean sprouts*

*2 medium-size garlic cloves, crushed*

Rinse the rice and place in a large saucepan filled with water. Bring to a boil, and cook for 30 minutes. Drain, and season with salt and pepper to taste.

Again, make sure all ingredients are prepped and ready for stir-frying. Heat the wok on high, and then add the oil. Add the rice, bean sprouts, and garlic, and sauté for 2 to 3 minutes. Season with salt and pepper to taste. Place on 2 plates and spoon the stir-fried chicken and vegetables on top.

*Makes 2 servings.*

**ONE SERVING: 207** CALORIES, **11G** PROTEIN, **25G** CARBOHYDRATE **9G** FAT (**1G** SATURATED), **0MG** CHOLESTEROL, **10MG** SODIUM, **1G** FIBER

### shopping list

*TO BUY:*

- *10 ounces boneless, skinless chicken legs or thighs*
- *1 small package brown rice*
- *1 small bottle rice vinegar*
- *1 small bottle sesame oil*
- *1 jar Chinese 5-spice powder*
- *1 small package broccoli florets (1/4 pound needed)*
- *1/2 pound sliced button mushrooms*
- *1 small package fresh bean sprouts*

*STAPLES:*

- *Garlic*
- *Fat free, low-salt chicken broth*
- *Low-salt soy sauce*
- *Salt*
- *Black peppercorns*

# right carbs

## introduction

You're now entering the third and permanent phase of the low-carb lifestyle: great food that's good for you, too. This balanced approach to eating incorporates high-fiber carbohydrates into breakfast, lunch, and dinner menus.

As with the other sections, I have organized the menus into a meal-at-a-glance chart with some easy and quick meals mid-week, alongside more elaborate ones for the weekends. They are arranged to give variety throughout the day and over the course of the week. The meals are ordered in the chapter in the same sequence. Just follow the meals in the order given for an easy two-week plan.

## breakfast

The French Toast with Ham and the Ranchero Burrito are 2 of the 14 savory breakfasts you can choose from. Try them all to add variety to your morning repertoire.

## lunch

Choose from the wide selection to fit any appetite. When you're in a hurry, grab a Baby Spinach, Mushroom, and Canadian Bacon Salad with Pineapple and Toasted Pine Nuts. Most restaurant menus will have a shrimp or tuna salad, or a pasta salad with turkey (or chicken). Make the recipe provided here, and use it as a guide for proportions when ordering out. When you have more time, enjoy the Tomatoes with Tuscan Green Sauce and Garlic Bruschetta and Strawberry Smoothie, or a Ham, Mushroom, and Onion Pita Pizza with Fennel Salad.

## dinner

Enjoy these meals in the proportions given, and you won't have to study the numbers or question what you eat. Menus like Beef Stir-Fry with Oyster Sauce and Brown Rice with Minted Tangerines, Pork and Peach Salsa with Pasta Salad and Melon, and a Country Minestrone with Herbed Meatballs and Ginger-Spiced Applesauce will entice you to stay on this low-carbohydrate, balanced style of eating.

Following the Right Carb 14-day plan, you will consume an average of 125 to 135 grams of carbohydrates per day. Carbohydrate percentage is based on carbohydrates less fiber consumed—the standard way to calculate carbohydrate consumption. The balance of these meals is 38 percent of calories from carbohydrates, 30 percent of calories from lean protein, 22 percent of calories from monounsaturated fat, and 7 percent of calories from saturated fat.

# right carbs 14-day menu plan

| week 1 | breakfast | lunch | dinner |
|---|---|---|---|
| sunday | Smoked Salmon Crêpes with Bran Cereal . . .150 | Layered Crab Salad with Parmesan Crostini and Grapes and Yogurt . .165 | Japanese Beef Sukiyaki and Fresh Peaches in Kirsch . . . . . . . . . .184 |
| monday | Grilled Ham and Cheddar Breakfast Sandwich with Oatmeal . . . . . . . .151 | Tomatoes with Tuscan Green Sauce and Garlic Bruschetta and Strawberry Smoothie . . . . . . . .167 | Sole in a Pouch with Garlic Zucchini Couscous . . . . . . . .185 |
| tuesday | Spinach and Parmesan Omelette with Bran-Yogurt Parfait . . . . . . . . . .152 | Shrimp Caesar Wrap with Pears and Yogurt . . . . . . .169 | Chicken Parmesan, Pasta, and Broccoli with Poached Spiced Pears . . . . .186 |
| wednesday | Ranchero Burrito with Bran Cereal . . . . . .153 | Smoked Turkey Pita with Avocado and Fresh Berries Yogurt . . . . .171 | Cioppino (Seafood Stew) with Sliced Beet Salad and Watermelon Spritzer . . . . . . . . .188 |
| thursday | Western Omelette with Oatmeal . . . . . . . .154 | Salmon Burgers with Cantaloupe Yogurt . .172 | Pork Souvlaki Kabobs with Bulghur Wheat Salad . . . . .190 |
| friday | Mediterranean Meze Platter with Bran Cereal and Fresh Berries . .155 | Chicken Tostada and Cilantro Tomatoes . . . . . . . .173 | Mediterranean Veal and Olives with Orange Barley . . . . . . . . . .191 |
| saturday | Vietnamese Pancakes with Bran Cereal . . . . . .156 | Caribbean Shrimp Salad and Mango Yogurt . . . .174 | Country Minestrone with Herbed Meatballs and Ginger-Spiced Applesauce . . . . . .193 |

| week 2 | breakfast | lunch | dinner |
|---|---|---|---|
| sunday | French Toast with Ham, Bran Cereal, and Vegetable Juice . . . .157 | Ham, Mushroom, and Onion Pita Pizza with Fennel Salad . . . . .175 | Curried Shrimp and Lentil Salad . . . . . .195 |
| monday | Shiitake and Swiss Cheese Scramble with Spiced Oatmeal . . .158 | Fresh Tuna Salad on a Bed of Spring Greens with Fresh Peach Yogurt . . . . .176 | Southwestern Chicken Fajitas with Tipsy Grapefruit . . . . . . .197 |
| tuesday | Chevre and Hearts of Palm Omelette with Oatmeal . . . . . . . .159 | Baby Spinach, Mushroom, and Canadian Bacon Salad with Pineapple and Toasted Pine Nuts . .177 | Roast Beef Hash with Shiitake Mushrooms and Cinnamon-Walnut Baked Apples . . . . . . . . .199 |
| wednesday | Cottage Cheese and Cucumber Sandwich with Yogurt Crunch . . . . .160 | Turkey and Asparagus Penne Salad with Tangerine and Orange Yogurt . . . . . . . . . .179 | Bahamian Fish Boil with Chayote Salad . . . .201 |
| thursday | Warm Smoked Turkey Sandwich with Grapefruit and Bran Cereal . . .161 | Waldorf Salad with Open-Faced Roast Beef Sandwich and Fresh Berry Yogurt . . . . . . . . . .180 | Winter Casserole Soup and Grilled Cinnamon Oranges . . . . . . . .203 |
| friday | Egg-in-the-Hole with Bran Cereal . . . . . .162 | Grouper Sandwich and Tomato Tapenade Salad with Orange Vanilla Yogurt . . . . . . . . . .181 | Beef Stir-Fry with Oyster Sauce and Brown Rice with Minted Tangerines . .204 |
| saturday | Frittata Primavera with Bran Cereal . . . . . .163 | Chicken Sandwich with Sun-Dried Tomato Sauce and Apple Yogurt . .182 | Pork and Peach Salsa with Pasta Salad and Melon . . . . . . . . . .206 |

# right carb breakfasts

# smoked salmon crêpes with bran cereal

## helpful hint

- *If using dried dill, make sure the bottle is less than 6 months old. The leaves should be green, not gray.*

## countdown

- *Preheat broiler.*
- *Make crêpe and fill.*
- *Assemble cereal.*

## shopping list

*TO BUY:*

*1 small carton reduced-fat sour cream*
*1/4 pound sliced smoked salmon*
*1 medium tomato*
*1 small bunch fresh dill or 1 jar dried*
*1 banana*

*STAPLES:*

*Eggs*
*Olive oil spray*
*High-fiber, no-sugar-added bran cereal*
*Skim milk*
*Salt*
*Black peppercorns*

*This is perfect for a weekend breakfast or parties.*

## smoked salmon crêpes

*2 whole eggs*
*4 egg whites*
*1/2 cup snipped fresh dill or 3 tablespoons dried*
*Salt and freshly ground black pepper to taste*
*Olive oil spray*
*1/4 pound sliced smoked salmon*
*1 medium tomato, sliced*
*2 tablespoons reduced-fat sour cream*
*Several sprigs fresh dill for garnish (optional)*

Preheat the broiler. Whisk the eggs, egg whites, and dill in a medium-size bowl. Season with salt and pepper to taste. Set an 8- to 9-inch nonstick skillet over medium-high heat. Spray with olive oil. Add half the egg mixture, and swirl in the skillet to form a thin layer. Cook 1 minute and place under broiler for 1 minute, or until the crêpe is cooked on top. Remove from broiler. Slide the crêpe onto a plate and repeat for the second one. Place the smoked salmon and tomato slices on one half of each crêpe, letting some of the salmon peek out from the edge. Spoon sour cream over the salmon and add sprigs of dill, again letting them peek out from the crêpes. Fold the crêpes in half once, and then in half again to form a triangle. Serve hot.
*Makes 2 servings.*

## bran cereal

*1 cup high-fiber, no-sugar-added bran cereal*
*1 cup skim milk*
*1 sliced banana (1 1/2 cups)*

Divide the cereal between 2 bowls and add the milk and banana to each.
*Makes 2 servings.*

TOTAL BREAKFAST **ONE SERVING: 428** CALORIES, **33G** PROTEIN, **61G** CARBOHYDRATE, **15G** FAT (**4G** SATURATED), **237MG** CHOLESTEROL, **832MG** SODIUM, **15G** FIBER

# grilled ham and cheese breakfast sandwich with oatmeal

*This is a simple ham and cheese melted sandwich. It's a quick breakfast that can be made in 5 minutes and taken with you for breakfast-on-the-run.*

## grilled ham and cheese breakfast sandwich

*4 slices whole wheat bread*
*Olive oil spray*
*½ pound sliced lean ham (about 4 slices)*
*¼ cup shredded, reduced-fat sharp cheddar cheese*
*2 small tomatoes, sliced*

Preheat the broiler. Line a baking tray with foil. Place the bread on the tray and spray with olive oil. Place under the broiler for 1 minute. Top each slice with ham and sprinkle with cheese. Return to the broiler for 2 minutes, or until the cheese melts. Serve as an open-faced sandwich with a sliced tomato on the side. Or, if taking it with you, place the tomato slices on one slice, and cover with another slice to make a complete sandwich.
*Makes 2 servings.*

## oatmeal

*1 cup oatmeal*
*2 cups water*
*1 cup skim milk*
*2 (.035-ounce) envelopes sugar substitute (optional)*

To prepare in the microwave, combine the oatmeal and water in a microwave-safe bowl. Microwave on high for 4 minutes. Stir in the milk and sugar substitute, divide between 2 bowls, and serve warm.

Alternatively, to prepare on the stovetop, combine the oatmeal and water in a small saucepan over medium-high heat, and bring to a boil. Reduce the heat to medium, and cook about 5 more minutes, stirring occasionally. Stir in the milk and sugar substitute, divide between 2 bowls, and serve warm.
*Makes 2 servings.*

TOTAL BREAKFAST **ONE SERVING: 488** CALORIES, **39G** PROTEIN, **60G** CARBOHYDRATE, **14G** FAT (**5G** SATURATED), **52MG** CHOLESTEROL, **116MG** SODIUM, **10G** FIBER

### helpful hints

- *The sandwich can be made in a toaster oven.*
- *Any type of whole grain bread can be used.*

### countdown

- *Preheat broiler.*
- *Make ham and cheese melt.*
- *Assemble cereal.*

### shopping list

*TO BUY:*

*1 small package shredded, reduced-fat sharp cheddar cheese*
*½ pound sliced lean ham*
*2 small tomatoes*

*STAPLES:*

*Oatmeal*
*Skim milk*
*Whole wheat bread*
*Olive oil spray*
*Sugar substitute*

# spinach and parmesan omelette with bran-yogurt parfait

*My husband made this breakfast one very hurried morning before going to work. His comment? "I can't believe it took me only 15 minutes—start to finish!"*

## spinach and parmesan omelette

*2 whole eggs*
*4 egg whites*
*Salt and freshly ground black pepper to taste*
*4 cups washed, ready-to-eat fresh spinach (5 ounces)*
*2 teaspoons olive oil*
*2 tablespoons freshly grated Parmesan cheese*

Preheat the oven to 400 degrees. Lightly beat the whole eggs and egg whites together in a medium-size bowl. Season with salt and pepper to taste. Set a medium-size nonstick skillet over medium heat. Add the spinach and sauté 3 minutes, or until wilted. Stir the cooked spinach into the egg mixture. In the same skillet, heat the oil on medium. Pour the egg mixture into skillet, and let set for 1 minute. Sprinkle with Parmesan, and place in the oven for 3 minutes, or until eggs are set to desired consistency. Serve immediately. *Makes 2 servings.*

## bran-yogurt parfait

*1 ½ cups blueberries*
*2 (.035-ounce) envelopes sugar substitute*
*1 cup light blueberry-flavored yogurt*
*1 cup high-fiber, no-sugar-added bran cereal*

Purée blueberries in a food processor or press through a strainer. Stir in the sugar substitute. Divide ½ cup of the yogurt between 2 bowls or parfait glasses, and sprinkle each with bran. Pour some blueberry purée over the bran in each bowl. Spoon the remaining yogurt over the purée and drizzle with the remaining blueberry purée before serving. *Makes 2 servings.*

TOTAL BREAKFAST **ONE SERVING: 366** CALORIES, **26G** PROTEIN, **53G** CARBOHYDRATE, **14G** FAT (**3G** SATURATED), **220MG** CHOLESTEROL, **564MG** SODIUM, **20G** FIBER

### helpful hints

- *Buy good quality Parmesan cheese and ask the grocer to grate it for you or chop it in the food processor yourself. Freeze extra for quick use later—simply spoon out what you need and leave the rest frozen.*
- *Washed, ready-to-eat fresh spinach is available in most supermarkets. It makes using fresh spinach a dream.*

### countdown

- *Preheat oven to 400 degrees.*
- *Prepare all ingredients.*
- *Make omelette.*
- *Assemble cereal.*

### shopping list

*TO BUY:*

*1 carton light blueberry-flavored yogurt*
*1 bag washed, ready-to-eat fresh spinach*
*1 small carton blueberries*

*STAPLES:*

*Eggs*
*Olive oil*
*Parmesan cheese*
*Sugar substitute*
*High-fiber, no-sugar-added bran cereal*
*Salt*
*Black peppercorns*

# ranchero burrito with bran cereal

*This burrito is quick to make and easy to eat. Black bean pâté, shredded Monterey jack cheese, and smoked turkey breast—all supermarket products designed to make our life easier—make this a 5-minute meal. Black bean pâté is usually found in the snack section near the chips in the supermarket. You can choose hot, medium, or mild. Look for one that does not have added sugar.*

## ranchero burrito

- *2 (6-inch) whole wheat tortillas*
- *¼ cup black bean pâté*
- *¼ pound sliced smoked turkey breast*
- *½ cup shredded, reduced-fat Monterey jack cheese*
- *1 medium tomato, sliced*

Warm the tortillas in a microwave oven for 10 seconds or place in a toaster oven for 15 to 20 seconds to make them easier to roll. Spread the warmed tortillas with the black bean pâté, top with turkey, and sprinkle with Monterey Jack cheese. Roll up, and microwave for 45 seconds on high, or until the cheese melts. Or, place in toaster oven for 2 minutes. Cut in half crosswise and serve with tomato slices on the side.

*Makes 2 servings.*

## bran cereal

- *1 cup high-fiber, no-sugar-added bran cereal*
- *1 cup skim milk*

Divide the cereal and milk between 2 bowls.

*Makes 2 servings.*

## tomato juice

- *1 cup low-sodium tomato juice*

Divide between 2 glasses.

*Makes 2 servings.*

TOTAL BREAKFAST **ONE SERVING: 353** CALORIES, **34G** PROTEIN, **51G** CARBOHYDRATE, **9G** FAT (**4G** SATURATED), **52MG** CHOLESTEROL, **939MG** SODIUM, **14G** FIBER

## helpful hint

- *If you like your food hot and spicy, buy a hot black bean pâté and hot pepper jack cheese.*

## countdown

- *Preheat broiler or toaster oven.*
- *Make burrito.*
- *Slice tomato.*
- *Prepare bran cereal and juice.*

## shopping list

*TO BUY:*

- *1 small package shredded, reduced-fat Monterey jack cheese*
- *¼ pound sliced smoked turkey breast*
- *1 package whole wheat tortillas*
- *1 jar black bean pâté*
- *1 medium tomato*

*STAPLES:*

- *Low-sodium tomato juice*
- *High-fiber, no-sugar-added bran cereal*
- *Skim milk*

# western omelette with oatmeal

## helpful hints

- *Use skillet with ovenproof handle.*
- *Frozen onion and green bell peppers are used to cut down on preparation time. Use fresh red onion and green bell pepper instead if you have a few extra minutes.*

## countdown

- *Preheat broiler.*
- *Make oatmeal.*
- *Make omelette.*

## shopping list

*TO BUY:*

*1/4 pound sliced lean ham*
*1 small jar or can roasted red bell pepper*

*STAPLES:*

*Olive oil*
*Egg substitute*
*Frozen, diced onion*
*Frozen, diced green bell pepper*
*Cayenne pepper*
*Sugar substitute*
*Oatmeal*
*Skim milk*
*Salt*

*Also known as a Denver omelette, this dish was said to be part of the chuck wagon legends in the Old West. Apparently they used plenty of onions to disguise old eggs. This is a modern version that takes about 10 minutes to make—and uses fresh eggs!*

## western omelette

*1 cup egg substitute*
*1/4 teaspoon cayenne pepper*
*Salt to taste*
*2 teaspoons olive oil*
*1/2 cup frozen, diced onion*
*2 cups frozen, diced green bell pepper*
*1 cup canned roasted red bell pepper, drained and diced*
*1/4 pound sliced lean ham, diced (1 cup)*

Preheat the broiler. Season the egg substitute with cayenne and salt to taste. Heat the oil in a medium-size nonstick skillet on medium high. Add the onion and green bell pepper, and sauté for 2 minutes. Add the roasted red pepper and ham, and sauté for another minute. Add the egg mixture, and let set for 2 minutes. Place under the broiler 5 minutes, or until desired consistency. Slide out of the skillet and serve. *Makes 2 servings.*

## oatmeal

*1 cup oatmeal*
*2 cups water*
*1 cup skim milk*
*2 (.035-ounce) envelopes sugar substitute (optional)*

To prepare in the microwave, combine the oatmeal and water in a microwave-safe bowl. Microwave on high for 4 minutes. Stir in the milk and sugar substitute, divide between 2 bowls, and serve warm.

Alternatively, to prepare on the stovetop, combine the oatmeal and water in a small saucepan over medium-high heat, and bring to a boil. Reduce the heat to medium and cook about 5 more minutes, stirring occasionally. Stir in the milk and sugar substitute, divide between 2 bowls, and serve warm. *Makes 2 servings.*

TOTAL BREAKFAST **ONE SERVING: 385** CALORIES, **31G** PROTEIN, **54G** CARBOHYDRATE, **12G** FAT (**4G** SATURATED), **93MG** CHOLESTEROL, **782MG** SODIUM, **16G** FIBER

# mediterranean meze platter with bran cereal and fresh berries

*Sun-dried tomatoes, oranges, and strawberries bring thoughts of a sunny Mediterranean morning. Better yet, it takes only a few minutes to assemble this breakfast.*

## mediterranean meze platter

- *1/2 cup low-fat ricotta cheese*
- *1/4 cup sun-dried tomatoes, drained and sliced*
- *1 medium cucumber, peeled and sliced*
- *2 medium oranges, peeled and sliced*
- *1/4 pound sliced roasted boneless chicken breast*
- *2 slices low-carbohydrate whole wheat bread*

Combine the ricotta cheese with the sun-dried tomatoes. Place on 2 plates. Arrange the cucumber, oranges, and chicken slices around the ricotta mixture. Toast the bread and serve on the side. *Makes 2 servings.*

## bran cereal and fresh berries

- *1 cup high-fiber, no-sugar-added bran cereal*
- *1 cup skim milk*
- *1 cup sliced strawberries*

Divide the cereal between 2 bowls and add milk to each. Sprinkle with the strawberries. *Makes 2 servings.*

TOTAL BREAKFAST **ONE SERVING: 482** CALORIES, **40G** PROTEIN, **69G** CARBOHYDRATE, **13G** FAT (**5G** SATURATED), **80MG** CHOLESTEROL, **443MG** SODIUM, **22G** FIBER

### helpful hint

- *Any type of whole grain bread can be used.*

### countdown

- *Make platter.*
- *Assemble cereal.*

### shopping list

*TO BUY:*

- *1 carton low-fat ricotta cheese*
- *1/4 pound sliced roasted boneless chicken breast*
- *1 small jar sun-dried tomatoes*
- *1 medium cucumber*
- *1 small carton strawberries*
- *2 medium oranges*

*STAPLES:*

- *High-fiber, no-sugar-added bran cereal*
- *Skim milk*
- *Low-carbohydrate whole wheat bread*

# vietnamese pancakes with bran cereal

*This paper-thin crêpe is topped with mushrooms, onion, roasted pork shoulder, and bean sprouts. When you are looking for a delicious variation from more traditional omelettes and frittatas, this version will fill the bill. It takes about 10 minutes to make and is worth every minute.*

### helpful hints

- *If pressed for time, use presliced mushrooms and frozen, diced onion.*
- *Lean ham can be substituted if pork shoulder is unavailable.*

### countdown

- *Prepare ingredients.*
- *Make pancakes.*
- *Assemble cereal.*

### shopping list

*TO BUY:*

*1/4 pound lean roasted pork shoulder*
*1/2 pound portobello mushrooms*
*1 package bean sprouts*
*1 bunch scallions (4 scallions needed)*

*STAPLES:*

*Eggs*
*Yellow onion*
*Skim milk*
*Whole wheat flour*
*High-fiber, no-sugar-added bran cereal*
*Canola oil*
*Low-sodium soy sauce*

## vietnamese pancakes

*2 eggs*
*4 egg whites*
*2 tablespoons whole wheat flour*
*2 tablespoons low-sodium soy sauce*
*4 scallions, thinly sliced (1/2 cup)*
*2 teaspoons canola oil*
*1/4 pound lean roasted pork shoulder, cut into thin strips (about 1/2 cup)*
*1/2 pound portobello mushrooms, sliced (3 cups)*
*1/2 cup diced yellow onion*
*2 cups bean sprouts*

With a wire whisk, mix the eggs, egg whites, whole wheat flour, and soy sauce together in a small bowl until smooth. Add the scallions and set aside. Heat the oil in a 9- to 10-inch nonstick skillet on medium high. Add the pork, mushrooms, onion, and bean sprouts. Sauté until the onion turns golden, about 4 minutes. Remove to a bowl, and add half the egg mixture to the hot pan. Swirl the mixture around the pan to form a thin crêpe. Cook 3 minutes, or until the center is cooked and the sides of the pancake start to curl up. Slide onto a plate. Repeat with the second half of the mixture. Divide the pork and vegetable mixture between both crêpes and serve.
*Makes 2 servings.*

## bran cereal

*1 cup high-fiber, no-sugar-added bran cereal*
*1 cup skim milk*

Divide cereal between 2 bowls and add milk to each.
*Makes 2 servings.*

TOTAL BREAKFAST **ONE SERVING: 349** CALORIES, **29G** PROTEIN, **50G** CARBOHYDRATE, **9G** FAT (**2G** SATURATED), **55MG** CHOLESTEROL, **851MG** SODIUM, **15G** FIBER

# french toast with ham, bran cereal, and vegetable juice

*For a change from scrambled eggs or omelettes, try this delicious French Toast. You can cook it with cheese or meat to vary the flavor, and it takes only minutes to make.*

## french toast with ham

- *½ cup egg substitute*
- *Salt and freshly ground black pepper to taste*
- *2 slices low-carbohydrate whole wheat bread*
- *2 teaspoons olive oil*
- *¼ pound sliced lean ham, cubed (1 cup)*

Pour the egg substitute into a small bowl, and season with salt and pepper to taste. Add the bread and let soak.

Heat the olive oil in a small skillet on medium high. Remove the bread from egg substitute and add to the skillet. Cook for 1 minute, then turn. Add the ham to the cooked sides, cover with a lid, and cook 2 more minutes before serving.

*Makes 2 servings.*

## bran cereal

- *1 cup high-fiber, no-sugar-added bran cereal*
- *1 cup skim milk*

Divide the cereal and milk between 2 bowls.

*Makes 2 servings.*

## vegetable juice

- *1½ cups low-salt, no-sugar-added V-8 or tomato juice*

Divide between 2 glasses.

*Makes 2 servings.*

TOTAL BREAKFAST **ONE SERVING: 340** CALORIES, **28G** PROTEIN, **49G** CARBOHYDRATE, **10G** FAT (**2G** SATURATED), **29MG** CHOLESTEROL, **1019MG** SODIUM, **17G** FIBER

## helpful hint

- *Look for low-sodium V-8 juice*

## countdown

- *Pour juice.*
- *Make French toast.*
- *Assemble cereal*

## shopping list

*TO BUY:*

*1 small package sliced lean ham (¼ pound needed)*

*1 bottle low-salt, no-sugar-added V-8 or tomato juice*

*STAPLES:*

*Egg substitute*

*Olive oil*

*Low-carbohydrate whole wheat bread*

*High-fiber, no-sugar-added bran cereal*

*Skim milk*

*Salt*

*Black peppercorns*

# shiitake and swiss cheese scramble with spiced oatmeal

*Shiitake mushrooms and sautéed onions form the base for these scrambled eggs. Although originally from Japan and Korea, shiitakes are now grown in the United States and available in most supermarkets. To speed preparation, use frozen, diced onion to save chopping time.*

## helpful hint

- *Any type of mushroom can be substituted.*

## countdown

- *Make oatmeal.*
- *Make eggs.*

## shopping list

*TO BUY:*

*1 small package shredded, reduced-fat Swiss cheese*

*1 small package shiitake mushrooms (1 ounce needed)*

*STAPLES:*

*Frozen, diced onion*
*Eggs*
*Olive oil*
*Oatmeal*
*Skim milk*
*Low-carbohydrate whole wheat bread*
*Ground ginger*
*Sugar substitute*
*Salt*
*Black peppercorns*

## shiitake and swiss cheese scramble

*2 teaspoons olive oil*
*½ cup frozen, diced onion*
*½ cup sliced shiitake mushrooms*
*2 eggs*
*4 egg whites*
*Salt and freshly ground black pepper to taste*
*¼ cup shredded, reduced-fat Swiss cheese*
*2 slices low-carbohydrate whole wheat bread*

Heat the oil in a medium-size nonstick skillet on medium high. Add the onion and mushrooms, and sauté for 3 minutes. Whisk the eggs and egg whites together lightly, and season with salt and pepper to taste. Add the eggs to the skillet and scramble with the vegetables about 1 minute. Sprinkle with the cheese, cover, and let sit until cheese melts, about 30 seconds. Toast the bread and place on 2 plates. Top each piece of toast with the scrambled eggs and serve immediately.

*Makes 2 servings.*

## spiced oatmeal

*1 cup oatmeal*
*2 cups water*
*2 (.035-ounce) envelopes sugar substitute (optional)*
*½ teaspoon ground ginger*
*1 cup skim or 1% milk*

To prepare in the microwave, combine the oatmeal and water in a microwave-safe bowl. Microwave on high for 4 minutes. Stir in the sugar substitute and ginger. Stir in the milk, divide between 2 bowls, and serve warm.

Alternatively, to prepare on the stovetop, combine the oatmeal and water in a small saucepan over medium-high heat, and bring to a boil. Reduce the heat to medium, and cook about 5 more minutes, stirring occasionally. Stir in the sugar substitute and ginger. Stir in the milk, divide between 2 bowls, and serve warm.

*Makes 2 servings.*

TOTAL BREAKFAST **ONE SERVING: 446** CALORIES, **33G** PROTEIN, **49G** CARBOHYDRATE, **17G** FAT (**4G** SATURATED), **223MG** CHOLESTEROL, **377MG** SODIUM, **7G** FIBER

# chevre and hearts of palm omelette with oatmeal

*Hearts of palm are the tender heart of the Sabal palm tree. If you can find fresh hearts of palm, they're really a treat. Otherwise, they are sold in cans or jars in the supermarket.*

## chevre and hearts of palm omelette

*Olive oil spray*
*2 cups sliced hearts of palm*
*1 cup egg substitute*
*2 ounces herbed goat cheese, broken into small pieces*
*Salt and freshly ground black pepper to taste*
*2 slices whole grain bread*

Set a medium-size nonstick skillet over medium-high heat, and spray with olive oil. Add the hearts of palm. Combine the egg substitute with the goat cheese. Pour into the skillet, cover with a lid, and cook 3 to 4 minutes. Sprinkle with salt and pepper to taste. Cut the omelette in half, and slide onto 2 plates with a spatula. Serve with toasted whole grain bread. *Makes 2 servings.*

## oatmeal

*1 cup oatmeal*
*2 cups water*
*1 cup skim milk*
*2 (.035-ounce) envelopes sugar substitute, (optional)*

To prepare in the microwave, combine the oatmeal and water in a microwave-safe bowl. Microwave on high for 4 minutes. Stir in the milk and sugar substitute, divide between 2 bowls, and serve warm.

Alternatively, to prepare on the stovetop, combine the oatmeal and water in a small saucepan over medium-high heat, and bring to a boil. Reduce the heat to medium, and cook about 5 more minutes, stirring occasionally. Stir in the milk and sugar substitute, divide between 2 bowls, and serve warm. *Makes 2 servings.*

TOTAL BREAKFAST **ONE SERVING: 461** CALORIES, **35G** PROTEIN, **53G** CARBOHYDRATE, **15G** FAT (**7G** SATURATED), **24**MG CHOLESTEROL, **1166MG** SODIUM, **11G** FIBER

### helpful hint

- *Any type of goat cheese can be used.*

### countdown

- *Make oatmeal.*
- *Make omelette.*

### shopping list

*TO BUY:*

*1 package herbed goat cheese (2 ounces needed)*
*1 small can or jar of hearts of palm*

*STAPLES:*

*Egg substitute*
*Olive oil spray*
*Sugar substitute*
*Oatmeal*
*Skim milk*
*Whole grain bread*
*Salt*
*Black peppercorns*

# cottage cheese and cucumber sandwich with yogurt crunch

## helpful hint

- *Any type of whole grain bread can be used.*

## countdown

- *Make sandwich.*
- *Assemble cereal.*

## shopping list

*TO BUY:*

*1 small carton light fruit-flavored yogurt*

*1 small carton low-fat cottage cheese*

*1 medium cucumber*

*STAPLES:*

*Olive oil spray*

*High-fiber, no-sugar-added bran cereal*

*Rye bread*

*This is a quick and simple breakfast to make. Be sure to read the label on the cottage cheese to make sure it is low-fat with no sugar added.*

## cottage cheese and cucumber sandwich

*2 slices rye bread*
*Olive oil spray*
*1 cup low-fat cottage cheese*
*1 medium cucumber, sliced*

Toast the bread. Spray with olive oil. Place the toast on 2 plates, spread each toast with cottage cheese, and top with cucumber slices. Serve the remaining cucumber slices on the side.

*Makes 2 servings.*

## yogurt crunch

*1 cup light fruit-flavored yogurt*
*1 cup high-fiber, no-sugar-added bran cereal*

Divide the yogurt between 2 bowls. Sprinkle with the bran cereal and stir together.

*Makes 2 servings.*

TOTAL BREAKFAST **ONE SERVING: 285** CALORIES, **24G** PROTEIN, **51G** CARBOHYDRATE, **6G** FAT (**2G** SATURATED), **13MG** CHOLESTEROL, **651MG** SODIUM, **17G** FIBER

# warm smoked turkey sandwich with grapefruit and bran cereal

*Sliced smoked turkey, tomato, and cream cheese on toast make a quick, 10-minute breakfast.*

## warm smoked turkey sandwich

*2 slices low-carbohydrate whole wheat bread*
*Olive oil spray*
*2 tablespoons reduced-fat cream cheese*
*1/4 pound sliced lean smoked turkey breast (1 1/2 cups)*
*1 medium tomato, sliced*
*Salt and freshly ground black pepper to taste*

Preheat the broiler. Spray the bread with olive oil and toast until golden brown. Spread the toast with cream cheese; top with the turkey and tomato slices. Season with salt and pepper to taste. Serve on 2 plates.
*Makes 2 servings.*

## grapefruit

*1 medium grapefruit, halved*

With a serrated knife, cut around the edge of the grapefruit to separate the flesh from the skin. Cut between the segments, and serve on 2 plates.
*Makes 2 servings.*

## bran cereal

*1 cup high-fiber, no-sugar-added bran cereal*
*1 cup skim milk*

Divide the cereal between 2 bowls and add milk to each.
*Makes 2 servings.*

TOTAL BREAKFAST **ONE SERVING: 338** CALORIES, **29G** PROTEIN, **53G** CARBOHYDRATE, **9G** FAT (**3G** SATURATED), **53MG** CHOLESTEROL, **411MG** SODIUM, **17G** FIBER

## countdown

- *Preheat broiler.*
- *Prepare grapefruit.*
- *Make sandwich.*
- *Assemble cereal.*

## shopping list

*TO BUY:*

*1 small package reduced-fat cream cheese*
*1/4 pound sliced lean smoked turkey breast*
*1 medium tomato*
*1 medium grapefruit*

*STAPLES:*

*Olive oil spray*
*Low-carbohydrate whole wheat bread*
*High-fiber, no-sugar-added bran cereal*
*Skim milk*
*Salt*
*Black peppercorns*

# egg-in-the-hole with bran cereal

## helpful hints

- *It doesn't matter if the egg spills over onto the bread or pan.*
- *To determine the weight of each slice of cheese, divide the package weight by the number of slices. With most brands, 1 slice equals 3/4 ounce.*
- *If you like your egg yolk firm, gently flip the bread and egg over before adding the cheese. Place the cheese on the top side.*

## countdown

*Prepare grapefruit.*

*Make egg.*

*Assemble cereal.*

## shopping list

*TO BUY:*

*1 small package sliced, reduced-fat Swiss cheese (1 1/2 ounces, needed)*

*1 grapefruit*

*STAPLES:*

*Olive oil spray*

*Eggs*

*High-fiber, no-sugar-added bran cereal*

*Skim milk*

*Low-carbohydrate whole wheat bread*

*Salt*

*Black peppercorns*

*We used to call it Hole-in-the-Middle. Some call it Egg-in-the-Hole and others call it Toad-in-the-Hole. Regardless, it's an old American favorite. I remember my father making this for breakfast; my job was to tear the hole out of the bread. Somehow I never got the hole to be the same size as the egg, but it was still very delicious. Whether the egg neatly fits the hole or runs over the bread, this is a quick and easy and fun breakfast.*

## egg-in-the-hole

*2 slices low-carbohydrate whole wheat bread*

*Olive oil spray*

*2 eggs*

*2 slices reduced-fat Swiss cheese (1 1/2 ounces)*

*Salt and freshly ground black pepper to taste*

Tear a hole in each slice of bread about 2 inches in diameter. Heat a nonstick skillet over low heat and spray with olive oil. Add the bread and the cutout pieces to the skillet. Cook until golden, about 2 minutes. Turn the bread and cutouts over, and break one egg into each hole. Cook 1 minute, turn over, and place the cheese slices over the eggs. Season with salt and pepper to taste. Cover with a lid and cook 2 to 3 minutes or until eggs set to the desired consistency. Serve with the cutouts.

*Makes 2 servings.*

## bran cereal

*1 cup high-fiber, no-sugar-added bran cereal*

*1 cup skim milk*

Divide the cereal and milk between 2 bowls.

*Makes 2 servings.*

## grapefruit

*1 medium grapefruit, halved*

With a serrated knife, cut around the edge of the grapefruit to separate the flesh from the skin. Cut between the segments, and serve on 2 plates.

*Makes 2 servings.*

TOTAL BREAKFAST **ONE SERVING: 340** CALORIES, **25G** PROTEIN, **51G** CARBOHYDRATE, **13G** FAT (**4G** SATURATED), **226MG** CHOLESTEROL, **414MG** SODIUM, **17G** FIBER

# frittata primavera with bran cereal

*A frittata is an Italian omelette that is cooked slowly so that it becomes thick, more like a quiche than an omelette.*

## frittata primavera

- *1 cup egg substitute*
- *2 cups fresh purple basil leaves*
- *Salt and freshly ground black pepper to taste*
- *8 large spears asparagus or 16 thin (2 ounces)*
- *4 teaspoons olive oil*
- *1 cup yellow squash, sliced*
- *½ cup sliced red onion*
- *½ pound whole portobello mushrooms, sliced thinly (2 cups)*
- *¼ cup shredded, reduced-fat, aged cheddar cheese*

Combine the egg substitute and basil in a medium-size bowl. Season with salt and pepper to taste. Cut or snap off the 1-inch fibrous stem on the asparagus and discard. Slice the remaining asparagus into 1-inch pieces. Heat the oil in a medium-size nonstick skillet on medium high, and add the squash, onion, mushrooms, and asparagus. Sauté 5 minutes. Pour the egg mixture into the skillet, and swirl around the vegetables. Sprinkle the frittata with cheese. Cover, reduce heat to low, and cook 10 minutes more before serving.

*Makes 2 servings.*

## bran cereal

- *1 cup high-fiber, no-sugar-added bran cereal*
- *1 cup skim milk*

Divide the cereal and milk between 2 bowls.

*Makes 2 servings.*

TOTAL BREAKFAST **ONE SERVING: 359** CALORIES, **25G** PROTEIN, **45G** CARBOHYDRATE, **14G** FAT (**3G** SATURATED), **12MG** CHOLESTEROL, **542MG** SODIUM, **15G** FIBER

## helpful hints

- *Zucchini can be substituted for the yellow squash.*
- *Regular green basil can be substituted for purple.*

## countdown

- *Start frittata.*
- *While frittata cooks, assemble cereal.*

## shopping list

*TO BUY:*

- *1 small package shredded, reduced-fat aged cheddar cheese*
- *1 small yellow squash*
- *½ pound whole portobello mushrooms*
- *1 small bunch asparagus*
- *1 package purple basil*

*STAPLES:*

- *Egg substitute*
- *Red onion*
- *Olive oil*
- *High-fiber, no-sugar-added bran cereal*
- *Skim milk*
- *Salt*
- *Black peppercorns*

# right carb lunches

# layered crab salad with parmesan crostini and grapes and yogurt

*Layering sweet crabmeat with fresh vegetables and light vinaigrette dressing makes this a colorful salad. It's perfect for a weekend lunch or entertaining. There is no cooking required, so this meal can be assembled in mere minutes. Cooked crabmeat is sold frozen or in cans. Look for jumbo lump or backfin. These names refer to large pieces of white meat from the body of the crab. The meat should be white with a little pink coloring. There are many brands and qualities available. Try different ones to find one that suits your palate. This salad is also great for any type of leftover cooked seafood. • Sherry wine vinegar has a very subtle flavor that perfectly complements the crab. • The Italians like to cover sliced bread with leftover cheese or vegetables and heat it in a wood fire. The resulting crostini or "little crusts" are used to garnish salads and appetizers. My version uses freshly grated Parmesan cheese.*

## layered crab salad

*2 tablespoons sherry wine vinegar*
*4 teaspoons Dijon mustard*
*4 teaspoons olive oil*
*2 tablespoons water*
*½ cup chopped red onion*
*2 tablespoons fresh tarragon or 2 teaspoons dried tarragon*
*Salt and freshly ground black pepper to taste*
*¼ pound jumbo lump cooked crabmeat*
*1 bag ready-to-eat mixed baby greens (about 5 cups)*
*1 medium cucumber, peeled and sliced*
*2 medium tomatoes, sliced*

Whisk the sherry wine vinegar and mustard together in a medium-size bowl. Whisk in the olive oil and water until smooth. Add the onion and tarragon, and season with salt and pepper to taste. Mix half the dressing with the crabmeat. Arrange the salad greens in the bottom of a glass salad bowl. Layer the cucumber slices on top. Drizzle the remaining dressing over the salad. Spoon the crabmeat over the cucumber. Arrange the sliced tomatoes around the edge of the bowl, sprinkle with salt and pepper to taste, and serve.

*Makes 2 servings.*

**ONE SERVING: 259** CALORIES, **25G** PROTEIN, **15G** CARBOHYDRATE, **11G** FAT (**1G** SATURATED), **88MG** CHOLESTEROL, **592MG** SODIUM, **1G** FIBER

### helpful hints

- *Bottled, no-sugar-added oil and vinegar dressing can be used instead of the recipe provided. Add tarragon and onion to the bottled dressing.*
- *Buy good quality Parmesan cheese and ask the grocer to grate it for you or chop it in the food processor yourself. Freeze extra for quick use later—simply spoon out what you need and leave the rest frozen.*
- *Any type of salad greens can be used.*
- *If using dried tarragon, make sure the bottle is less than 6 months old.*
- *Red wine or balsamic vinegar can be used.*

### countdown

- *Preheat broiler or toaster oven.*
- *Make dressing.*
- *Make crab salad.*
- *Make crostini.*

# layered crab salad with parmesan crostini and grapes and yogurt *continued*

## shopping list

*TO BUY:*

*1 carton light fruit-flavored yogurt*

*1/4 pound jumbo lump cooked crabmeat (fresh, canned or frozen)*

*1 small bottle sherry wine vinegar*

*1 small bunch fresh tarragon or 1 jar dried*

*1 medium cucumber*

*2 medium tomatoes*

*1 bag ready-to-eat, mixed baby greens*

*1 small bunch grapes (30 needed)*

*STAPLES:*

*Olive oil*

*Olive oil spray*

*Red onion*

*Multigrain bread*

*Parmesan cheese*

*Dijon mustard*

*Salt*

*Black peppercorns*

## parmesan crostini

*Olive oil spray*

*2 slices multigrain bread*

*2 tablespoons freshly grated Parmesan cheese*

Preheat the broiler or toaster oven. Spray olive oil over the bread. Sprinkle with Parmesan cheese. Place in broiler about 6 inches from the heat for 2 to 3 minutes, or until the cheese starts to melt. Serve with the salad.

*Makes 2 servings.*

**ONE SERVING: 83** CALORIES, **6G** PROTEIN, **10G** CARBOHYDRATE, **4G** FAT (**1G** SATURATED), **4MG** CHOLESTEROL, **221MG** SODIUM, **3G** FIBER

## grapes and yogurt

*1 cup light fruit-flavored yogurt*

*30 grapes (2/3 cup)*

Spoon the yogurt into 2 dessert bowls and sprinkle with grapes.

*Makes 2 servings.*

**ONE SERVING: 79** CALORIES, **4G** PROTEIN, **16G** CARBOHYDRATE, **0G** FAT (**0G** SATURATED), **3MG** CHOLESTEROL, **59MG** SODIUM, **0G** FIBER

# tomatoes with tuscan green sauce and garlic bruschetta and strawberry smoothie

*Tomatoes with Green Sauce is a recipe given to me by a friend from Tuscany. It always reminds me of sitting on her porch looking out on the rolling green hills and heavily laden olive trees. This light lunch can be made in minutes and enjoyed in your own backyard. • Serve this lunch on the weekend or when you're having friends for lunch. • Bruschetta is a Roman garlic bread. When testing the season's first pressing of olive oil, the Romans would taste it on a slice of bread that was sometimes rubbed with fresh garlic. If you like a lot of garlic, crush the garlic clove onto the bread instead of rubbing.*

## tomatoes with tuscan green sauce

- *6 eggs (only the whites are used)*
- *2 ripe tomatoes, stemmed and halved crosswise*
- *2 anchovy fillets, drained and rinsed*
- *4 teaspoons capers, drained*
- *2 tablespoons bread crumbs (whole wheat if possible)*
- *2 tablespoons balsamic vinegar*
- *½ cup chopped fresh parsley, divided*
- *4 teaspoons olive oil*
- *Salt and freshly ground black pepper to taste*

Place the eggs in a small saucepan and cover with cold water. Bring to a boil, then reduce the heat to a very gentle simmer. Cook 12 minutes. Drain and rinse eggs under cold water. When cool enough to handle, peel the eggs. Cut in half, and remove and discard the yolks.

Hollow out the tomatoes with a spoon, reserving the pulp. Mash the anchovy fillets with a fork and place in the bowl of a food processor. Add the capers, tomato pulp (about 1 cup), and egg whites; coarsely chop. If you don't have a food processor, chop by hand. In a small bowl, soak the bread crumbs in the vinegar. Set aside 4 tablespoons parsley for garnish. Add the remaining parsley and egg white mixture to the bread crumbs. Stir in the olive oil, and season with salt and pepper to taste. Combine well. Fill the tomatoes with the mixture, sprinkle with the reserved parsley, and serve. *Makes 2 servings.*

**ONE SERVING: 173** CALORIES, **16G** PROTEIN, **8G** CARBOHYDRATE, **10G** FAT (**1G** SATURATED), **0MG** CHOLESTEROL, **489MG** SODIUM, **0G** FIBER

### helpful hints

- *To save time, first chop the parsley in the food processor, remove, and measure. Then add the rest of the ingredients.*
- *Try not to overprocess the filling: Coarsely chop using the pulse button.*
- *Keep hard-boiled eggs on hand for a quick snack, breakfast, or lunch.*
- *Frozen strawberries can be used for the smoothie. Make sure they are not packed in a sugar syrup.*

### countdown

- *Hard boil the eggs.*
- *Assemble bruschetta.*
- *Make tomatoes and green sauce.*
- *Toast bruschetta.*

# tomatoes with tuscan green sauce and garlic bruschetta and strawberry smoothie *continued*

## shopping list

*TO BUY:*

- *1 carton light strawberry-flavored yogurt*
- *1 small tin anchovies packed in olive oil*
- *1 small jar capers*
- *1 small container bread crumbs*
- *2 ripe tomatoes*
- *1 small bunch fresh parsley*
- *1 container fresh strawberries*

*STAPLES:*

- *Eggs*
- *Garlic*
- *Olive oil*
- *Olive oil spray*
- *Balsamic vinegar*
- *Multigrain bread*
- *Vanilla extract*
- *Sugar substitute*
- *Salt*
- *Black peppercorns*

## garlic bruschetta

*Olive oil spray*
*1 small garlic clove, halved*
*2 slices crusty country multigrain bread*

Spray the bread with olive oil, and rub the cut side of the garlic on the bread. Toast the bread, and serve with the tomatoes.

*Makes 2 servings.*

**ONE SERVING: 61** CALORIES, **4G** PROTEIN, **11G** CARBOHYDRATE, **2G** FAT (**0G** SATURATED), **0MG** CHOLESTEROL, **115MG** SODIUM, **3G** FIBER

## strawberry smoothie

*1½ cups strawberries*
*1 cup light strawberry-flavored yogurt*
*2 teaspoons vanilla extract*
*2 (.035-ounce) envelopes sugar substitute*
*4 cups ice cubes*

Place the strawberries, yogurt, vanilla extract, and sugar substitute in a blender. Blend until smooth. Add the ice cubes, and blend until thick. Pour into 2 glasses.

*Makes 2 servings.*

**ONE SERVING: 96** CALORIES, **5G** PROTEIN, **18G** CARBOHYDRATE, **0.5G** FAT (**0G** SATURATED), **3MG** CHOLESTEROL, **59MG** SODIUM, **2G** FIBER

# shrimp caesar wrap with pears and yogurt

*Caesar Salad, one of America's most popular salads, is said to have been created in 1924 in Tijuana, Mexico, by a restaurateur named Caesar Cardini. I don't think he ever dreamed that 70 years later, his combination of anchovies, garlic, lemon juice, croutons, and lettuce would be on nearly every restaurant menu in the United States.*

## shrimp caesar wrap

*8 anchovies, rinsed*
*2 small garlic cloves, crushed*
*2 tablespoons freshly squeezed lemon juice (1 lemon)*
*4 teaspoons olive oil, divided*
*4 teaspoons Worcestershire sauce*
*½ pound large shrimp, shelled and deveined*
*2 (12-inch) whole wheat flour tortillas*
*6 large romaine lettuce leaves, torn into bite-size pieces*
*2 tablespoons freshly grated Parmesan cheese*
*Freshly ground black pepper to taste.*

To make the dressing, put the anchovies, garlic, lemon juice, 2 teaspoons of the olive oil, and the Worcestershire sauce in a food processor and blend thoroughly, or mix and mash together well by hand. Heat the remaining 2 teaspoons of olive oil in a small nonstick skillet on medium high. Add the shrimp and sauté 2 minutes. Remove the skillet from the heat, leaving the shrimp in skillet to finish cooking. Wrap the tortillas in paper towels and microwave on high for 20 seconds to soften. Remove from the microwave, discard the paper towel, and place the tortillas on a countertop. Spread the dressing over each tortilla. Place lettuce evenly over dressing, and sprinkle with Parmesan cheese. Cut the shrimp in half and place on lettuce, making sure to add any juices from the skillet. Season with black pepper to taste. Fold up the top and bottom edges of the tortilla, then tightly roll up to make a neat package. Slice in half and serve.

*Makes 2 servings.*

**ONE SERVING: 333** CALORIES, **33G** PROTEIN, **18G** CARBOHYDRATE **15G** FAT (**3G** SATURATED), **178MG** CHOLESTEROL, **1076MG** SODIUM, **5G** FIBER

### helpful hints

- *1 tablespoon low-sugar (less than .5 grams per 2 tablespoons) Caesar salad dressing can be substituted for this homemade one.*
- *Buy shelled shrimp or ask for the shrimp to be shelled while you complete your shopping. Most stores will do this for a small fee—well worth the time saved in shelling them yourself.*
- *Any type of lettuce can be used.*
- *Buy good quality Parmesan cheese and ask the grocer to grate it for you or chop it in the food processor yourself. Freeze extra for quick use later—simply spoon out what you need and leave the rest frozen.*

### countdown

- *Make dressing.*
- *Make wrap.*
- *Assemble yogurt and pear.*

# shrimp caesar wrap with pears and yogurt *continued*

## shopping list

*TO BUY:*

- *1 carton light fruit-flavored yogurt*
- *1/2 pound large shrimp*
- *1 small tin anchovies packed in olive oil*
- *1 package (12-inch) whole wheat flour tortillas*
- *1 small head romaine lettuce*
- *1 lemon*
- *2 medium pears*

*STAPLES:*

- *Garlic*
- *Olive oil*
- *Worcestershire sauce*
- *Parmesan cheese*
- *Black peppercorns*

## pears and yogurt

*1 cup light fruit-flavored yogurt*
*2 medium pears, cored and sliced*

Spoon the yogurt into 2 dessert bowls and top with the pear slices.

*Makes 2 servings.*

**ONE SERVING: 148** CALORIES, **5G** PROTEIN, **34G** CARBOHYDRATE, **1G** FAT (**0G** SATURATED), **3MG** CHOLESTEROL, **59MG** SODIUM, **4G** FIBER

# smoked turkey pita with avocado and fresh berries yogurt

*Turkey, crunchy sprouts, and nutty avocado blend together for a fresh taste in this pita pocket sandwich. It's sometimes hard to find a ripe avocado, but you can ripen one quickly by removing the small stem and storing in a paper bag in a warm spot until soft to the touch.*

## smoked turkey pita with avocado

- *1 whole wheat pita bread, halved*
- *1/4 pound sliced smoked turkey breast, cut into 1/2-inch strips*
- *1/2 small ripe avocado, pitted, peeled, and sliced*
- *1 cup alfalfa sprouts, tops only*
- *1 small tomato, sliced*
- *1 tablespoon no-sugar-added oil and vinegar dressing*

Preheat the broiler. Place the pita halves on a foil-lined tray. Broil or toast 1 minute or until the bread is warm. Place the turkey, avocado slices, alfalfa sprouts, and tomato slices in the pockets of the pita bread and spoon dressing over the turkey and vegetables before serving.

*Makes 2 servings.*

**ONE SERVING: 339** CALORIES, **25G** PROTEIN, **29G** CARBOHYDRATE **15G** FAT (**3G** SATURATED), **40MG** CHOLESTEROL, **154MG** SODIUM, **6G** FIBER

## fresh berries yogurt

- *1 cup light mixed berry-flavored yogurt*
- *1 1/2 cups fresh raspberries*

Place the yogurt in 2 small dessert dishes and sprinkle with the berries.

*Makes 2 servings.*

**ONE SERVING: 81** CALORIES, **5G** PROTEIN, **16G** CARBOHYDRATE, **0.5G** FAT (**0G** SATURATED), **3MG** CHOLESTEROL, **58MG** SODIUM, **3G** FIBER

## helpful hints

- *Any type of sprouts can be used.*
- *Any flavor light yogurt can be used.*

## countdown

- *Preheat broiler or toaster oven.*
- *Peel avocado.*
- *Make sandwich.*
- *Assemble yogurt and berry cup.*

## shopping list

*TO BUY:*

- *1 carton light mixed berry-flavored yogurt*
- *1/4 pound sliced smoked turkey breast*
- *1 small package whole wheat pita bread*
- *1 small ripe avocado*
- *1 carton alfalfa sprouts*
- *1 small tomato*
- *1 small carton fresh raspberries*

*STAPLES:*

- *No-sugar-added oil and vinegar dressing*

# salmon burgers with cantaloupe yogurt

## helpful hint

- *Buy no-salt-added tomato purée in a can. You can keep the unused portion in a plastic container or self-seal bag in the refrigerator or freezer.*

## countdown

- *Make salmon burgers.*
- *Assemble cantaloupe and yogurt cup.*

## shopping list

*TO BUY:*

*1 carton light fruit-flavored yogurt*
*6 ounces salmon fillet*
*1 small container whole wheat bread crumbs*
*1 small can no-salt-added tomato purée*
*1 small bunch scallions (8 scallions needed)*
*1 small tomato*
*1 small cantaloupe*

*STAPLES:*

*Eggs*
*Multigrain bread*
*Mayonnaise made with olive or soybean oil*
*Salt*
*Black peppercorns*

*My sons have given me a strong warning, "Don't mess with my burgers." The fact is that this all-American dish is changing. I've recently noticed salmon burgers on several menus and decided to create this quick salmon burger lunch. The flavorful salmon meat requires very little fish for a rich-tasting burger. • The salmon can be chopped in a food processor. However, it is very soft and takes only a few minutes to chop by hand if you don't have a processor.*

## salmon burgers

*6 ounces salmon fillet*
*8 scallions, sliced (divided) (1 cup)*
*¼ cup whole wheat bread crumbs*
*1 tablespoon no-salt-added tomato purée*
*2 egg whites*
*Salt and freshly ground black pepper to taste*
*2 tablespoons mayonnaise made with olive or soybean oil*
*2 slices multigrain bread*
*1 small tomato, sliced*

Remove any fat or dark meat from the salmon. Cut the pink meat into 2-inch cubes and chop in food processor or by hand. Add half the scallions to the salmon along with the bread crumbs, tomato purée, and egg whites. Season with salt and pepper to taste. Form into 2 burgers about 4 inches in diameter and ½ inch thick. Set a nonstick skillet over medium-high heat and brown the burgers on one side, about 1 minute. Reduce the heat to medium and cook 3 minutes. Turn over, raise the heat to medium high, and cook another 2 minutes. Meanwhile, mix the mayonnaise and remaining scallions together in a small bowl. Season with salt and pepper to taste. Toast the bread. To serve, place the salmon burgers on the toasted bread and top with mayonnaise. Serve tomato slices alongside the salmon burger.
*Makes 2 servings.*

**ONE SERVING: 350** CALORIES, **31G** PROTEIN, **19G** CARBOHYDRATE, **17G** FAT (**3G** SATURATED), **65MG** CHOLESTEROL, **341MG** SODIUM, **3G** FIBER

## cantaloupe yogurt

*1 cup light fruit-flavored yogurt*
*1 cantaloupe, cubed (4 cups)*

Spoon the yogurt into 2 dessert bowls and top with the cantaloupe.
*Makes 2 servings.*

**ONE SERVING: 127** CALORIES, **6G** PROTEIN, **27G** CARBOHYDRATE, **1G** FAT (**0G** SATURATED), **3MG** CHOLESTEROL, **77MG** SODIUM, **3G** FIBER

# chicken tostada and cilantro tomatoes

*Crisp tortillas, smooth beans, hot flavors, and cool tomatoes make this tostada recipe a favorite, quick meal. A tostada is simply a crisp tortilla. Here it is topped with chicken and vegetables, but the variations are endless. • This meal is really a snap if you have a food processor. To save washing the processor bowl during preparation, chop all of the vegetables first, and then mash the beans. If you don't have a processor, simply chop the vegetables by hand and mash the beans with a fork.*

## chicken tostadas

- *2 (8-inch) whole wheat tortillas*
- *Olive oil spray*
- *2 tablespoons no-sugar-added oil and vinegar dressing*
- *2 teaspoons ground cumin, divided*
- *2 medium-size jalapeño peppers, seeded and sliced (divided)*
- *½ cup chopped red onion*
- *2 medium-size garlic cloves, crushed*
- *½ cup canned dark red kidney beans, rinsed and drained*
- *4 tablespoons water*
- *Salt and freshly ground black pepper to taste*
- *¼ pound sliced roasted chicken breast, skin removed and meat cut into ½-inch strips*
- *2 cups washed, ready-to-eat lettuce, shredded*

Preheat the oven to 400 degrees. Line a baking tray with foil. Place the tortillas on the tray, and spray both sides of the tortillas with olive oil. Bake for 5 minutes in the oven. Remove from the oven, turn, and bake 5 more minutes. Place on 2 plates.

Combine the dressing with 1 teaspoon cumin and 1 tablespoon chopped jalapeño, and toss with the chicken.

If using a food processor, chop the onion and set aside 2 tablespoons for garnish. Add the garlic and remaining jalapeños to onion in the processor bowl. Add the beans, remaining teaspoon ground cumin, and water; purée to a smooth paste. Season with salt and pepper to taste.

Spread the tortillas with the bean paste. Place the chicken on top of the beans, and top with the lettuce. Sprinkle with remaining chopped red onion and serve. *Makes 2 servings.*

**ONE SERVING: 332** CALORIES, **25G** PROTEIN, **33G** CARBOHYDRATE **14G** FAT (**2G** SATURATED), **48MG** CHOLESTEROL, **402MG** SODIUM, **1G** FIBER

## cilantro tomatoes

- *2 medium tomatoes, diced (about 2 cups)*
- *4 tablespoons chopped fresh cilantro*
- *Salt and freshly ground black pepper to taste*

Combine the tomatoes and cilantro and season with salt and pepper to taste. Serve with the tostadas. *Makes 2 servings.*

**ONE SERVING: 31** CALORIES, **2G** PROTEIN, **6G** CARBOHYDRATE, **0G** FAT (**0G** SATURATED), **0MG** CHOLESTEROL, **13MG** SODIUM, **0G** FIBER

## helpful hints

- *The tortilla can be baked in a toaster oven.*
- *Red onion is used for the beans and as a garnish. Chop it all at one time and divide accordingly.*
- *For best flavor, make sure the ground cumin is less than 6 months old.*

## countdown

- *Preheat oven to 400 degrees.*
- *Bake tortilla.*
- *Prepare tomatoes.*

## shopping list

*TO BUY:*

- *¼ sliced roasted chicken breast*
- *1 package (8-inch) whole wheat tortillas*
- *1 small can dark red kidney beans (4 ounces needed)*
- *2 medium tomatoes*
- *1 small bunch cilantro*
- *2 medium jalapeño peppers*
- *1 bag washed, ready-to-eat shredded lettuce*

*STAPLES:*

- *Red onion*
- *Garlic*
- *Olive oil spray*
- *No-sugar-added oil and vinegar dressing*
- *Ground cumin*
- *Salt*
- *Black peppercorns*

# caribbean shrimp salad and mango yogurt

## helpful hint

- *Any type of bean, such as red or white kidney beans can be used.*

## countdown

- *Make yogurt cup.*
- *Make shrimp salad.*

## shopping list

*TO BUY:*

*1 carton light tropical fruit-flavored yogurt*
*½ pound cooked shrimp*
*1 small can black beans (8 ounces needed)*
*1 medium-size green bell pepper*
*1 small tomato*
*1 small head lettuce*
*1 mango*
*2 limes*

*STAPLES:*

*Red onion*
*Celery*
*Mayonnaise made with olive or soybean oil*
*Hot pepper sauce*
*Salt*
*Black peppercorns*

*Emerald waters and crystal-clear blue skies create the backdrop for this tropical lunch. Shrimp, hot pepper sauce, and black beans are staples throughout the Caribbean. • Based on total worldwide consumption, mangoes are second in popularity only to bananas. They can be found in most supermarkets. They can be messy to cube, but I offer an easy method below.*

## caribbean shrimp salad

*2 tablespoons mayonnaise made with olive or soybean oil*
*2 tablespoons warm water*
*Several drops hot pepper sauce*
*2 tablespoons freshly squeezed lime juice*
*½ cup canned black beans, rinsed and drained*
*1 medium-size green bell pepper, diced (1 cup)*
*2 celery stalks, diced (1 cup)*
*½ cup red onion, diced*
*1 small tomato, diced*
*½ pound cooked shrimp, cubed*
*Salt and freshly ground black pepper to taste*
*Several lettuce leaves, washed and torn into bite-size pieces*

Combine the mayonnaise, water, hot pepper sauce, and lime juice in a medium-size bowl. Add the black beans, bell pepper, celery, onion, tomato, and shrimp. Toss well. Season with salt and pepper to taste. Place the lettuce leaves on a plate and spoon the shrimp salad on top of the lettuce to serve.
*Makes 2 servings.*

**ONE SERVING: 346** CALORIES, **31G** PROTEIN, **27G** CARBOHYDRATE, **14G** FAT (**2G** SATURATED), **178MG** CHOLESTEROL, **341MG** SODIUM, **3G** FIBER

## mango yogurt

*1 mango*
*½ cup light tropical fruit-flavored yogurt*

Slice off each side of the mango as close to the seed as possible. Take the mango half in your hand, skin- side down. Score the fruit in a cross-hatch pattern through to the skin. Bend the skin backwards so that the cubes pop up similar to a porcupine. Slice the cubes off the skin. Score and slice any fruit left on the pit.

Divide the yogurt between 2 cups and top with the mango cubes.
*Makes 2 servings.*

**ONE SERVING: 117** CALORIES, **5G** PROTEIN, **26G** CARBOHYDRATE, **0.3G** FAT (**0G** SATURATED), **3MG** CHOLESTEROL, **60G** SODIUM, **1** FIBER

# ham, mushroom, and onion pita pizza with fennel salad

*When a friend walked into my kitchen and saw this pizza sitting on the counter, she insisted on eating it immediately. It's covered with onion, mushrooms, peppers, and ham—and it can be made faster than ordering out for pizza. • A secret to cooking the pizza fast is to heat the baking tray in the oven. When the pizza is placed on the hot tray, the bottom heat helps the pizza cook from underneath.*

## ham, mushroom, and onion pita pizza

*Olive oil spray*
*1 medium-size green bell pepper, sliced (about 1 cup)*
*4 slices red onion (1/2 cup)*
*2 small portobello mushrooms, sliced (about 1 cup)*
*1 whole-wheat pita bread*
*1 medium tomato sliced*
*1/4 pound sliced lean ham, torn into bite-sized pieces*
*1 cup shredded, reduced-fat mozzarella cheese (4 ounces)*

Preheat the broiler. Line a baking tray with foil and place under the broiler. Set a nonstick skillet over medium-high heat, and spray with olive oil. Add the pepper, onion, and mushrooms, and sauté for 5 minutes. Slice open the pita bread so that you have 2 round pizza bases. Remove the baking tray from broiler and place pita halves on the foil, cut-side up. Spray the pita bread with olive oil and place the tomato slices on top. Spoon the pepper mixture over the tomatoes and top with the ham and cheese. Broil for 3 minutes, or until the cheese is bubbly. Serve hot.
*Makes 2 servings.*

**ONE SERVING: 354** CALORIES, **36G** PROTEIN, **35G** CARBOHYDRATE **8G** FAT (**3G** SATURATED), **35MG** CHOLESTEROL, **1009MG** SODIUM, **5G** FIBER

## fennel salad

*1 small fennel bulb, sliced (2 cups)*
*1 tablespoon no-sugar-added oil and vinegar dressing*
*Salt and freshly ground black pepper to taste*

Remove the stem and fern-like leaves from the fennel. Wash and reserve the leaves. Thinly slice the fennel. Toss the fennel with the dressing. Snip small pieces from the fennel leaves with scissors (about 1/4 cup) and sprinkle on top as garnish. Season with salt and pepper to taste. Serve with the pizza.
*Makes 2 servings.*

**ONE SERVING: 53** CALORIES, **0G** PROTEIN, **0G** CARBOHYDRATE, **4G** FAT (**1G** SATURATED), **0MG** CHOLESTEROL, **38MG** SODIUM, **0G** FIBER

## banana

*1 medium banana*

Slice the banana in half and serve.
*Makes 2 servings.*

**ONE SERVING: 70** CALORIES, **1G** PROTEIN, **18G** CARBOHYDRATE, **0.5G** FAT (**0G** SATURATED), **0MG** CHOLESTEROL, **1MG** SODIUM, **1G** FIBER

### helpful hint

- *Any type of washed, ready-to-eat salad can be substituted for the fennel salad.*
- *The fennel bulb can be sliced with a mandolin or in a food processor fitted with a thin-slicing blade.*

### countdown

- *Preheat broiler.*
- *Prepare all ingredients.*
- *Make pizza.*
- *While pizza bakes, make salad.*

### shopping list

*TO BUY:*

*1 small package shredded, reduced-fat mozzarella cheese (4 ounces needed)*
*1/4 pound lean ham*
*1 small package whole wheat pita bread*
*1 medium-size green bell pepper*
*2 portobello mushrooms (2 ounces needed)*
*1 medium tomato*
*1 small fennel bulb*
*1 medium banana*

*STAPLES:*

*Olive oil spray*
*Red onion*
*No-sugar-added oil and vinegar dressing*
*Salt*
*Black peppercorns*

# fresh tuna salad on a bed of spring greens with fresh peach yogurt

## helpful hints

- *Try not to overcook the tuna, or it will become very dry. Note that it will continue to cook in its own heat when removed from the saucepan.*
- *Make double if you have time, and store in the refrigerator for another lunch.*
- *Any type of lettuce can be used.*
- *Any type of whole grain bread can be used.*

## countdown

- *Cook tuna.*
- *Make salad.*
- *Toast bread.*

## shopping list

*TO BUY:*

*1 carton light fruit-flavored yogurt*
*6 ounces fresh yellow or black fin tuna*
*1 package crab boil*
*2 medium tomatoes*
*1 bunch fresh parsley*
*1 bag washed, ready-to-eat mesclun salad*
*2 medium peaches*

*STAPLES:*

*Celery*
*Olive oil spray*
*Yellow onion*
*Mayonnaise made with olive or soybean oil*
*Rye bread*
*Salt*
*Black peppercorns*

*A salad made from fresh tuna rather than canned is a treat. In fact, if you have any leftover cooked fish, it can be used in this salad. • Crab boil, also called shrimp boil, is a mixture of herbs and spices that are added to water to flavor fish. It usually includes bay leaves, peppercorns, mustard seeds, allspice, cloves, and dried ginger.*

## fresh tuna salad on a bed of spring greens

*6 ounces fresh yellow or black fin tuna*
*2 teaspoons crab boil seasoning (optional)*
*2 celery stalks, diced (1 cup)*
*2 medium tomatoes, chopped*
*1/2 cup chopped yellow onion*
*1/4 cup chopped fresh parsley*
*2 tablespoons mayonnaise made with olive or soybean oil*
*Salt and freshly ground black pepper to taste*
*2 cups washed, ready-to-eat mesclun salad*
*2 slices rye bread*
*Olive oil spray*

Place the tuna in a medium saucepan and cover with cold water. Add the crab boil seasoning. Bring to a simmer and gently cook until the tuna turns opaque or white, about 3 to 5 minutes. Reserve 2 tablespoons of the poaching liquid; drain the fish and pat dry with a paper towel. Gently combine the celery, tomatoes, onion, parsley, mayonnaise, and poaching liquid in a medium-size bowl. Flake in the tuna. Season with salt and pepper to taste, and stir to incorporate the tuna and seasonings. Place the mesclun salad on 2 plates and top with the tuna salad. Spray the bread with olive oil and toast. Serve with the salad.

*Makes 2 servings.*

**ONE SERVING: 339** CALORIES, **28G** PROTEIN, **23G** CARBOHYDRATE **18G** FAT (**3G** SATURATED), **37MG** CHOLESTEROL, **318MG** SODIUM, **4G** FIBER

## fresh peach yogurt

*1 cup light fruit-flavored yogurt*
*2 medium peaches, pitted and sliced*

Divide the yogurt between 2 dessert bowls and top with the peach slices.

*Makes 2 servings.*

**ONE SERVING: 87** CALORIES, **5G** PROTEIN, **18G** CARBOHYDRATE, **0G** FAT (**0G** SATURATED), **3MG** CHOLESTEROL, **58MG** SODIUM, **1G** FIBER

# baby spinach, mushroom, and canadian bacon salad with pineapple and toasted pine nuts

*Baby spinach leaves and mushrooms topped with warm bacon is a popular, flavorful lunch salad. This version uses lean Canadian bacon and takes only minutes to make. There are several brands of lean Canadian bacon available, and they vary considerably in fat content. Look for the one with the lowest fat content.*

## baby spinach, mushroom, and canadian bacon salad

*6 ounces sliced lean Canadian bacon, cut into thin strips*
*1 cup chickpeas*
*2 tablespoons no-sugar-added oil and vinegar dressing*
*8 scallions, sliced (1 cup)*
*Salt and freshly ground black pepper to taste*
*1/4 pound button mushrooms, sliced (about 1 1/2 cups)*
*4 cups washed, ready-to-eat fresh baby spinach, torn into bite-size pieces*
*1 cup fresh bean sprouts, rinsed and drained*

Place the Canadian bacon and chickpeas on a foil-lined baking tray, and broil 10 minutes or until crisp. Combine the dressing and scallions together in a medium-size bowl. Season with salt and pepper to taste. Add mushrooms, spinach, and sprouts. Toss well. Sprinkle with the Canadian bacon strips and chickpeas and serve.

*Makes 2 servings.*

**ONE SERVING: 387** CALORIES, **29G** PROTEIN, **35G** CARBOHYDRATE **15G** FAT (**3G** SATURATED), **40MG** CHOLESTEROL, **911MG** SODIUM, **9G** FIBER

### helpful hints

- *The Canadian bacon and chickpeas can be browned in a toaster oven.*
- *The pine nuts for the dessert can be toasted at the same time as the bacon. Watch them carefully, as they burn easily.*
- *To clean whole mushrooms, wipe them gently with a damp paper towel.*
- *If spinach leaves are large, tear them into smaller pieces.*
- *Buy fresh pineapple cubes in the produce section of the supermarket.*

### countdown

- *Preheat broiler.*
- *Broil Canadian bacon.*
- *Toast pine nuts.*
- *Make salad.*
- *Toss pineapple and pine nuts together.*

# baby spinach, mushroom, and canadian bacon salad with pineapple and toasted pine nuts *continued*

## shopping list

*TO BUY:*

- *6 ounces sliced lean Canadian bacon*
- *1 small can chickpeas*
- *1 small container pine nuts*
- *1 small bunch scallions (8 scallions needed)*
- *1 small package button mushrooms (4 ounces needed)*
- *1 bag washed, ready-to-eat fresh spinach*
- *1 package fresh bean sprouts (1 cup needed)*
- *1 small container fresh pineapple cubes*

*STAPLES:*

- *No-sugar-added oil and vinegar dressing*
- *Salt*
- *Black peppercorns*

## pineapple and toasted pine nuts

*2 tablespoons pine nuts*
*1 cup fresh pineapple cubes*

Place the pine nuts on a foil-lined tray under the broiler or in toaster oven for 1 minute. Toss the pineapple and pine nuts together, and divide between 2 dessert bowls.

*Makes 2 servings.*

**ONE SERVING: 72** CALORIES, **0.5G** PROTEIN, **10G** CARBOHYDRATE, **0.5G** FAT (**0G** SATURATED), **0MG** CHOLESTEROL, **1MG** SODIUM, **1**G FIBER

# turkey and asparagus penne salad with tangerine and orange yogurt

*This turkey, asparagus, tomato, and basil pasta salad can be assembled in the time it takes to boil water and cook the pasta. My first experience with whole wheat pasta was a surprise. It has a nutty flavor, very good texture, and can be used like regular pasta.*

## turkey and asparagus penne salad

- *1/2 cup whole wheat penne or other short-cut pasta (2 ounces)*
- *1/4 pound asparagus*
- *1/2 cup sliced carrots*
- *1 medium tomato, cut into 1-inch cubes (1 cup)*
- *1/4 pound sliced smoked turkey breast*
- *1/2 cup fresh basil, snipped with scissors*
- *3 tablespoons no-sugar-added oil and vinegar dressing*
- *Salt and freshly ground black pepper to taste*

Bring a large saucepan filled with water to a boil. Add the pasta and cook 10 minutes, or according to package instructions. Do not overcook. While the pasta is cooking, cut or snap off the 1-inch fibrous stem on the asparagus and discard. Slice the remaining asparagus into 1-inch pieces (you should have about 1 cup). Add the asparagus and carrots for the last 2 minutes of cooking. Drain. Place the pasta, asparagus, carrots, tomato, turkey, and basil in a bowl. Add the dressing and toss well. Season with salt and pepper if needed and serve warm.

*Makes 2 servings.*

**ONE SERVING: 334** CALORIES, **23G** PROTEIN, **26G** CARBOHYDRATE **15G** FAT (**3G** SATURATED), **40MG** CHOLESTEROL, **170MG** SODIUM, **5G** FIBER

## tangerine and orange yogurt

- *1 cup light orange-flavored yogurt*
- *2 medium tangerines, peeled and segmented*

Divide the yogurt into 2 dessert bowls, and top with tangerine slices.

*Makes 2 servings.*

**ONE SERVING: 87** CALORIES, **5G** PROTEIN, **18G** CARBOHYDRATE, **0.2G** FAT (**0G** SATURATED), **3MG** CHOLESTEROL, **59MG** SODIUM, **0G** FIBER

### helpful hints

- *Whole wheat pasta can be found in the pasta section of most markets.*
- *A quick way to chop basil is to cut it with a scissors.*
- *To save time and saucepans, add carrots and asparagus to pasta while cooking.*

### countdown

- *Cook pasta.*
- *Prepare turkey salad.*
- *Prepare yogurt and tangerine.*

### shopping list

*TO BUY:*

- *1 carton light orange-flavored yogurt*
- *1/4 pound smoked turkey breast*
- *1 box whole wheat short-cut pasta (penne or macaroni)*
- *1/4 pound asparagus*
- *1 medium tomato*
- *1 small bunch fresh basil*
- *2 medium tangerines*

*STAPLES:*

- *Carrots*
- *No-sugar-added oil and vinegar dressing*
- *Salt*
- *Black peppercorns*

# waldorf salad with open-faced roast beef sandwich and fresh berry yogurt

## helpful hints

- *Any type of lettuce can be used.*
- *Toasting pecans can be tricky, as they burn quickly. Watch them carefully.*

## countdown

- *Make salad.*
- *Make sandwich.*
- *Assemble yogurt.*

## shopping list

*TO BUY:*

*1 carton light fruit-flavored yogurt*

*1/4 pound sliced lean roast beef*

*1 small package pecan halves (1/2 ounce needed)*

*1 small tomato*

*1 small head romaine lettuce*

*1 lemon*

*1 small red apple*

*STAPLES:*

*Celery*

*Mayonnaise made with olive or soybean oil*

*Dijon mustard*

*Rye bread*

*Salt*

*Black peppercorns*

*Salad greens with crisp apples and nuts were first served at the Waldorf Astoria Hotel in Manhattan in 1893, and it's been a standard on menus ever since. Add a roast beef sandwich to the spread and enjoy an all-American lunch.*

## waldorf salad

*1 tablespoon mayonnaise made with olive or soybean oil*

*1 tablespoon freshly squeezed lemon juice (about 1/2 lemon)*

*Salt and freshly ground black pepper to taste*

*4 pecan halves, broken into pieces (1 tablespoon)*

*2 celery stalks, sliced (1 cup)*

*1 small red apple, cored and cut into 1/2-inch cubes (about 1 1/2 cups)*

*Several romaine lettuce leaves, washed and dried*

Combine the mayonnaise and lemon juice in a medium-size bowl. Season with salt and pepper to taste. Toast the pecans in a toaster oven for 1 minute, or until brown to bring out their flavor (optional). Be careful: They burn easily. Toss the celery, apple, and pecans in the mayonnaise mixture. Place lettuce leaves on 2 plates and spoon the salad onto the leaves to serve.

*Makes 2 servings.*

**ONE SERVING: 151** CALORIES, **2G** PROTEIN, **16G** CARBOHYDRATE, **10G** FAT (**1G** SATURATED), **3MG** CHOLESTEROL, **116MG** SODIUM, **4G** FIBER

## open-faced roast beef sandwich

*2 slices rye bread*

*1 tablespoon Dijon mustard*

*1/4 pound sliced lean roast beef, sliced*

*1 small tomato, sliced*

Spread the bread with mustard. Divide the roast beef between each slice of bread. Top with the tomato slices. Serve any extra tomato slices on the side.

*Makes 2 servings.*

**ONE SERVING: 179** CALORIES, **22G** PROTEIN, **13G** CARBOHYDRATE, **6G** FAT (**2G** SATURATED), **46MG** CHOLESTEROL, **337MG** SODIUM, **3G** FIBER

## fresh berry yogurt

*1 cup light fruit-flavored yogurt*

Divide the yogurt between 2 dessert bowls.

*Makes 2 servings.*

**ONE SERVING: 50** CALORIES, **4G** PROTEIN, **9G** CARBOHYDRATE, **0G** FAT (**0G** SATURATED), **51MG** CHOLESTEROL, **511**MG SODIUM, **6G** FIBER

# grouper sandwich and tomato tapenade salad with orange-vanilla yogurt

*This dish of fresh fish sautéed with onions and served on melted cheese toast reminds me of the lunches we have sitting on the docks watching the boats come in with their fresh catch. A tapenade is a thick paste made from capers, olives, oil, and vinegar. It is a great hors d'oeuvre or topping, in this case, to dress fresh sliced tomatoes.*

## grouper sandwich

*6 ounces grouper fillet*
*2 teaspoons olive oil*
*Salt and freshly ground black pepper to taste*
*½ cup diced red onion*
*2 slices reduced-fat cheddar cheese (1½ ounces)*
*2 slices whole wheat bread*

Rinse the fillet and pat dry with paper towel. Heat the oil in a small nonstick skillet on medium high. Add the fillet, and sauté 5 minutes. Turn; salt and pepper the cooked side. Add the onion to the skillet, and sauté 3 more minutes. Place the cheese on the bread and toast in a toaster oven until the cheese melts. Divide the grouper in half, place on top of the melted cheese, and spoon the onion over the fillet to serve. *Makes 2 servings.*

**ONE SERVING: 249** CALORIES, **26G** PROTEIN, **13G** CARBOHYDRATE **11G** FAT (**4G** SATURATED), **46MG** CHOLESTEROL, **341MG** SODIUM, **3G** FIBER

## tomato tapenade salad

*2 medium-size garlic cloves, crushed*
*2 tablespoons drained capers*
*4 pitted green olives*
*2 teaspoons balsamic vinegar*
*1 medium tomato, sliced*
*Salt and freshly ground black pepper to taste*

Place garlic, capers, olives, and balsamic vinegar in a food processor and purée. Alternatively, finely chop by hand. Divide the tomato slices between 2 plates. Sprinkle with salt and pepper to taste, and spoon the tapenade on top. Serve at room temperature. *Makes 2 servings.*

**ONE SERVING: 27** CALORIES, **1G** PROTEIN, **4G** CARBOHYDRATE, **1G** FAT (**0G** SATURATED), **0MG** CHOLESTEROL, **410MG** SODIUM, **0G** FIBER

## orange-vanilla yogurt

*2 medium-size oranges*
*1 cup light vanilla-flavored yogurt*

Peel and segment the oranges. Divide the yogurt between 2 dessert bowls, and top with the orange segments.

*Makes 2 servings.*

**ONE SERVING: 174** CALORIES, **6G** PROTEIN, **39G** CARBOHYDRATE, **0.5G** FAT (**0G** SATURATED), **3MG** CHOLESTEROL, **0MG** SODIUM, **6G** FIBER

### helpful hints

- *Ask to have skin removed when you buy grouper.*
- *To determine the weight of each slice of cheese, divide the package weight by the number of slices. With most brands, 1 slice equals ¾ ounce.*

### countdown

- *Make tomato tapenade.*
- *Make grouper sandwich.*

### shopping list

*TO BUY:*

*1 carton light vanilla-flavored yogurt*
*1 small package sliced, reduced-fat cheddar cheese (1½ ounces needed)*
*6 ounces grouper fillet*
*1 small bottle capers*
*1 small container pitted green olives*
*1 medium tomato*
*2 medium oranges*

*STAPLES:*

*Garlic*
*Red onion*
*Olive oil*
*Balsamic vinegar*
*Whole-wheat bread*
*Salt*
*Black peppercorns*

# chicken sandwich with sun-dried tomato sauce and apple yogurt

## helpful hint

- *The sauce can be made several days ahead and refrigerated.*

## countdown

- *Make chicken.*
- *Assemble dessert.*

## shopping list

*TO BUY:*

*1 carton light fruit-flavored yogurt*
*2 (3-ounce) boneless, skinless chicken breasts*
*1 bottle diced sun-dried tomatoes in olive oil*
*1 small jar capers*
*1 small loaf 8-grain bread*
*1 small head red-leaf lettuce*
*1 lemon*
*2 apples*

*STAPLES:*

*Garlic*
*Mayonnaise made with olive or soybean oil*
*Salt*
*Black peppercorns*

*Sun-dried tomatoes and capers make a great sauce for chicken breasts. The chicken can be sautéed in minutes in garlic and lemon juice, or buy roasted or rotisserie chicken to save time. • People often ask me what a caper is. There are many types of capers in the supermarket with varying degrees of flavor. Capers are the small, unopened flower bud from a bush that grows in the Mediterranean region. Capers are picked, dried, and then pickled in a vinegar brine. They vary from the small, nonpareil type from southern France to larger versions. The flavor depends largely on the brining and pickling process. Buy a good quality, well-known brand for the best results.*

## chicken sandwich with sun-dried tomato sauce

*2 (3-ounce) boneless, skinless chicken breasts*
*2 teaspoons freshly squeezed lemon juice (½ small lemon)*
*4 medium-size garlic cloves, crushed*
*¼ teaspoon freshly ground black pepper*
*2 slices 8-grain bread*
*2 tablespoons diced sun-dried tomatoes, drained*
*3 tablespoons drained capers*
*2 tablespoons mayonnaise made with olive or soybean oil*
*Several leaves red-leaf lettuce*

Remove any visible fat from the chicken and pound it flat to about ¼ inch with a meat mallet or the bottom of a sturdy frying pan. Combine lemon juice, garlic, and black pepper in a small bowl. Set a medium-size nonstick skillet over medium-high heat. Add the lemon mixture and chicken. Cook 3 minutes. Turn, and cook 3 more minutes. Toast the bread. Combine the sun-dried tomatoes and capers with the mayonnaise. (Use the same bowl as for the lemon mixture.) Place the bread on 2 plates; place the lettuce leaves on the bread. Top with the chicken, and spread with sauce to serve.

*Makes 2 servings.*

**ONE SERVING: 327** CALORIES, **32G** PROTEIN, **16G** CARBOHYDRATE **17G** FAT (**2G** SATURATED), **77MG** CHOLESTEROL, **596MG** SODIUM, **4G** FIBER

## apple yogurt

*1 cup light fruit-flavored yogurt*
*2 apples, cored and sliced*

Divide the yogurt between 2 bowls and top with the apple slices.

**ONE SERVING: 131** CALORIES, **4G** PROTEIN, **30G** CARBOHYDRATE, **0.5G** FAT (**0G** SATURATED), **3MG** CHOLESTEROL, **58MG** SODIUM, **4G** FIBER

# right carb dinners

# japanese beef sukiyaki and fresh peaches in kirsch

## helpful hints

- *Any type of liqueur or brandy can be substituted for the kirsch*
- *To keep from having to look back at the recipe as you stir-fry the ingredients, line them up on a cutting board or plate in the order of use so you know which ingredient comes next.*

## countdown

- *Cook noodles.*
- *Prepare remaining ingredients.*
- *Bring to table and cook.*

## shopping list

*TO BUY:*

*6 ounces beef sirloin*
*1 can sliced water chestnuts*
*1 bottle sesame oil*
*1 box angel hair or thin whole wheat spaghetti (2 ounces needed)*
*1 small bottle dry sherry*
*1 small bottle kirsch*
*1 container sliced mushrooms (4 ounces needed)*
*1 bunch scallions (8 scallions needed)*
*1 bag washed, ready-to-eat fresh spinach (5 ounces needed)*
*2 medium peaches*

*STAPLES:*

*Celery*
*Yellow onion*
*Fat-free, low-salt chicken broth*
*Low-salt soy sauce*
*Sugar substitute*
*Black peppercorns*

*This is a fun meal that's cooked at the table with an electric frying pan or wok. You can also cook the entire meal in the kitchen and bring it to the table. The meal is for two servings, but can easily be doubled or tripled.*

## japanese beef sukiyaki

*1 cup angel hair or thin whole wheat spaghetti (1 ounce)*
*¼ cup fat-free, low-salt chicken broth*
*¼ cup low-salt soy sauce*
*½ cup dry sherry*
*2 (.035-ounce) envelopes sugar substitute*
*4 teaspoons sesame oil*
*1 cup sliced yellow onion*
*4 celery stalks, sliced (2 cups)*
*6 ounces beef sirloin, cut into strips about 4 inches long and 1 inch wide*
*¼ pound mushrooms, sliced (¾ cup)*
*5 ounces washed, ready-to-eat fresh spinach (4 cups)*
*1 cup sliced water chestnuts drained*
*8 scallions, sliced (about 1 cup)*
*Freshly ground black pepper to taste*

Bring a large saucepan filled with water to a boil. When the water boils, add the noodles and boil 5 minutes, or according to package instructions. Do not overcook. Drain and divide between 2 dinner plates.

Combine the chicken broth, soy sauce, sherry, and sugar substitute in a small bowl. Make sure all ingredients are prepped and ready for stir-frying. Heat the sesame oil in nonstick skillet or electric frying pan. Add the onion and celery and cook 3 minutes. Add the beef and cook for 1 minute, tossing constantly. Add half of the sauce and stir. Add the mushrooms and cook 30 seconds. Add the spinach, water chestnuts, and scallions and cook 1 minute. Add the remaining sauce and cook 30 seconds more, continuing to stir. Season with black pepper to taste. Remove immediately from the pan and serve over the noodles. Spoon the sauce on top.

*Makes 2 servings.*

**ONE SERVING: 666** CALORIES, **46G** PROTEIN, **68G** CARBOHYDRATE, **18G** FAT (**6G** SATURATED), **76MG** CHOLESTEROL, **1604MG** SODIUM, **14G** FIBER

## fresh peaches in kirsch

*2 medium peaches, pitted and sliced*
*2 tablespoons kirsch*

Divide the peach slices between 2 dessert bowls and sprinkle with kirsch.

*Makes 2 servings.*

**ONE SERVING: 69** CALORIES, **1G** PROTEIN, **10G** CARBOHYDRATE, **0G** FAT (**0G** SATURATED), **0MG** CHOLESTEROL, **0MG** SODIUM, **1G** FIBER

# sole in a pouch with garlic zucchini couscous

*A burst of aroma escapes when you open the pouch of this simple fish meal. The ingredients are placed on a piece of foil that is folded into a pouch. The natural juices are sealed in as the fish steams. You can assemble the pouch about an hour in advance and then place it in the oven when needed. • There's a large variety of flavored or infused olive oils available. Using them is an easy way to add flavor to a dish.*

## sole in a pouch

*10 ounces thin fish fillet (sole or snapper)*
*2 (10-inch) squares foil*
*Salt and freshly ground black pepper to taste*
*1 cup sliced mushrooms (3 ounces)*
*½ cup diced and drained sun-dried tomatoes*
*½ teaspoon dried thyme*
*¼ cup dry white wine or fat-free, low-salt chicken broth*

Preheat the broiler. Line a baking tray with foil and place in the oven about 5 inches from the broiler to heat. Place the foil squares on the counter, and center the fish on each piece. Season with salt and pepper to taste. Spread the mushrooms and sun-dried tomatoes over the fish. Sprinkle with the thyme, and pour the wine or chicken broth on top. Fold the edges of foil together, making sure they are tightly sealed to keep from leaking. Place the packets on a baking tray and broil 15 minutes. Serve the fish in the pouch or remove to plates and spoon the sauce and vegetables on top. *Makes 2 servings.*

**ONE SERVING: 213** CALORIES, **31G** PROTEIN, **6G** CARBOHYDRATE, **6G** FAT **(0G** SATURATED), **52MG** CHOLESTEROL, **169MG** SODIUM, **2G** FIBER

## garlic zucchini couscous

*1 cup water*
*2 cups zucchini, sliced (½ pound)*
*⅔ cup couscous*
*4 teaspoons garlic-infused olive oil*
*Salt and freshly ground black pepper to taste*

Combine the water and zucchini in a medium saucepan, and bring to a boil over high heat. Remove from the heat, add the couscous, cover, and let sit 5 minutes. Add the infused oil and toss with a fork. Season with salt and pepper to taste, and serve. *Makes 2 servings.*

**ONE SERVING: 263** CALORIES, **8G** PROTEIN, **38G** CARBOHYDRATE, **10G** FAT **(1G** SATURATED), **0MG** CHOLESTEROL, **8MG** SODIUM, **2G** FIBER

## grapes

*30 grapes (2 cups)*

Divide the grapes between 2 dessert plates. *Makes 2 servings.*

**ONE SERVING: 58** CALORIES, **1G** PROTEIN, **16G** CARBOHYDRATE, **0G** FAT **(0G** SATURATED), **0MG** CHOLESTEROL, **2MG** SODIUM, **0G** FIBER

### helpful hints

- *Buy diced sun-dried tomatoes to save time from dicing the whole ones.*
- *Olive oil with a small crushed garlic clove works fine as a substitute for garlic-infused oil.*
- *For the best flavor, make sure the dried thyme is less than 6 months old.*
- *Fat-free, low-salt chicken broth can be substituted for the dry white wine.*

### countdown

- *Preheat broiler.*
- *Make fish.*
- *While fish cooks, make couscous.*

### shopping list

*TO BUY:*

*10 ounces thin fish fillet (snapper or sole)*
*1 jar diced sun-dried tomatoes*
*1 small bottle dry white wine or 1 can fat-free, low-salt chicken broth*
*1 small box couscous*
*1 bottle garlic-infused olive oil*
*1 small package sliced mushrooms, (3 ounces needed)*
*½ pound zucchini*
*1 small bunch grapes*

*STAPLES:*

*Dried thyme*
*Foil*
*Salt*
*Black peppercorns*

# chicken parmesan, pasta, and broccoli with poached spiced pears

## helpful hints

- *Buy good quality Parmesan cheese and ask the grocer to grate it for you or chop it in the food processor yourself. Freeze extra for quick use later—simply spoon out what you need and leave the rest frozen.*
- *When draining pasta, leave a little water on the pasta for added sauce.*
- *If pressed for time, omit the poached spiced pears and serve 1 medium pear per person.*

## countdown

- *Place water for pasta on to boil.*
- *Make poached spiced pears.*
- *Make pasta and broccoli.*
- *Make chicken.*

*This quick dinner takes only 20 minutes to make. The pasta and broccoli are cooked in the same saucepan to save washing an extra pan.*

## chicken parmesan

*Olive oil spray*

*1/2 pound boneless, skinless chicken breast, visible fat removed*

*Salt and freshly ground pepper to taste*

*1/2 cup low-sugar, low-fat pasta sauce*

*2 tablespoons freshly grated Parmesan cheese*

Set a medium-size nonstick skillet over medium-high heat. Spray with olive oil, and brown the chicken 2 minutes on each side. Season each cooked side with salt and pepper to taste. Add the pasta sauce and let simmer for 4 minutes. Sprinkle with Parmesan cheese, cover with a lid, and let sit 1 minute. Divide between 2 plates and serve with the pasta and broccoli.

*Makes 2 servings.*

**ONE SERVING: 248** CALORIES, **39G** PROTEIN, **4G** CARBOHYDRATE, **9G** FAT (**3G** SATURATED), **100MG** CHOLESTEROL, **390MG** SODIUM, **1G** FIBER

## pasta and broccoli

*2 ounces whole wheat spaghetti (1/2 cup uncooked)*

*2 cups broccoli florets (4 ounces)*

*2 teaspoons olive oil*

*Salt and freshly ground black pepper to taste*

Bring a large pot of water to a boil and add the pasta. Cook 5 minutes, add broccoli, and continue to cook 4 minutes. Drain and toss with the olive oil; season with salt and pepper to taste.

*Makes 2 servings.*

**ONE SERVING: 206** CALORIES, **9G** PROTEIN, **30G** CARBOHYDRATE, **6G** FAT (**1G** SATURATED), **0MG** CHOLESTEROL, **28MG** SODIUM, **6G** FIBER

# chicken parmesan, pasta, and broccoli with poached spiced pears *continued*

## italian-style salad

*4 cups washed, ready-to-eat, Italian-style salad*
*1 cup frozen corn kernels*
*2 tablespoons no-sugar-added salad dressing*

Toss the salad and corn with the dressing.
*Makes 2 servings.*

**ONE SERVING: 151** CALORIES, **3G** PROTEIN, **19G** CARBOHYDRATE, **9G** FAT (**1G** SATURATED), **0MG** CHOLESTEROL, **85MG** SODIUM, **2G** FIBER

## poached spiced pears

*2 cups water*
*2 (.035-ounce) envelopes sugar substitute*
*8 whole cloves*
*8 strips lemon peel from 1 lemon*
*2 ripe pears*
*2 sprigs fresh mint*

Place the water, sugar substitute, cloves, and lemon peel in a medium-size saucepan. Peel the pears over pan to catch the juice. Core and slice the pears. Add the pear slices to the saucepan. Bring to a simmer and poach gently for 10 minutes. Remove the pear slices, and arrange in a circle on 2 dessert plates. Place a sprig of mint in the center of each plate.
Makes 2 servings.

**ONE SERVING: 98** CALORIES, **1G** PROTEIN, **26G** CARBOHYDRATE, **1G** FAT (**0G** SATURATED), **0MG** CHOLESTEROL, **1MG** SODIUM, **4G** FIBER

## shopping list

*TO BUY:*

- *1/2 pound boneless, skinless chicken breast*
- *1 bottle whole cloves*
- *1 small bottle low-sugar, low-fat pasta sauce (4 ounces needed)*
- *1 small box whole wheat spaghetti (2 ounces needed)*
- *1 small bag frozen corn kernels*
- *1 small package broccoli florets (4 ounces needed)*
- *1 bag washed, ready-to-eat, Italian-style salad*
- *1 small bunch fresh mint*
- *2 ripe pears*
- *1 lemon*

*STAPLES:*

- *Olive oil spray*
- *Olive oil*
- *No-sugar-added salad dressing*
- *Parmesan cheese*
- *Sugar substitute*
- *Salt*
- *Black peppercorns*

# cioppino (seafood stew) with sliced beet salad and watermelon spritzer

## helpful hints

- *Any type of firm, non-oily white fish can be substituted.*
- *Several drops hot pepper sauce can be substituted for red pepper flakes.*
- *Look for watermelon cut into cubes in the produce section of the supermarket or at a salad bar.*
- *If pressed for time, omit the Watermelon Spritzer and serve 1 cup of watermelon cubes per person.*

## countdown

- *Make soup.*
- *While soup simmers, make salad.*
- *Make watermelon spritzer.*

*Cioppino is a 20-minute, one-pot meal that is great winter or summer. Italian immigrants are credited with bringing this soup—a hearty combination of seafood and vegetables—to San Francisco.*

## cioppino

*½ pound fresh sea scallops*
*6 ounces grouper fillet*
*3 teaspoons olive oil*
*Salt and freshly ground black pepper to taste*
*1 cup red onion, sliced*
*2 medium-size green bell peppers, sliced (2 cups)*
*5 medium-size garlic cloves, crushed (divided)*
*¼ pound unpeeled red potatoes, washed, halved, and sliced (1 cup)*
*2 cups low-salt, no-sugar-added canned whole tomatoes (including juice)*
*2 cups bottled clam juice*
*¼ teaspoon red pepper flakes*
*2 tablespoons balsamic vinegar*
*½ cup chopped fresh basil*
*2 slices multigrain bread*
*Olive oil spray*

Wash the scallops and grouper and pat dry with a paper towel. Cut the grouper into 1-inch pieces about the same size as the scallops. Heat the olive oil in a medium-size nonstick skillet on high. Add the fish and scallops, and sauté 2 minutes. Remove to a large soup bowl, and season with salt and pepper to taste. In the same skillet, sauté the onion, bell pepper, and 4 garlic cloves over high heat for 3 minutes. Add the potatoes, tomatoes, clam juice, and red pepper flakes, breaking up the whole tomatoes with a spoon. Bring to a simmer, cover and simmer 15 minutes. Add the balsamic vinegar; season with salt and pepper to taste. Spoon over the fish in the soup bowl, and sprinkle with the basil. Spray the bread with olive oil. Cut the remaining garlic clove in half, and rub the bread with the cut sides of the garlic. Place in toaster oven or under broiler to toast. Serve the cioppino with the toast.

*Makes 2 servings.*

**ONE SERVING: 502** CALORIES, **46G** PROTEIN, **50G** CARBOHYDRATE, **14G** FAT (**2G** SATURATED), **67MG** CHOLESTEROL, **966MG** SODIUM, **8G** FIBER

# cioppino (seafood stew) with sliced beet salad and watermelon spritzer *continued*

## sliced beet salad

- *2 cups canned sliced beets, drained*
- *½ cup sliced red onion*
- *2 tablespoons no-sugar-added oil and vinegar dressing*
- *Salt and freshly ground black pepper to taste*

Divide the sliced beets between 2 plates. Sprinkle with the onion, and drizzle with the dressing. Season with salt and pepper to taste and serve with the cioppino.

*Makes 2 servings.*

**ONE SERVING: 129** CALORIES, **2G** PROTEIN, **13G** CARBOHYDRATE, **9G** FAT (**1G** SATURATED), **0MG** CHOLESTEROL, **159MG** SODIUM, **0G** FIBER

## watermelon spritzer

- *2 cups no-sugar-added lemon-lime or citrus-flavored seltzer, chilled*
- *2 tablespoons freshly squeezed lime juice*
- *2 (.035-ounce) envelopes sugar substitute*
- *2 cups watermelon cubes*

Place the seltzer, lime juice, sugar substitute, and watermelon cubes in a blender. Blend until smooth. Pour into 2 glasses and serve immediately.

*Makes 2 servings.*

**ONE SERVING: 53** CALORIES, **1G** PROTEIN, **13G** CARBOHYDRATE, **0.6G** FAT ( **0G** SATURATED), **0MG** CHOLESTEROL, **3MG** SODIUM, **1G** FIBER

## shopping list

*TO BUY:*

- *½ pound fresh sea scallops*
- *6 ounces grouper fillet*
- *1 bottle no-sugar-added lemon-lime or citrus-flavored seltzer (16 ounces needed)*
- *1 small bottle red pepper flakes*
- *1 can no-sugar-added whole tomatoes*
- *2 bottles clam juice (18 ounces needed)*
- *1 can or jar sliced beets*
- *2 medium-size green bell peppers*
- *¼ pound red potatoes*
- *1 small bunch fresh basil*
- *1 container watermelon cubes or ¼ whole watermelon (10 ounces needed)*
- *2 limes*

*STAPLES:*

- *Red onion*
- *Garlic*
- *Olive oil*
- *Olive oil spray*
- *Balsamic vinegar*
- *No-sugar-added oil and vinegar dressing*
- *Multigrain bread*
- *Sugar substitute*
- *Salt*
- *Black peppercorns*

# pork souvlaki kabobs with bulghur wheat salad

## helpful hints

- *If using wooden skewers, soak in water before using.*
- *To make marinating the pork easier, place it in self-seal bags. You only need to flip the bag over to turn the meat in the marinade—and there's no bowl to wash.*

## countdown

- *Preheat broiler or stove top grill*
- *Marinate pork.*
- *Make salad.*
- *Cook kabobs.*

## shopping list

*TO BUY:*

*1/2 pound pork tenderloin*
*1 box bulghur or cracked wheat*
*1 small container pine nuts*
*1 small box raisins*
*2 small green bell peppers*
*2 lemons*
*8 medium-size fresh apricots*

*STAPLES:*

*Yellow onion*
*Garlic*
*Olive oil*
*Dried oregano*
*Fat free, low-salt chicken broth*
*Salt*
*Black peppercorns*

*Barbecued, skewered meats called souvlaki are sold as a quick meal on many street corners in Athens. A simple Greek marinade of lemon juice, olive oil, oregano, and garlic flavors the meat. • Bulghur is wheat kernels that have been steamed, dried, and crushed. It has a chewy texture and tastes delicious in salads.*

## pork souvlaki kabobs

*1/4 cup freshly squeezed lemon juice (2 lemons)*
*2 teaspoons olive oil*
*2 teaspoons dried oregano*
*2 medium-size garlic cloves, crushed*
*1/2 pound pork tenderloin, visible fat removed and meat cut into 1 1/2-inch cubes*
*2 small green bell peppers, cut into 2-inch square pieces*
*1/2 small yellow onion, cut into pieces about 1/2 inch wide and 2 inches long*
*2 kabob skewers*

Preheat the broiler. Combine the lemon juice, oil, oregano, and garlic in a medium-size bowl or large ziplock bag. Add the pork and marinate 15 minutes. Remove the pork from the marinade and thread onto skewers, alternating with the bell pepper and onion pieces. If using the broiler, line a baking tray with foil and place the kabobs on the tray. Or, place on pre-heated stove-top grill. Broil or grill 5 minutes. Turn and cook 5 more minutes. Serve over the bulghur wheat.
*Makes 2 servings.*

**ONE SERVING: 299** CALORIES, **36G** PROTEIN, **16G** CARBOHYDRATE, **10G** FAT (**3G** SATURATED), **106MG** CHOLESTEROL, **82MG** SODIUM, **1G** FIBER

## bulghur wheat salad

*1 cup fat-free, low-salt chicken broth*
*1/2 cup coarse bulghur or cracked wheat*
*Salt and freshly ground black pepper to taste*
*1/4 cup raisins*
*1/4 cup pine nuts*
*2 teaspoons olive oil*

Bring the broth to a boil in a small saucepan over high heat. Add the bulghur wheat and a pinch of salt and pepper. Lower the heat, stir, and cover with a lid. Gently simmer for 10 minutes, or until the liquid is absorbed. Stir the raisins, pine nuts, and olive oil into the cooked bulghur. Season with additional salt and pepper to taste.
*Makes 2 servings.*

**ONE SERVING: 245** CALORIES, **5G** PROTEIN, **32G** CARBOHYDRATE, **5G** FAT (**1G** SATURATED), **0MG** CHOLESTEROL, **553MG** SODIUM, **4G** FIBER

## apricots

*8 medium-size fresh apricots*

Divide between 2 plates.
*Makes 2 servings.*

**ONE SERVING: 67** CALORIES, **2G** PROTEIN, **16G** CARBOHYDRATE, **0.5G** FAT (**0G** SATURATED), **0MG** CHOLESTEROL, **1MG** SODIUM, **3G** FIBER

# mediterranean veal and olives with orange barley

*Olives and pine nuts give this 20-minute veal stew a rich Mediterranean flavor. • Warm, bright sunshine, rolling hills touched with varying shades of green from the rows of olive trees, good food, thoughts of Italy and Greece. . .these memories inspired this quick, Mediterranean dinner.*

## mediterranean veal and olives

*Olive oil spray*

*½ pound veal stewing meat, visible fat trimmed and meat cut into 1-inch cubes*

*1 cup diced yellow onion*

*2 medium-size garlic cloves, crushed*

*½ cup dry white wine*

*1 cup low-salt, no-sugar-added canned crushed tomatoes*

*3 to 4 cups broccoli florets (½ pound)*

*8 black olives, pitted and halved*

*2 tablespoons pine nuts*

*½ cup fresh basil, torn into bite-size pieces*

*Salt and freshly ground black pepper to taste*

Set a nonstick skillet over medium-high heat and spray with olive oil. Brown the veal on all sides for 3 minutes. Remove the veal; add the onion and garlic to the skillet, and cook 2 minutes. Add the wine and cook another minute. Add the tomatoes and broccoli. Reduce the heat to medium low, and return the veal to the pan. Cover and simmer 15 minutes. Add the olives and pine nuts. Cook 5 more minutes. Add basil, season with salt and pepper to taste, and serve.

*Makes 2 servings.*

**ONE SERVING: 409** CALORIES, **38G** PROTEIN, **22G** CARBOHYDRATE **13G** FAT (**4G** SATURATED), **100MG** CHOLESTEROL, **497MG** SODIUM, **5G** FIBER

### helpful hints

- *Look for quick-cooking barley in the supermarket.*
- *Most supermarkets sell veal stew meat that is already cut into small pieces. Buy lean veal, or cut as much fat off the meat as possible before you cook it.*
- *Pine nuts are also called pignoli. They can be found in the spice, nut, or gourmet section of your market. Store any leftover pine nuts in your freezer.*

### countdown

- *Prepare veal.*
- *While veal cooks, make barley.*

# mediterranean veal and olives with orange barley *continued*

## shopping list

*TO BUY:*

- *½ pound veal stewing meat*
- *1 can low-salt, no-sugar-added canned crushed tomatoes (8 ounces needed)*
- *1 small can pitted black olives*
- *1 small package pine nuts*
- *1 small box quick-cooking pearl barley*
- *1 small bottle dry white wine*
- *1 small container orange juice*
- *½ pound broccoli florets*
- *1 small bunch fresh basil*

*STAPLES:*

- *Yellow onion*
- *Garlic*
- *Olive oil*
- *Olive oil spray*
- *Fat free, low-salt chicken broth*
- *Salt*
- *Black peppercorns*

## orange barley

*½ cup fat-free, low-salt chicken broth*

*½ cup quick-cooking pearl barley*

*2 teaspoons olive oil*

*1 tablespoon orange juice*

*Salt and freshly ground black pepper to taste*

Bring the broth to a boil in a medium saucepan and add the barley. Boil 10 minutes, uncovered. Drain and add the oil and orange juice. Season with salt and pepper to taste and serve with the veal. *Makes 2 servings.*

**ONE SERVING: 222** CALORIES, **5G** PROTEIN, **41G** CARBOHYDRATE, **5G** FAT (**1G** SATURATED), **0MG** CHOLESTEROL, **142MG** SODIUM, **0G** FIBER

# country minestrone with herbed meatballs and ginger-spiced applesauce

*Minestra is Italian for soup, and minestrone is a hearty vegetable soup. This meatball minestrone is a complete meal in one pot. The recipe can be doubled easily, so if you have time, make extra to use for another meal. • Spices can add exciting flavors with very little effort. Fennel seeds are oval, green-brown seeds that come from the common fennel plant. They have an anise taste and are used in many liqueurs. They can be found in the spice section of your market and will keep for 6 months. Here, combined with oregano, they give the meatballs a unique flavor.*

## country minestrone with herbed meatballs

- *2 teaspoons fennel seeds*
- *1 teaspoon dried oregano*
- *1/4 pound lean ground beef sirloin*
- *Salt and freshly ground black pepper to taste*
- *2 teaspoons olive oil*
- *1/2 cup sliced yellow onion*
- *2 celery stalks, sliced (about 1 cup)*
- *4 medium-size garlic cloves, crushed*
- *1 cup canned low-sodium, no-sugar-added diced tomatoes*
- *2 cups fat-free, low-salt chicken broth*
- *2 cups water*
- *1/2 cup whole wheat spaghetti or linguine, broken into small pieces (2 ounces)*
- *8 cups washed, ready-to-eat fresh spinach (10 ounces)*
- *1/2 cup canned small navy beans, rinsed and drained*
- *2 tablespoons freshly grated Parmesan cheese*

Mix the fennel seeds and oregano into the ground beef. Add a little salt and pepper to taste. Roll into meatballs about 1 1/2 to 2 inches in diameter. Heat the oil in a medium-size nonstick saucepan on medium high. Brown the meatballs on all sides, about 5 minutes, or until cooked through. Remove to a plate, and add the onion and celery to the saucepan. Sauté for 3 minutes without letting them brown. Add the garlic, tomatoes, chicken broth, and water. Bring to a boil. Add the pasta and cook gently for 8 or 9 minutes, stirring once or twice to make sure the pasta rolls freely in the liquid. Add the spinach and beans to the cooking pasta. Return the meatballs to the soup and cook until heated through, about 2 minutes. Season with salt and pepper to taste. Serve in 2 large soup bowls with Parmesan cheese sprinkled on top.

*Makes 2 servings.*

**ONE SERVING: 510** CALORIES, **45G** PROTEIN, **62G** CARBOHYDRATE **14G** FAT (**5G** SATURATED), **55MG** CHOLESTEROL, **965MG** SODIUM, **21G** FIBER

## helpful hints

- *If you are not serving the soup immediately or are making some to freeze later, cook the pasta in a separate pot of water for 10 minutes. Drain, reserving 3 tablespoons of the cooking liquid. Add 1/2 teaspoon olive oil to the liquid and toss with the pasta to keep it from sticking. Add the pasta to the soup a few minutes before serving to warm through. The pasta will absorb the soup liquid if left to sit for any length of time.*
- *Cannellini beans or chickpeas can be substituted for navy beans.*
- *Frozen spinach can be used instead of fresh. Defrost and squeeze dry before using.*
- *Buy good quality Parmesan cheese and ask the grocer to grate it for you or chop it in the food processor yourself. Freeze extra for quick use later—simply spoon out what you need and leave the rest frozen.*
- *If pressed for time, omit the Ginger Spiced Applesauce and serve 1 medium apple per person.*

## countdown

- *Make minestrone.*
- *Core, peel, and cook apples.*
- *Assemble salad.*
- *Complete applesauce.*

# country minestrone with herbed meatballs and ginger-spiced applesauce *continued*

## shopping list

*TO BUY:*

- *1/4 pound lean ground beef sirloin*
- *1 can low-sodium, no-sugar-added diced tomatoes (16 ounces needed)*
- *1 small can small navy beans (4 ounces needed)*
- *1 jar fennel seeds*
- *1 box whole wheat spaghetti or linguine (2 ounces needed)*
- *1 bag washed, ready-to-eat fresh spinach (10 ounces needed)*
- *1 bag washed, ready-to-eat, Italian-style salad*
- *1-inch piece fresh ginger*
- *2 Granny Smith apples*
- *1 lemon*

*STAPLES:*

- *Celery*
- *Yellow onion*
- *Garlic*
- *Parmesan cheese*
- *Olive oil*
- *No-sugar-added oil and vinegar dressing*
- *Dried oregano*
- *Fat-free, low-salt chicken broth*
- *Ground cinnamon*
- *Sugar substitute*
- *Salt*
- *Black peppercorns*

## italian salad

*2 cups washed, ready-to-eat, Italian-style salad*

*2 tablespoons no-sugar-added oil and vinegar dressing*

Toss the salad with the dressing and serve.

*Makes 2 servings.*

**ONE SERVING: 79** CALORIES, **0G** PROTEIN, **1G** CARBOHYDRATE, **8G** FAT (**1G** SATURATED), **0MG** CHOLESTEROL, **78MG** SODIUM, **0G** FIBER

## ginger-spiced applesauce

*2 Granny Smith apples, cored and cut into eighths*

*1/2 cup water*

*2 tablespoons freshly squeezed lemon juice (1 lemon)*

*2 (.035-ounce) envelopes sugar substitute*

*2 tablespoons grated fresh ginger*

*1/2 teaspoon ground cinnamon*

Place the apples and water in a medium saucepan. Cover with a lid and bring to a boil. Cook for 10 minutes. Alternatively, place the apples and water in a microwave-safe bowl. Cover and microwave on high for 5 minutes. Let stand 2 to 3 minutes.

Place the cooked apples and water in the bowl of a food processor, and add the lemon juice and sugar substitute. Grate the ginger over the bowl, making sure to catch any ginger juice. Process until thoroughly mixed. Spoon into 2 dessert bowls. Sprinkle the applesauce with a little cinnamon and serve.

*Makes 2 servings.*

**ONE SERVING: 90** CALORIES, **0.5G** PROTEIN, **24G** CARBOHYDRATE, **0.5G** FAT, (**0G** SATURATED), **0MG** CHOLESTEROL, **1MG** SODIUM, **4G** FIBER

# curried shrimp and lentil salad

*Juicy shrimp cooked in a light curry sauce produces a flavor-packed, ethnic meal. This meal takes a little more time, about 30 minutes, but is very much worth the effort. Try it when you want something with a zing. • Authentic curries are made with a blend of about 15 spices. I have used store-bought curry powder to shorten the preparation time for this meal. This type of powder loses its flavor quickly and should be not used if more than three to four months old.*

## curried shrimp

- *1 tablespoon olive oil*
- *2 medium-size garlic cloves, crushed*
- *1-inch piece fresh ginger, chopped (2 tablespoons)*
- *2 tablespoons whole wheat flour*
- *2 teaspoons ground cumin*
- *1 ½ tablespoons curry powder*
- *1 cup fat-free, low-salt chicken broth*
- *½ pound broccoli florets (about 2 cups)*
- *½ cup sliced red onion*
- *¼ cup raisins*
- *¾ pound large shrimp, shelled and deveined*
- *Salt and freshly ground black pepper to taste*
- *2 tablespoons heavy whipping cream*

Heat the olive oil in a nonstick skillet on medium. Add the garlic, ginger, whole wheat flour, cumin, and curry, stirring to blend well. Add the chicken broth. Cook until sauce begins to thicken, about 1 minute. Add the broccoli florets, onion, and raisins. Cover and simmer 5 minutes. Add the shrimp and cook, uncovered, for 2 minutes, or until shrimp are cooked. Season with salt and pepper to taste. Remove from the heat and blend in the cream. Divide between 2 plates and serve.

*Makes 2 servings.*

**ONE SERVING: 451** CALORIES, **42G** PROTEIN, **36G** CARBOHYDRATE **17G** FAT (**5G** SATURATED), **281MG** CHOLESTEROL, **564MG** SODIUM, **1G** FIBER

## helpful hints

- *Buy shelled shrimp or ask for the shrimp to be shelled while you complete your shopping. Most stores will do this for a small fee—well worth the time saved in shelling them yourself.*
- *To chop fresh ginger quickly, cut it into small cubes and press through a garlic press with large holes. If using a press with small holes, just capture the juice that is squeezed out; it will give enough flavor for the recipe.*
- *Lentil salad can be made a day ahead and served warm or at room temperature. Make extra if you have time for a great lunch or snack*
- *To shorten preparation time for this meal, omit the lentil salad and serve a quick-cooking brown rice instead.*

## countdown

- *Start lentil salad.*
- *Prepare ingredients for curried shrimp.*
- *Make shrimp.*
- *Finish lentil salad.*

# curried shrimp and lentil salad *continued*

## shopping list

*TO BUY:*

*1 small carton heavy whipping cream*

*3/4 pound large shrimp, peeled*

*1 can litchis*

*1 jar curry powder*

*1 small package dried lentils*

*1 small package raisins (1/4 cup needed)*

*1/2 pound broccoli florets*

*1 small bunch scallions (4 scallions needed)*

*1-inch piece fresh ginger*

*STAPLES:*

*Olive oil*

*No-sugar-added oil and vinegar dressing*

*Red onion*

*Garlic*

*Whole wheat flour*

*Fat-free, low-salt chicken broth*

*Ground cumin*

*Salt*

*Black peppercorns*

## lentil salad

*1 cup fat-free, low-salt chicken broth*

*1 cup water*

*1/2 cup lentils*

*2 whole garlic cloves*

*4 scallions, thinly sliced (1/2 cup)*

*2 tablespoons no-sugar-added oil and vinegar dressing*

*Salt and freshly ground black pepper to taste*

Bring the broth and water to a boil in a medium saucepan. Rinse the lentils and slowly pour into the boiling broth so that the broth continues to boil. Add the garlic and reduce the heat to medium low. Simmer for 20 minutes, or until lentils are cooked through but still firm. Meanwhile, mix the scallions with the dressing. Add salt and pepper to taste. Drain the lentils and remove the garlic cloves. Mix the dressing with the lentils while still warm.

*Makes 2 servings.*

**ONE SERVING: 147** CALORIES, **6G** PROTEIN, **13G** CARBOHYDRATE, **9G** FAT (**1G** SATURATED), **0MG** CHOLESTEROL, **357MG** SODIUM, **2G** FIBER

## litchis

*1 cup drained, canned litchis*

Divide the litchis between 2 dessert bowls and serve.

*Makes 2 servings.*

**ONE SERVING: 63** CALORIES, **1G** PROTEIN, **16G** CARBOHYDRATE, **0.5G** FAT (**0G** SATURATED), **0MG** CHOLESTEROL, **1MG** SODIUM, **1G** FIBER

# southwestern chicken fajitas with tipsy grapefruit

*Southwestern Fajitas make deliciously light meals. Served with an array of colorful vegetables and wrapped in warm tortillas, these little Mexican sandwiches are an entire meal in themselves.*

## southwestern chicken fajitas

- *¼ cup freshly squeezed lemon juice (2 lemons)*
- *3 teaspoons canola oil, divided*
- *1 teaspoon ground cumin*
- *Pinch ground cayenne*
- *½ pound boneless, skinless chicken breast, very thinly sliced*
- *4 (8-inch) whole wheat tortillas*
- *1 cup sliced red onion*
- *2 medium-size red bell peppers, sliced (4 cups)*
- *2 medium-size green bell peppers, sliced (2 cups)*
- *4 garlic cloves, crushed*
- *2 medium tomatoes, diced*
- *½ cup shredded, reduced-fat Monterey Jack cheese*
- *½ cup chopped fresh cilantro*

Preheat the oven to 350 degrees. Mix the lemon juice, 1 teaspoon of the oil, the cumin, and cayenne together in a microwave-safe bowl. Microwave for 30 seconds on high. Alternatively, place in a small saucepan, bring to a boil, and then immediately remove from the heat. Place the chicken in the warm marinade for 15 minutes, stirring to make sure all of the chicken is covered. Tightly wrap the tortillas in 2 foil packages and place in the preheated oven for 10 minutes. Remove and leave wrapped in foil.

Heat the remaining 2 teaspoons of oil in a skillet until the oil begins to smoke. Remove the chicken from marinade, being sure to save any marinade that remains (most will be absorbed by the chicken), and sauté the chicken in the hot pan for about 1 minute. Add the onion, bell peppers, and garlic. Sauté for 2 minutes. Add the marinade, and toss with the chicken and vegetables for another minute, or until the sauce reduces and just coats the chicken.

To serve, arrange the diced tomatoes, shredded cheese, and chopped cilantro in small bowls. Spoon the chicken and vegetables onto a warm serving dish along with the wrapped tortillas. Fill the tortillas with the chicken and vegetables, sprinkle with the tomatoes, grated cheese, and cilantro, and fold to eat.

*Makes 2 servings.*

**ONE SERVING: 630** CALORIES, **63G** PROTEIN, **56G** CARBOHYDRATE **23G** FAT (**8G** SATURATED), **116MG** CHOLESTEROL, **614MG** SODIUM, **2G** FIBER

### helpful hints

- *Red, yellow, and green bell peppers make this a colorful dish, but you can use one or any combination of peppers you like.*
- *Heating dried spices releases their oils, increasing their flavor.*
- *Triple Sec and other orange liqueurs can be bought in small splits of about 2 ounces at most liquor stores.*

### countdown

- *Preheat oven to 350 degrees.*
- *Make fajitas.*
- *Make grapefruit.*

# southwestern chicken fajitas with tipsy grapefruit *continued*

## shopping list

*TO BUY:*

- *1 small package shredded, reduced-fat Monterey Jack cheese*
- *1/2 pound boneless, skinless, chicken breast*
- *1 small package whole wheat tortillas*
- *1 small bottle Triple Sec*
- *2 medium-size red bell peppers*
- *2 medium-size green bell peppers*
- *2 medium tomatoes*
- *1 small bunch fresh cilantro*
- *2 lemons*
- *1 small grapefruit*

*STAPLES:*

- *Red onion*
- *Garlic*
- *Canola oil*
- *Ground cumin*
- *Cayenne pepper*

## tipsy grapefruit

- *1 grapefruit*
- *1 tablespoon Triple Sec or other orange liqueur*

Separate the grapefruit segments with a serrated knife and scoop out onto 2 dessert plates. Sprinkle with the Triple Sec and serve.

*Makes 2 servings.*

**ONE SERVING: 101** CALORIES, **1G** PROTEIN, **17G** CARBOHYDRATE, **0G** FAT (**0G** SATURATED), **0MG** CHOLESTEROL, **1MG** SODIUM, **1G** FIBER

# roast beef hash with shiitake mushrooms and cinnamon-walnut baked apples

*Roast beef, shiitake mushrooms, and fresh thyme transform a 1950s-style hash to a modern version that takes only 20 minutes to make. I've shortened the cooking time by using lean roast beef from the deli and making a light gravy with chicken broth. The gravy just coats the hash. I've updated the flavor using shiitake mushrooms, pine nuts, and fresh thyme. This hash keeps well, so make double if you have time.*

## roast beef hash with shiitake mushrooms

- *2 teaspoons olive oil*
- *¼ pound unpeeled red potatoes, washed and cut into 1-inch cubes (about 1 cup)*
- *½ cup diced red onion*
- *2 medium-size red bell peppers, diced (4 cups)*
- *¼ pound shiitake mushrooms, diced (1½ cups)*
- *½ pound sliced lean roast beef, diced (2 cups)*
- *2 tablespoons whole wheat flour*
- *1 cup fat-free, low-salt chicken broth*
- *Salt and freshly ground black pepper to taste*

Heat the oil in a nonstick skillet on medium high. Add the potatoes, and sauté 5 minutes, tossing to turn halfway through. Add the onion, bell peppers, and mushrooms. Sauté 10 minutes, tossing after 5 minutes. Add the roast beef and toss for 1 minute. Push ingredients to the sides of the skillet, leaving a hole in the center. Add the flour, then the broth, and stir until the sauce thickens. Toss with the ingredients to lightly bind the hash. Season with salt and pepper to taste. Divide between 2 plates and serve.

*Makes 2 servings.*

**ONE SERVING: 409** CALORIES, **39G** PROTEIN, **29G** CARBOHYDRATE **14G** FAT (**4G** SATURATED), **93MG** CHOLESTEROL, **364MG** SODIUM, **1G** FIBER

## green salad

- *4 cups washed, ready-to-eat salad*
- *½ cup cannellini beans*
- *2 tablespoons no-sugar-added oil and vinegar salad dressing*
- *Salt and freshly ground black pepper to taste*

Place salad and beans in a bowl and drizzle with the dressing. Season with salt and pepper to taste and toss. Serve with the hash.

*Makes 2 servings.*

**ONE SERVING: 136** CALORIES, **4G** PROTEIN, **14G** CARBOHYDRATE, **9G** FAT (**1G** SATURATED), **0MG** CHOLESTEROL, **82MG** SODIUM, **3G** FIBER

## helpful hints

- *Ask the deli to cut the roast beef in one piece to make it easier to cube.*
- *Pecans or almonds can be substituted for the walnuts.*
- *If pressed for time, substitute 1 medium apple (per person) for the Cinnamon Walnut Baked Apples*

## countdown

- *Make hash.*
- *While hash cooks, make salad.*
- *Make baked apples.*

## shopping list

*TO BUY:*

- *½ pound sliced lean roast beef diced*
- *1 can cannellini beans (4 ounces needed)*
- *1 small package broken walnuts (about 1 ounce needed)*
- *¼ pound red potatoes*
- *2 medium-size red bell peppers*
- *1 container shiitake mushrooms (4 ounces needed)*
- *1 bag washed, ready-to-eat lettuce*
- *2 Red Delicious apples*

# roast beef hash with shiitake mushrooms and cinnamon-walnut baked apples *continued*

*STAPLES:*
- *Olive oil*
- *Red onion*
- *Whole wheat flour*
- *Fat-free, low-salt chicken broth*
- *Ground cinnamon*
- *Sugar substitute*
- *No-sugar-added oil and vinegar salad dressing*
- *Salt*
- *Black peppercorns*

## cinnamon-walnut baked apples

*2 tablespoons broken walnuts*
*1 teaspoon ground cinnamon*
*2 (.035-ounce) envelopes sugar substitute*
*2 Red Delicious apples, cored*

Chop the walnuts with the cinnamon and sugar substitute in a mini chop or food processor. Place the apples in 2 small dessert bowls, and fill the core of each apple with the cinnamon-walnut mixture. (Some of the mixture may spill over the top. This is fine.) Cover each bowl with another bowl or microwave-safe plastic wrap. Microwave on high 4 minutes. Remove and let stand, covered, 2 minutes. Serve in the dessert bowls.

*Makes 2 servings.*

**ONE SERVING: 159** CALORIES, **2G** PROTEIN, **24G** CARBOHYDRATE, **8G** FAT, (**0.8G** SATURATED), **0MG** CHOLESTEROL, **1MG** SODIUM, **4G** FIBER

# bahamian fish boil with chayote salad

*This 20-minute meal is made in one pot. With excellent fresh fish available all year round, the Bahamian natives are masters at cooking it. The fish for this dinner should be cooked just long enough so that it is tender and juicy. One secret to this dish is to be sure to season the fish well before it cooks. • For an interesting change, try this chayote salad. Chayote, also called mirliton or christophene, looks like a gnarled pear. It has a flavor similar to zucchini, but retains its crisp texture when cooked.*

## bahamian fish boil

*1/4 pound sweet potatoes or yams, peeled and cut into 1/2-inch pieces (1/2 cup)*
*4 celery stalks, sliced (2 cups)*
*1/2 cup sliced yellow onion*
*8 sprigs fresh thyme or 2 teaspoons dried*
*3 cups cold water*
*3/4 pound mahi mahi fillet cut into 1-inch pieces*
*2 tablespoons freshly squeezed lemon juice (1 lemon)*
*Salt and freshly ground black pepper to taste*
*Several drops hot pepper sauce*
*1 tablespoon olive oil*
*2 slices country-style, multigrain bread*

Place the potatoes, celery, onion, thyme, and water in a saucepan. Cover and cook over medium-high heat for 15 minutes. Meanwhile, season both sides of the fish with the lemon juice, salt, and pepper, pressing the seasoning into the fillet. Lower the heat and add the fish to the saucepan. Cover and gently simmer for 5 minutes. Add the pepper sauce and olive oil; season with additional salt and pepper to taste. Meanwhile, toast the bread. Serve the soup in large soup bowls with the toasted bread.
*Makes 2 servings.*

**ONE SERVING: 353** CALORIES, **38G** PROTEIN, **34G** CARBOHYDRATE **10G** FAT (**1G** SATURATED), **126MG** CHOLESTEROL, **418MG** SODIUM, **6G** FIBER

## helpful hints

- *Fresh thyme works best in this dish. If using dried, make sure the bottle is less than 6 months old.*
- *Any type of white fish can be used. A delicate, flaky fish such as sole will need only 2 minutes to cook.*
- *Any type of hot pepper sauce can be used.*
- *Any type of washed, ready-to-eat lettuce can be used instead of the chayote salad.*

## countdown

- *Start vegetables boiling in the broth.*
- *Season fish and add to broth.*
- *While fish cooks, make salad.*

## shopping list

*TO BUY:*
*3/4 pound mahi mahi fillet*
*1/4 pound sweet potatoes or yams*
*1 bunch fresh thyme or 1 jar dried*
*2 small chayotes*
*1 bag washed, ready-to-eat lettuce*
*1 medium mango*
*1 lemon*

## bahamian fish boil with chayote salad *continued*

*STAPLES:*

*Celery*
*Yellow onion*
*Garlic*
*Hot pepper sauce*
*Olive oil*
*No-sugar-added oil and vinegar dressing*
*Multigrain bread*
*Salt*
*Black peppercorns*

### chayote salad

*2 tablespoons no-sugar-added oil and vinegar dressing*
*2 medium-size garlic cloves, crushed*
*2 small chayotes, peeled and sliced (about 2 cups)*
*Salt and freshly ground black pepper to taste*
*Several lettuce leaves, washed and dried*

Heat the dressing in a medium-size nonstick skillet on medium high, and add garlic and chayote slices. Toss 3 to 4 minutes. Season with salt and pepper to taste. Place the lettuce leaves on a plate, and spoon the chayote on top before serving.

*Makes 2 servings.*

**ONE SERVING: 126** CALORIES, **2G** PROTEIN, **11G** CARBOHYDRATE, **9G** FAT (**1G** SATURATED), **0MG** CHOLESTEROL, **83MG** SODIUM, **0G** FIBER

### mango

*1 medium mango*

Slice off each side of the mango as close to the seed as possible. Take the mango half in your hand, skin- side down. Score the fruit in a cross-hatch pattern through to the skin. Bend the skin backwards so that the cubes pop up similar to a porcupine. Slice the cubes off the skin. Score and slice any fruit left on the pit.

Divide the mango cubes between 2 dessert bowls.

*Makes 2 servings.*

**ONE SERVING: 67** CALORIES, **1G** PROTEIN, **18G** CARBOHYDRATE, **0G** FAT (**0G** SATURATED), **0MG** CHOLESTEROL, **2MG** SODIUM, **1G** FIBER

# winter casserole soup and grilled cinnamon oranges

*This flavorful soup takes only 30 minutes to make and is a whole meal in one bowl. It's more of a casserole than a soup and light enough to enjoy year-round.*

## winter casserole soup

*3 cups fat-free, low-salt chicken broth*
*2 cups low-salt, no-sugar-added, canned diced tomatoes (including juice)*
*1 cup sliced red onion*
*2 celery stalks, sliced (1 cup)*
*1 cup sliced white cabbage*
*½ cup whole wheat fusille pasta (2 ounces)*
*1 tablespoon horseradish*
*1 tablespoon balsamic vinegar*
*8 cups washed, ready-to-eat fresh spinach*
*2 slices whole wheat bread*
*2 ounces shredded, reduced-fat Swiss cheese (½ cup)*
*Salt and freshly ground black pepper to taste*

Bring the chicken broth and tomatoes to a boil in a large saucepan over medium-high heat. Add the onion and celery. Cover, lower heat to medium, and cook on a slow boil for 10 minutes. Add the cabbage and fusille. Boil, uncovered, 10 minutes. Combine the horseradish and vinegar. Add to the soup, and stir in the spinach. Simmer 2 minutes, until the spinach is just wilted. Toast the bread. Add the cheese to the soup. Season with salt and pepper to taste. Serve with the toasted bread.

*Makes2 servings.*

**ONE SERVING: 434** CALORIES, **36G** PROTEIN, **66G** CARBOHYDRATE **7G** FAT (**3G** SATURATED), **15MG** CHOLESTEROL, **1289MG** SODIUM, **22G** FIBER

## grilled cinnamon oranges

*2 medium oranges*
*½ teaspoon ground cinnamon*
*2 tablespoons slivered almonds*
*2 (.035-ounce) envelopes sugar substitute*

Preheat the broiler. Line a baking tray with foil or use a small oven-to-table dish. Peel the oranges over a bowl to catch the juice. With a serrated knife, cut the oranges into circular ½-inch slices. (Add any juice to bowl of reserved juice.) Place the orange slices in a single layer in the baking dish. Sprinkle with the cinnamon and almonds, and broil for 3 minutes. Combine the sugar substitute with the reserved orange juice. Pour the juice over the grilled oranges and serve.

*Makes 2 servings.*

**ONE SERVING: 129** CALORIES, **4G** PROTEIN, **19G** CARBOHYDRATE, **6G** FAT (**0.5G** SATURATED), **0MG** CHOLESTEROL, **0MG** SODIUM, **4G** FIBER

### helpful hints

- *Any type of short-cut whole wheat pasta can be used.*
- *If pressed for time, omit the grilled cinnamon oranges and serve 1 orange per person.*

### countdown

- *Preheat broiler.*
- *Prepare all ingredients.*
- *Make casserole soup.*
- *While soup cooks, toast bread.*
- *Make grilled oranges.*

### shopping list

*TO BUY:*

*1 small package shredded, reduced-fat Swiss cheese (2 ounces needed)*
*1 can low-salt, no-sugar-added, canned diced tomatoes (16 ounces needed)*
*1 small jar horseradish*
*1 small package slivered almonds*
*1 box whole wheat fusille pasta (2 ounces needed)*
*¼ head white cabbage*
*1 bag washed, ready-to-eat fresh spinach*
*2 medium oranges*

*STAPLES:*

*Celery*
*Red onion*
*Fat-free, low-salt chicken broth*
*Balsamic vinegar*
*Whole wheat bread*
*Ground cinnamon*
*Sugar substitute*
*Salt*
*Black peppercorns*

# beef stir-fry with oyster sauce and brown rice with minted tangerines

### helpful hints

- *Look for meat that has already been cut for stir-frying.*
- *Oyster sauce can be found in the Oriental section of the supermarket. Look for a low-sodium one, about 260 mg per tablespoon.*
- *I call for regular brown rice instead of quick-cooking brown rice because it contains more nutrients. If you're really pressed for time, the quick-cooking brown rice will work fine.*
- *Quick-cooking brown rice can be found in most supermarkets. Be careful not to buy the type that comes with a sauce packet.*
- *Any type of mint (such as spearmint) can be used.*
- *I like to cook my rice like pasta, using a pot of boiling water that's large enough for the rice to roll freely. Use the method given here or follow the directions on the package of rice.*
- *To keep from having to look back at the recipe as you stir-fry the ingredients, line them up on a cutting board or plate in the order of use so you know which ingredient comes next.*
- *For crisp, not steamed, stir-fried vegetables, start with a very hot wok or skillet.*

*You can make a beef, broccoli, and water chestnut stir-fry in less time than it takes to send out for Chinese food. The popularity of Chinese food in America has made this a classic "American" dish.*

## beef stir-fry with oyster sauce

*1/4 cup bottled oyster sauce*
*1/4 cup dry sherry or water*
*2 teaspoons sesame oil, divided*
*1/2 pound broccoli florets (4 cups)*
*1/2 pound lean beef (tenderloin, sirloin, strip, flank, or skirt) cut into stir-fry strips (2 x 1/2 inches)*
*1 1/2 cups sliced water chestnuts*
*Salt and freshly ground black pepper to taste*

Combine the oyster sauce, sherry, and 1 teaspoon of the sesame oil in a small bowl. Make sure all ingredients are prepped and ready for stir-frying. Heat the remaining teaspoon of sesame oil in a wok or skillet until smoking. Add the broccoli and stir-fry 3 minutes. Add the beef, water chestnuts, and sauce. Stir fry 2 more minutes. Season with salt and pepper to taste, and serve over brown rice.

*Makes 2 servings.*

**ONE SERVING: 470** CALORIES, **47G** PROTEIN, **37G** CARBOHYDRATE **15G** FAT (**5G** SATURATED), **102MG** CHOLESTEROL, **675MG** SODIUM, **8G** FIBER

## brown rice

*1/2 cup brown rice*
*8 scallions, sliced (about 1 cup)*
*2 teaspoons sesame oil*
*Salt and freshly ground black pepper to taste*

Bring a large saucepan with about 2 to 3 quarts of water to a boil. Place the rice in a strainer and rinse under cold water. Add to the saucepan, stir once or twice, and let boil 30 minutes. Alternatively, follow the cooking instructions on the rice package. Drain leaving about 3 tablespoons water on the rice. Toss the scallions and sesame oil with the rice. Season with salt and pepper to taste.

*Makes 2 servings.*

**ONE SERVING: 140** CALORIES, **3G** PROTEIN, **20G** CARBOHYDRATE, **5G** FAT (**1G** SATURATED), **0MG** CHOLESTEROL, **2MG** SODIUM, **1G** FIBER

# beef stir-fry with oyster sauce and brown rice with minted tangerines *continued*

## minted tangerines

- *1 cup no-sugar-added lemon-lime or citrus-flavored seltzer, chilled*
- *2 sprigs fresh mint*
- *2 (.035-ounce) envelopes sugar substitute*
- *2 medium tangerines, peeled and divided into segments*

Pour the seltzer into a small bowl and add the mint sprigs, sugar substitute, and tangerine segments. Stir to dissolve the sugar substitute. Let marinate 15 minutes. Remove the tangerine segments and arrange on 2 small plates. Garnish with a sprig of mint on each plate. Pour a little of the marinade over the segments before serving.

*Makes 2 servings.*

**ONE SERVING: 37** CALORIES, **0.5G** PROTEIN, **10G** CARBOHYDRATE, **0. 2G** FAT (**0G** SATURATED), **0MG** CHOLESTEROL, **1MG** SODIUM, **0G** FIBER

*Let the vegetables sit a minute before tossing to allow the wok to regain its heat.*

- *If pressed for time, omit the Minted Tangerines and serve 1 tangerine per person.*

### countdown

- *Start rice.*
- *Marinate tangerines.*
- *Prepare beef ingredients.*
- *Stir-fry beef.*
- *Finish rice.*

### shopping list

*TO BUY:*

- *1/2 pound lean beef (tenderloin, sirloin, strip, flank, or skirt)*
- *1 can sliced water chestnuts (12 ounces needed)*
- *1 bottle oyster sauce*
- *1 small bottle sesame oil*
- *1 small package brown rice*
- *1 small bottle no-sugar-added lemon-lime or citrus-flavored seltzer (8 ounces needed)*
- *1 small bottle dry sherry*
- *1/2 pound broccoli florets*
- *1 small bunch scallions (8 needed)*
- *1 small bunch fresh mint*
- *2 medium tangerines*

*STAPLES:*

- *Sugar substitute*
- *Salt*
- *Black peppercorns*

# pork and peach salsa with pasta salad and melon

## helpful hints

- *If peaches are not available, use fresh pear or papaya.*
- *Store-bought salsa can be used instead of fresh peach salsa. Make sure there is no sugar added.*

## countdown

- *Preheat oven to 400 degrees.*
- *Start pork.*
- *Start pasta.*
- *Make salsa.*
- *Finish pasta.*

## shopping list

*TO BUY:*

*1/2 pound pork tenderloin*
*1 box whole wheat fusille or macaroni pasta (2 ounces needed)*
*1/2 pound zucchini*
*2 jalapeño peppers*
*1 small bunch fresh cilantro*
*2 ripe peaches*
*1 lime*
*1 cantaloupe*

*STAPLES:*

*Carrots*
*Olive oil*
*Olive oil spray*
*Dried oregano*
*Ground cumin*
*Sugar substitute*
*Salt*
*Black peppercorns*

*The delicate flavor of peaches goes well with roasted pork. For this dinner, I made a fresh peach salsa to spoon over the sliced meat. For best results, the peaches should be ripe—look for tree-ripened peaches at the supermarket. But don't be surprised if they are not yet ripe enough to eat. They will have more flavor than other peaches and should ripen within a couple of days. • Both the pork and pasta salad can be served warm or at room temperature.*

## pork and peach salsa

*1/2 pound pork tenderloin*
*Olive oil spray*
*1/2 teaspoon dried oregano*
*1/2 teaspoon ground cumin*
*2 ripe peaches, washed, halved, and pitted*
*2 teaspoons freshly squeezed lime juice*
*2 (.035-ounce) envelopes sugar substitute*
*2 tablespoons chopped fresh cilantro*
*2 jalapeño peppers, seeded and chopped (2 tablespoons)*
*Salt and freshly ground black pepper to taste*

Preheat the oven to 400 degrees. Line a baking tray with foil. Remove any visible fat from the pork, place on the foil, and spray both sides with olive oil. Sprinkle the pork with the oregano and cumin. Place in the oven and roast 25 minutes.

While the pork roasts, dice the peaches. Combine the lime juice and sugar substitute in a small bowl. Add the peaches, cilantro, and jalapeños. Toss well, and season with salt and pepper to taste.

When the pork is cooked, slice and serve immediately; or let cool to room temperature, and then slice. Serve with the salsa on the side.

*Makes 2 servings.*

**ONE SERVING: 278** CALORIES, **35G** PROTEIN, **19G** CARBOHYDRATE, **8G** FAT (**3G** SATURATED), **106MG** CHOLESTEROL, **83MG** SODIUM, **1G** FIBER

# pork and peach salsa with pasta salad and melon *continued*

## pasta salad

- *½ cup whole wheat fusille or macaroni pasta (2 ounces)*
- *2 cups sliced carrots*
- *2 cups sliced zucchini*
- *4 teaspoons olive oil*
- *Salt and freshly ground black pepper to taste*

Bring a large saucepan filled with water to a boil. Add the pasta and boil 7 minutes. Add the carrots and zucchini. Continue to boil 2 minutes, or until the pasta is cooked through, but firm. Drain the pasta and vegetables, and toss with the olive oil. Season with salt and pepper to taste. Serve with the pork. *Makes 2 servings.*

**ONE SERVING: 285** CALORIES, **9G** PROTEIN, **40G** CARBOHYDRATE, **10G** FAT (**2G** SATURATED), **0MG** CHOLESTEROL, **51MG** SODIUM, **7G** FIBER

## melon

- *1 cantaloupe, cubed (4 cups)*

Divide the cantaloupe between 2 dessert bowls. *Makes 2 servings.*

**ONE SERVING: 77** CALORIES, **2G** PROTEIN, **18G** CARBOHYDRATE, **1G** FAT (**0G** SATURATED), **0MG** CHOLESTEROL, **20MG** SODIUM, **2G** FIBER

# desserts

## introduction

With this chapter at hand, there's no need to go off your healthy eating lifestyle when you want a special treat or guests come over.

Most desserts, unfortunately, are laden with carbohydrates. I created these recipes for those times when you want something sweet at the end of a meal and still stay within the lifestyle guidelines.

Desserts have not been included as part of the Quick Start section, but the Strawberry Pecan Whip and Coffee Latte Whip are two desserts that you can enjoy during the Quick Start phase (and subsequent phases). They're satisfying at the end of a meal and have limited carbohydrate content.

A few desserts are included in the Which Carb section because they fit the nutritional guidelines for that menu.

But most desserts have been included in the Right Carb meals. I have created some additional temptations as alternatives to a simple fruit dessert. The Mocha Fudge Soufflé and the Raspberry Parfait are winners and can be proudly served for guests.

## dessert index

# strawberry pecan whip

*Whipped Jell-O was a favorite of mine when I was young. Here is an updated version that fits perfectly into a low-carb lifestyle—and can be eaten in Quick Start, Which Carbs, and Right Carbs.*

## strawberry pecan whip

- *1 (0.3-ounce) package sugar-free, low-calorie strawberry Jell-O gelatin*
- *1 cup boiling water*
- *1 cup cold water*
- *1 teaspoon vanilla extract*
- *2 tablespoons pecan pieces, toasted*
- *¼ cup part-skim ricotta cheese*

Dissolve the Jell-O in boiling water, stirring for 2 minutes. Add the cold water and place in refrigerator to set for 1½ hours. Stir the vanilla extract and pecans into the ricotta cheese. Whip into the partially set Jell-O with an electric beater. Spoon into 4 dessert bowls. Refrigerate to set again before serving.
*Makes 4 servings.*

**ONE SERVING: 147** CALORIES, **8G** PROTEIN, **3G** CARBOHYDRATE, **11G** FAT (**3G** SATURATED), **15MG** CHOLESTEROL, **45MG** SODIUM, **1G** FIBER

### helpful hints

- *Any fruit-flavored, sugar-free Jell-O gelatin can be used.*
- *Be careful toasting pecans, as they burn easily.*

### countdown

- *Place water on to boil.*
- *Make recipe.*

### shopping list

*TO BUY:*

*1 (0.3-ounce) package sugar-free, low-calorie strawberry Jell-O gelatin*

*1 small carton part-skim ricotta cheese*

*1 small package pecan pieces*

*STAPLES:*

*Vanilla extract*

# coffee latte whip

## helpful hint

- *Instant decaffeinated coffee can be used.*

## countdown

- *Prepare ingredients.*
- *Make recipe.*

## shopping list

*TO BUY:*

*1 box gelatin (1 envelope needed)*

*1 container unsweetened cocoa powder*

*1 small container heavy whipping cream*

*STAPLES:*

*Sugar substitute*

*Decaffeinated coffee*

*This recipe was created for the Quick Start phase and can be used during any phase.*

## coffee latte whip

*1 tablespoon gelatin (1 envelope or 1/4 ounce)*

*1/4 cup cold water*

*1/2 cup boiling water*

*3 (.035-ounce) envelopes sugar substitute*

*1/2 tablespoon unsweetened cocoa powder*

*1/4 cup strong, decaffeinated, black coffee*

*2 tablespoons heavy whipping cream*

Soak the gelatin in the cold water for 5 minutes. Pour the boiling water into the cold water–gelatin mixture to dissolve the gelatin. Stir in the sugar substitute, cocoa powder, and coffee. Pour into a bowl and refrigerate for 1 hour to set. Remove the gelatin from the refrigerator, and whip with an electric beater. Add the cream, and continue to whip until fluffy. Pour into 2 dessert dishes and refrigerate to gel, about 15 minutes.

*Makes 2 servings.*

**ONE SERVING: 74** CALORIES, **4G** PROTEIN, **3G** CARBOHYDRATE, **6G** FAT (**4G** SATURATED), **21MG** CHOLESTEROL, **12MG** SODIUM, **0.5G** FIBER

# apricot almond custard

*Good quality dried apricots add more flavor to this dish. Once reconstituted, they should look like apricots. This dessert can be eaten during Right Carbs.*

## apricot almond custard

*6 dried apricots*
*1/2 cup skim milk*
*1 (.035-ounce) envelope sugar substitute*
*1/4 teaspoon almond extract*
*1 egg*
*1 tablespoon slivered almonds*

Preheat the oven to 350 degrees. Bring a small saucepan of water to a boil and add the apricots. Let boil 3 to 4 minutes to reconstitute, then drain and coarsely chop. Combine the apricots, milk, sugar substitute, almond extract, and egg in a small bowl. Divide between 2 ovenproof ramekins or a bowl (3 x 1 3/4 inches deep). Sprinkle the almonds on top. Bake for 30 minutes, or until custard is firm.

*Makes 2 servings.*

**ONE SERVING: 143** CALORIES, **8G** PROTEIN, **17G** CARBOHYDRATE, **6G** FAT (**1G** SATURATED FAT), **3G** FIBER, **108MG** CHOLESTEROL, **64MG** sodium.

## countdown

- *Preheat oven to 350 degrees.*
- *Place a small saucepan of water on to boil.*
- *Complete recipe.*

## shopping list

*TO BUY:*

*1 package dried apricots (6 needed)*
*1 small bottle almond extract*
*1 small package slivered almonds (about 1/2 ounce needed)*

*STAPLES:*

*Skim milk*
*Sugar substitute*
*Egg*

# mocha fudge cake

## helpful hints

- *Buy high-quality chocolate for best results.*
- *Instant coffee can be used.*

## countdown

- *Preheat oven to 350 degrees.*
- *Melt chocolate.*
- *Whip egg whites.*
- *Complete recipe.*

## shopping list

*TO BUY:*

*2 ounces bittersweet chocolate*

*STAPLES:*

*Eggs*

*Decaffeinated coffee*

*Sugar substitute*

*Here's a scrumptious dessert for chocoholics in the Right Carbs stage. Melting the chocolate in a microwave takes only minutes.*

## mocha fudge cake

*2 ounces bittersweet chocolate*
*1 tablespoon strong, decaffeinated, black coffee*
*2 (.035-ounce) envelopes sugar substitute*
*4 egg whites*

Preheat the oven to 350 degrees. Place the chocolate in a microwave-safe bowl and microwave on high for 2 minutes to melt. Stir in the coffee and sugar substitute.

Beat the egg whites until stiff peaks form. Fold into the chocolate mixture. Spoon into 2 soufflé dishes (each 1⅓ high x 4 inches in diameter or a single Pyrex bowl 3 inches high x 6 inches in diameter). Bake in the oven for 8 minutes and serve warm. *Makes 2 servings.*

**ONE SERVING: 169** CALORIES, **11G** PROTEIN, **9G** CARBOHYDRATE, **15G** FAT (**9G** SATURATED), **0MG** CHOLESTEROL, **111MG** SODIUM, **0G** FIBER

# index